**GIANT LEAP**

*Apollo 11: Mankind's
first footprints on the
Moon fulfill the Apollo
commitment and mark
the culmination of a
great adventure.*

# Apollo

## THE EPIC JOURNEY TO THE MOON

BY DAVID WEST REYNOLDS

A TEHABI BOOK

HARCOURT, INC.

NEW YORK   SAN DIEGO   LONDON

**TEHABI BOOKS**

TEHABI BOOKS designed and produced *Apollo: The Epic Journey to the Moon* and has developed and published many award-winning books that are recognized for their strong literary and visual content. Tehabi works with national and international publishers, corporations, institutions, and nonprofit groups to identify, develop, and implement comprehensive publishing programs. Tehabi Books is located in San Diego, California.
www.tehabi.com

*President:* Chris Capen
*Senior Vice President:* Tom Lewis
*Vice President, Development:* Andy Lewis
*Editorial Director:* Nancy Cash
*Director, Sales and Marketing:* Tim Connolly
*Director, Trade Relations:* Marty Remmell
*Art Director:* Vicky Vaughn
*Editor:* Garrett W. Brown
*Panorama Compositor:* Mark Santos
*Copy Editor:* Ruth Goldberg
*Proofreader:* Bonnie Freeman
*Indexer:* Ken DellaPenta

Photography and illustration credits appear on page 272.

Cover photograph: Apollo 12 astronaut Alan Bean holds a vacuum-sealed sample container filled with moondust. Mission commander Pete Conrad took this photograph during their stop at Sharp Crater.

Back-cover photograph: The Apollo 11 cockpit stage, rising from the lunar surface, prepares to rendezvous with the orbiting command module.

Title-page panorama: In the bleak setting of the Moon's Fra Mauro highlands, the only color is provided by a U.S. flag and Apollo 14's hand-built lunar lander *Antares,* the third golden chariot to carry men to the Moon.

Table-of-contents photograph: Witnessed from the farthest frontier of human exploration, the planet Earth rises over a moonscape horizon in one of the extraordinary views that only Apollo made possible. Apollo 11 photographed this image some 69 miles above the lunar surface in July 1969.

www.HarcourtBooks.com

Harcourt Trade books may be purchased for educational use. For information, please write: Harcourt Trade Publishers, Attn: Director of Special Sales, 525 B Street, Suite 1900, San Diego, CA 92101. Specific, large quantity needs can also be met with special editions, including personalized covers and corporate imprints. For information, please write: Tehabi Books, Attn: Eric Pinkham, Director of Corporate Publishing and Promotions, 4920 Carroll Canyon Road, Suite 200, San Diego, CA 92121.

The paper used in this publication meets the minimum requirements of the American National Standard for Information Sciences—Permanence of Paper for Printed Library Materials, ANSI Z39.48-1992.

Library of Congress Cataloging-in-Publication Data

Reynolds, David West.
    Apollo : the epic journey to the moon / by David West Reynolds ; foreword by Wally Schirra ; introduction by Von Hardesty ; afterword by Gene Cernan.
        p. cm.
    Includes bibliographical references and index.
    ISBN 0-15-100964-3
    1. Project Apollo (U.S.)—History. 2. Space flight to the moon.  I. Title.

TL789.8.U6 A58113 2002
629.45'4'0973—dc21

                                                                                    2001051930

Printed by Dai Nippon Printing Co., Ltd., in Hong Kong

First edition
J I H G F E D C B A

WHEN you're sitting on top of a rocket like Apollo 7 there's a sense of anticipation that's finally rewarded by the "bolts firing," when the rocket is released from the pad. We used to laugh at comedian Bill Dana's fearful astronaut character José Jimenez who would look miserable and say, "Blast off? Oh, I hope not!" We all hoped it was *liftoff*. The real point is, on Apollo 7 we were taking off after the loss of what was called the Apollo 1 crew, who died during a test on the launch pad a year and a half earlier. (Technically, they were the Apollo 6 crew, but in their honor after the fire, we renamed their mission Apollo 1.) Gus Grissom, who commanded Apollo 1, had been a close friend and neighbor of mine. With our launch, the Apollo program was starting up again, getting back on track. So the Apollo 7 liftoff was pretty momentous to us, symbolically as well as for the fact that we were heading into space.

# Liftoff
## BY WALLY SCHIRRA
Mission Commander of Apollo 7

You're way up at the top of this thing. The cockpit is quivering around you. The couch is pretty well padded, and you're pretty well insulated, but you have all that length of rocket behind you. It's like you're at the tip of an arrow just as it's let go. It's airtight in the vehicle, you can't really hear it, but you can *feel* it. You're burning off tremendous amounts of fuel in those first few thousand feet. It takes tremendous energy to leave the Earth and get going.

On Apollo 7 we weren't supposed to launch if the winds would blow us back to a hard ground landing in an abort, but they violated that mission rule and launched us anyway. I was somewhat concerned about that. When you are given command, it means you *own* the vehicle. When they launched in spite of the mission rule, they usurped my command. The role of command means *you* protect your people, *you* make sure nothing happens that shouldn't happen. I think the civilian engineers in Mission Control didn't appreciate that aspect of the situation. And I've never heard of a flight controller risking his life falling out of a chair.

Launch is not really the rough part of the ride. Staging is the big event. When a stage disengages and drops off behind you, retro-rockets blow it backward and there's a lot of smoke and fire that goes past you. That's a "wow." I had been through

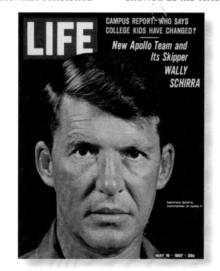

*This cover story ran a year and a half before Apollo 7's October 1968 launch.*

launch twice before, and I knew what to expect. That made the other two guys fun to watch—my shipmates Walt Cunningham and Donn Eisele. The jolt throws you hard against the belts, and they thought they were going right through the control panels.

The Apollo spacecraft was a big thing like a multi-engine passenger jet, compared to the jet fighter experience of the Gemini spacecraft or the experimental feeling of Mercury. By the time of Apollo the computer was a big part of everything, and we all had to become computer gurus to fly the ship. Back in Mercury we had a wristwatch and a wind-up clock. A lot happened in just a few years back then.

During Mercury, I remember when the seven of us went to Huntsville for the first time, before any of us had even had a flight. Wernher von Braun had us all to dinner at his home. Wernher was a team player, even more than some of the contractors we worked very closely with. He was very much liked by all of us astronauts. After dinner Wernher showed us spacecraft drawings and plans he had made years earlier for a manned version of his A-4 rocket. He had always been looking ahead. Then he took us out on his patio and showed us his telescope and some of the stars he was looking at. It was like a father teaching his kids about astronomy. After that I started going to planetariums. It was because of that night that I still have a Meade telescope in my home today.

People ask me how I see the Moon race in perspective. I think of Apollo as having won the Cold War. In accomplishing that goal, our technology proved to the Soviets that we could do what we said we could do. When the Strategic Defense Initiative came along, they believed we could do that, too. While they were competing with us, they were exhausting their technical strength; we were still improving ours. At the same time, Apollo also showed *us* what was possible. It was a beginning, a liftoff. We have yet to see where it is all headed. There are a lot of stars out there, and there will always be people looking ahead.

So now I'll hand you over to David West Reynolds and *Apollo: The Epic Story of the Journey to the Moon.* A lot of books have come out on space exploration. I look through them and just read the parts that interest me. I actually read David's book all the way through. That should tell you something.

*Wally Schirra*

"THE exploration of the planets," Arthur C. Clarke wrote in *The Saturday Review* in 1955, "is now closer to us in time than the exploration of Africa by Stanley and Livingstone." Clarke—British scientist, science-fiction writer, and visionary of the Space Age—fully comprehended that modern rocketry had made interplanetary exploration both feasible and imminent—so imminent that he predicted a human landing on the Moon by 1980, give or take 10 years. Such a stunning technical feat, in Clarke's mind, would not be an end but a beginning. The projected lunar landing would establish a trajectory for the human exploration of the solar system and beyond. Clarke's bold prophecy anticipated the actual time line for the Space Age: The Apollo 11 mission of 1969 saw two men, Neil Armstrong and Buzz Aldrin, walk on the Moon, the first visit by humans to another celestial body.

# The Space Frontier

BY VON HARDESTY

Smithsonian National Air and Space Museum

Clarke made this prophecy before Sputnik, before Gagarin, before NASA and the Mercury astronauts, before John F. Kennedy committed the United States to a lunar mission. Just half a century separated Clarke from the Wright brothers, who had inaugurated the Air Age with their awe-inspiring 12-second flight across the wind-swept sands of Kitty Hawk, North Carolina, in December 1903. The fragile Wright Flyer, fashioned of wood and fabric, was the first practical flying machine, rising into the air under its own power and completing a flight path of merely 120 feet. The Apollo astronauts—as heirs to the Wrights—traveled a quarter of a million miles to Earth's nearest neighbor, the Moon, having been catapulted into space by a powerful Saturn V rocket.

For Clarke, the Moon landing he foresaw in 1955 would represent more than another episode in the quest to fly "faster, farther, and higher." Such a feat would embody the human aspiration to explore the heavens, to become the harbinger for even bolder treks into the solar system. "The men of 500 or 1,000 years from now," he wrote, "will have motivations very different from ours, but if they are men at all, they will still burn with the restless curiosity which has driven us over the world and which is about to take us into space."

David West Reynolds, in *Apollo: The Epic Journey to the Moon*, captures in word and image the dramatic story of how humans fulfilled Clarke's prescient musings in 1955. The Apollo program demonstrated that old visions and modern engineering could indeed make space travel something more than the stuff of dreams.

As Reynolds shows, one cannot understand the Apollo journey to the Moon in the single time frame of the fast-paced 1950s and 1960s. The genesis of Apollo is a diverse and complex matter, one that includes visionaries of the past, the rocket societies, the pioneering scientists and engineers, the military planners and politicians (as both advocates and adversaries), and the men and women who flew atop rockets into space. Three nations, in particular, played pivotal roles in shaping the science and technique of space flight: the United States, Germany, and Russia. All these elements mix and overlap in the genealogy for Apollo.

A central figure of the American space program was Wernher von Braun. His work for America's civilian and military missile programs followed a controversial career in Nazi Germany. At heart a space visionary, von Braun nevertheless had to render to Caesar important service, if not his soul, to secure avenues for his rocket work. As with his counterpart, Sergei Korolev, in Soviet Russia, and so many other scientists in the 20th century, von Braun made more than one Faustian bargain. Historians debate—and will continue to debate—the moral issues of his role in space history, a mixed legacy of V-2 rockets bombing London and Saturn V rockets propelling astronauts to the Moon. Nevertheless, it is clear that von Braun's advocacy of a practical vision of space exploration, in particular his association with Chesley Bonestell and the Disney studios, inspired Americans in 1950s. The Apollo program came into being in this altered popular context, one where the idea of a trek to the Moon appeared feasible for the first time. Space science had overtaken space fantasy.

**ORIGINS**

*In 1930, the forefront of rocket experimentation was in Berlin, where the amateur rocket club VfR supported experiments based on Hermann Oberth's theories. Here, Oberth stands to the right of the large rocket, and a young Wernher von Braun looks on, third figure to Oberth's right. Von Braun's VfR efforts would lead to war rockets and Moon rockets alike.*

The story of Apollo cannot be understood without reference to the parallel universe of the Russian aerospace program. The Russians, in fact, provide the leitmotif for Reynold's lively narrative of America's Moon odyssey. And they had their own visionaries thinking about the future Space Age. Pioneer theorist Konstantin Tsiolkovsky had published his seminal essay, "The Exploration of the Cosmos in a Rocket-Powered Vehicle," in May 1903, several months *before* the Wrights launched the Air Age. Their space spectaculars, beginning with the launch of Sputnik in October 1957, came as a stunning surprise to Americans. The touchstones of the Russian space program—Sputnik, the Lunas and Vostoks, the orbiting dog Laika, and cosmonaut Gagarin and company, establishing a sequence of "space firsts"—gave an impression of monolithic purpose and technical prowess. Such popular images reflected concrete achievement, for certain, but Russian space activities were often less coherent and scripted than Westerners imagined. The space program, in reality, had been a stepchild to the missile program in the 1950s. Having perfected atomic weapons, the Soviets worked feverishly to develop a missile delivery system, one truly intercontinental in character and on par with the West. Korolev and others, however, took every opportunity to redirect Russia's finite resources into a genuine space program. The manifest propaganda potential of Soviet space achievements—always a powerful endorsement of the supposed superiority of communism—tempted Soviet leader Nikita Khrushchev to sponsor the nonmilitary use of his missile technology.

The Soviet exploitation of Sputnik for propaganda purposes had been foreshadowed in the 1930s, when Joseph Stalin used staged aerial spectaculars to showcase Soviet technical progress. Stalin's Falcons, in particular Valery Chkalov, established a series of air records in that turbulent decade of massive industrialization and purges. When Chkalov led a team of Soviet aviators in an historic flight over the North Pole in June 1937, Soviet propaganda mills began to talk about another transpolar flight, this time over the South Pole—a feat that would make "the Earth spin on a Bolshevik Axis." Such instincts to exploit technical achievements for propaganda purposes would be in place a generation later when Sputnik appeared in the night sky and Yuri Gagarin made his orbital path around the planet. For the Soviets, science and politics were always intertwined and mutually supportive, an expression of the Bolshevik self-image as the revolutionary instrument for modernity and technological progress.

Soviet rocket mastermind Sergei Korolev came of age in this Soviet context of technological breakthroughs. Trained as a mechanical engineer, Korolev flew gliders and moved in a circle of aviation experts that included Andrei Tupolev. Eventually Korolev acquired a passion for rockets—and the alluring possibility of interplanetary exploration. Korolev's own career led ultimately to a leadership role in the Soviet space program in the 1950s and 1960s, but his contributions were never publicly recognized. During his lifetime, he was known only as the "chief designer," because of the Soviet regime's policy of strict secrecy surrounding all missile and rocket programs. Since his death in 1966, however, Korolev has joined von Braun in history as one of the great organizers of space exploration in the 20th century.

In retrospect, it is important for us to see the Russian space triumphs as historical benchmarks in their own right, not merely as a catalyst for Americans to execute a lunar landing. I anticipate that future generations, say a hundred years from now, will view Russian space activities as distinct and memorable, the contributions of one space-faring nation to the saga of human exploration.

While *Apollo: The Epic Journey to the Moon* covers the eventual triumph of the Americans in the Space Race, Reynolds also sets the Moon landings in context, showing how the era came to an end in the

**ROBOT VIEW**

*Utopia Plain on Mars stretches two miles to the horizon in this Viking 2 view. The twin Viking probes sent back the first photographs of the surface of Mars in 1976, yet these have never become icons of history comparable to the Apollo astronaut images. Without a human proxy, space exploration can accomplish good science but achieves limited public engagement.*

1970s and revealing the Apollo planners' visions of what might have been with Skylab and beyond. In lieu of those visions the space shuttle and the effort to build the International Space Station, or I.S.S., have defined the nature of space activities in the last quarter of the 20th century. For many, especially those animated by the ideas of Arthur Clarke and other space visionaries, the near-Earth proximity of the shuttle flights and the I.S.S. suggest an abandonment of true space exploration. These programs continue to demonstrate technological skill and to foster multinational participation in space, but for their critics, they are unworthy of the larger potential of Apollo and its quantum leaps.

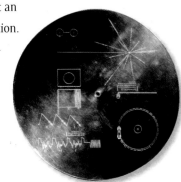

Voyagers 1 and 2, sent beyond our solar system, carried a technological "message in a bottle" about Earth for unknown beings to find—a purely exploratory gesture attached to these automated scientific probes.

Whether humans should continue to explore the cosmos is today a matter of dispute. The successful work of robotic space probes—for example, the Viking photos of Mars and the Voyager missions to the outer solar system—suggest the potential of this technology and approach. The less-costly robot probes offer significant contributions to science and clearly should continue. But, as Apollo showed us, there is something irreplaceably inspiring about a human presence on the frontier of exploration, and it is certainly the human dimension that captured the imagination of the world.

Arthur Clarke, as stated in his 1955 essay, saw an imperative for humans to explore the heavens, to leave their footprints on celestial bodies, just as the 12 Apollo astronauts left theirs on the lunar surface. This potential remains. Apollo points to the future even as it represents an epochal event in the first century of human flight.

VISIONARIES laid the groundwork for the Moon odyssey. A Cold War brought it to pass. For centuries men had dreamed of reaching Earth's pale companion in the night sky, but it was not until a novelist dramatized the possibilities of a new era that a way to reach upward became more than fantasy. Inspiration drove a generation of rocket theorists and experimenters to design new instruments and to build in their minds the way to the stars. A world war seized the power of these new instruments and filled them with strength. In the aftermath, two superpowers engaged in a duel for the world's imagination, and the arena became the realm beyond the clouds. Their weapons became the instruments of the visionaries, and their ultimate contest would drive both powers in an unprecedented race to set foot on the sky. The challenge was undertaken as a political gamble, but it would embark mankind upon an odyssey of the spirit.

# Dawn of the Space Age

## AUTHORS OF THE VISION

It began with imagination. French author Jules Verne wrote a novel in 1865 entitled *From the Earth to the Moon* and lit the fuse of the Space Age. Verne's story described the efforts of an American enterprise to create a gigantic cannon called *Columbiad* that could fire a manned projectile to the Moon. Verne marveled at the technological wonders of his day and believed that technology would empower mankind to overcome all obstacles. The book was his ringing manifesto that with "all the resources of art, science, and industry . . . one can do anything." *From the Earth to the Moon* made the first case that a journey into the heavens had become only a matter of determination. For so long a symbol of the unreachable, the Moon in Verne's hands illuminated a new era of human capability.

Verne's "Extraordinary Voyages," as the publisher called his novels, were far from flights of fancy; they were virtually expedition blueprints. Inspired by his planning for a real balloon journey across Africa, Verne had invented "a new genre, one all my own," he proudly claimed, of scientific adventure, filled with calculations and realistic preparation, which gave a new dimension to bold fantasy of exotic travels and miraculous machines. Verne's African balloon trip never came to pass, but the spark it gave his fiction burned brightly.

The crucial inspiration contained in *From the Earth to the Moon* was the way in which Verne framed the concept of sending a projectile to the Moon completely undaunted by the magnitudes of the figures and forces involved. He set his story in the young nation of America, where it seemed that the citizens could do anything they set their minds to, no matter how difficult. In this setting, Verne's characters attack the problem of launching a Moon rocket with straightforward calculation rather than dreamy musings. In a few short meetings, the Baltimore Gun Club determines the necessary force of the explosive power, the size of the gun they will need to build, and the size of the projectile, all using basic physics. From here it is only a matter of marshaling the resources and undertaking the construction.

Verne located his launch site prophetically in Florida, for exactly the same reason that it would later be chosen by NASA: Since the Earth's rotation is faster nearer the equator, a more equatorial latitude offers a launch vehicle more of an assist toward escape velocity. Verne's calculations were not fantasy. An interested reader can trace the demands of real physics by following along with Baltimore Gun Club president Barbicane's presentations. There were flaws in the fictional plan; it was not perfect nor completely realistic. But this was the first time that the Moon as a human goal had been approached with practicality, and it was the approach more than the specifics that galvanized many young readers and future scientists.

Verne declared that applied science could achieve the Moon. It is for this that he takes a place of honor in the saga of mankind's Moon odyssey. Jules Verne directly inspired the great pioneers of rocketry and thus wrote the prologue of the Space Age.

It had taken millennia for the familiar Moon to become a destination in the imagination of man. Understood as a sphere as early as classical antiquity, the Moon's size and distance were determined with remarkable accuracy by the Greek astronomer Hipparchus around 130 B.C. But the Moon, like all celestial bodies, was believed to be a flawless sphere (the heavens were, literally, the perfect realm of heaven) until Galileo Galilei

**VERNE'S COLUMBIAD**

*French novelist Jules Verne's giant cannon blasts a manned projectile* From the Earth to the Moon *in 1865. Verne's innovative, realistic approach inspired the theorists and engineers of the real Space Age.*

aimed a telescope in Padua, Italy, at the night's companion in 1609. To Galileo's eye, first of all mankind, the detail of the Moon was revealed. With a marveling gaze he explored an astonishing realm of mountains and craters. Today, a good pair of binoculars can afford anyone a similar experience, and when you first see the craters of the Moon this way, you can almost feel the wonder that transfixed Galileo at this revelation. The Moon was not an abstraction: It was a place. Galileo published his discoveries in a book called *Sidereus Nuncius,* or *Starry Messenger* (1610), which was an immediate sensation.

In time, men began to map the unexplored territories of the Moon. A generation after *Starry Messenger,* the lunar mountain chains were named after earthly prototypes

*Upon learning of the invention of the telescope, Galileo built an improved model of his own.*

such as the Alps and Apennines, but in 1651, Giovanni Baptista Riccioli captured the inspiration of the new world in the heavens by rendering into his detailed lunar atlas lyrical and haunting names for features across the rest of the lunar surface. Since the dark, flat areas resembled earthly waters, Riccioli saw in them the Sea of Tranquility, the Ocean of Storms, the Lake of Dreams, and the Bay of Rainbows, among others. Rendered into Latin, these became *maria,* the Mare Tranquilitatis, Oceanus Procellarum, Lacus Somnorum, and Sinus Iridium, their sounds and meanings forming the poetry of the Moon. Magnificent and beautiful, familiar yet otherworldly, the names were cast by Riccioli in a heritage rather than a national language, an elegant international solution that still serves the astronomical community today. Riccioli also began the tradition of naming craters after astronomers, scientists, and philosophers such as Tycho, Copernicus, and Plato.

*From the Earth to the Moon* thus looked back on a long tradition of science writing about the Earth's nighttime companion. And for all its fame and special influence, Verne's was not the only or even the first fictional account of a voyage to the Moon, which had figured as a fantasy location since Lucian's second-century A.D. satire *True History*. There were even a variety of contemporary Moon and planetary voyage novels in the Victorian period. But none of these had Verne's authentic approach, and of them all only latecomer H. G. Wells's *The First Men in the Moon* (1906) has stood the test of time.

### ENGINEERS OF THE DREAM

**O**ne of Verne's notable readers was a Russian theorist and teacher named Konstantin Tsiolkovsky, born in 1857. Driven inward by the isolation of deafness as a youth, Tsiolkovsky traveled like Verne did: in his imagination. Tsiolkovsky's mother gave him the book *From the Earth to the Moon* when he was nine years old, and he read it so many times that he "fairly memorized it," he later wrote. As a young man of very limited means, Tsiolkovsky taught himself physics and mathematics. This scientific background equipped the introspective Tsiolkovsky to calculate that Verne's massive cannon would not be a truly practical way to reach the Moon—the force of the explosion would have atomized the projectile. Rather, the method by which Verne's spaceship maneuvered near the Moon showed the real way to get there, and that was with rockets. The Russian theorist spent countless hours and many years mentally refining his ideas, until at the age of 46 he first put them into print.

In *Exploring Space with Reactive Devices* (1903), Tsiolkovsky presented an astonishing range of mathematical calculations and design concepts that laid out the foundations for liquid-fueled rocketry, from the use

of kerosene propellant and the configuration of thrust chambers and guidance systems to the use of multiple stages, space stations, and much more—a powerful debut. Tsiolkovsky eventually published hundreds of books and articles but was not an experimenter and never built a functioning rocket of his own. Instead, he made scale models of his designs and also used the concepts, as Verne did, in works of science fiction. Tsiolkovsky had taken his inspiration from Verne and responded with tremendous intellectual force. His works would in turn inspire German rocket pioneers and proud fellow Russians to emerge later as leaders in the enterprise of space flight. But the first modern rocket experimenter was born in America.

**P**hysics professor Robert Goddard experimented with solid-fuel (gunpowder-based) rockets in Massachusetts after earning his doctorate in 1911. His best early rockets made it not quite 500 feet into the air. He and Tsiolkovsky did not know about each other, but both independently reached the conclusion that liquid fuel would be the way to get a rocket anywhere interesting. In 1920, the Smithsonian Institution published Goddard's seminal work, *A Method of Reaching Extreme Altitudes*, in which he detailed the possibilities of both solid- and liquid-fueled rockets.

Unfortunately for Goddard, he mentioned within the proposal an experiment that would involve shooting a rocket to the Moon with a flash powder charge that could be seen through telescopes. The concept was merely an aside within the overall work, but it was this one item that seized

*Inspired by Jules Verne, physicist Hermann Oberth spurred rocket experimentation in Germany with his 1923 book,* The Rocket into Interplanetary Space. *Oberth's exciting theories were the catalyst to action for young engineers who would one day build the world's first large rockets.*

public attention. Newspapers across the United States trumpeted the invention of the "Rocket Which Will Hit Moon," and Goddard was immediately subjected to intense publicity and withering ridicule, including a famously snide *New York Times* editorial that described him as lacking even "the knowledge ladled out daily in high schools."

The disastrous experience burned Goddard, already shy by nature, and left him paranoid of publicity and permanently suspicious of interest in his work. Resentful but undaunted, Goddard kept working in secret, making the experimental debut of his great concept an event witnessed by almost no one. On March 16, 1926, Goddard launched the first working liquid-fueled rocket on his Aunt Effie's farm near Worcester, Massachusetts. Goddard's odd-looking contraption roared with a tiny throat and lifted from a tubular scaffolding, gaining speed quickly and tracing an arc 41 feet high and 184 feet long before it hit the ground. Humble beginnings, but this was a real rocket, and that is what invested the little flight with tremendous historical significance. No matter how brilliant all the theories were, this was the beginning of the real thing. In 1926, at the hands of Robert Goddard, the realization of rocket dreams and visions began.

Goddard would pursue the development of liquid-fuel rocketry with a few assistants on a remote ranch in Roswell, New Mexico, until his death in 1945. His work was funded by a grant from the Guggenheim Foundation, obtained through the support of aviation pioneer Charles Lindbergh. Goddard's reclusive ways, however, greatly limited his

direct legacy, and the rockets that would surpass those of the American physics professor would be built in Germany, thanks to a Romanian.

Romanian-born Hermann Oberth had been given Verne's *From the Earth to the Moon* by his mother when he was eleven years old, and like Tsiolkovsky, he came to know the book by heart. Oberth studied to become a physics professor but was denied his doctorate at Heidelberg, Germany, in 1922, when his dissertation advisor pronounced Oberth's work on rocket applications admirable and intriguing but too speculative for evaluation. Undeterred by this rejection, Oberth pushed on and found a publisher for what became his first book, *The Rocket into Interplanetary Space* (1923). Oberth's concepts for space travel and space stations were so bold that they generated interest even among the public. Tsiolkovsky had explored much of this territory before, but his work, published in small editions, was virtually unknown outside Russia. So it was Hermann Oberth who brought the thrill of rocket science to Europe. Popularized by German science writer Willy Ley and others, rocketry became a fashionable interest and sport in 1920s Germany. One result was that it crossed into the medium of film.

In 1929 the renowned German director Fritz Lang (of *Metropolis* and *M* fame) asked Hermann Oberth to serve as technical advisor for a realistic movie about the first rocket to the Moon. Lang's film *Frau im Mond (Woman in the Moon)* brought Oberth's concepts to the screen with remarkable visual effects and prophetically depicted events that would not come to pass for well over a generation. It was for *Frau im Mond* that the dramatic "ten . . . nine . . . eight . . ." countdown was invented. The film anticipated with amazing prescience much of what was to come, from the moonship assembly building and floodlit rocket rollout to space weightlessness. None of this was lost on certain awed members of the theater audience, some of whom were the men who would one day build the real things.

*In this sketch Oberth envisioned clustered liquid-fueled rocket engines powering a bullet-shaped rocket of multiple stages.*

## GODDARD

*While Tsiolkovsky and Oberth published visionary treatises on the physics and possibilities of liquid-fueled rockets, American professor Robert Goddard, left, pioneered experimentation with the real things. Goddard's first design, seen here in Massachusetts on the day of its first flight in 1926, featured a rocket with its engine near the nose to pull the weight of the fuel tanks behind it in a flight-stable arrangement.*

*Wernher von Braun, age 18 (right), shoulders a Mirak-series rocket for testing with his Society for Space Travel club fellows at the* Raketenflugplaz, *or rocket testing ground, in Berlin, 1929. Von Braun's boyhood experiments would lead directly to the first large-scale rockets.*

Amateur rocket enthusiasts began forming clubs, and the first and most important was Germany's Society for Space Travel—the *Verein für Raumschiffahrt,* or VfR—founded in 1927. The club members were dedicated to testing Oberth's theories with small-scale model rockets, and the most promising of these young experimenters was a highly intelligent engineering student named Wernher von Braun. A tall, blond, blue-eyed, and strongly built Prussian, von Braun was a natural leader with infectious enthusiasm. He had been experimenting with backyard rockets ever since he was a boy, encouraged by his mother and taught

discipline by his father. A dogged worker and a good organizer, von Braun had also been greatly inspired by Oberth's book, which led him to study mathematics and engineering. After corresponding with Oberth, von Braun eventually became his assistant in Berlin.

At the age of 19, von Braun was working with a small group of experimenters in the VfR. They built their rockets in a run-down shack and conducted their tests at a deserted munitions depot, turning Oberth's theory into their own metal reality and painstakingly learning from trial and error. But they could only go so far. During the depression of the 1930s, financial hard times stifled the VfR's experiments. The club's money ran out, and there were increasing concerns about the safety of the amateur group's rocket tests as the rockets traveled farther and higher. In 1932, von Braun found himself at a crossroads.

*Oberth's book, left, inspired young von Braun, who drew this cutaway view of a manned rocketship in his school notebook, right, at age 16.*

Fritz Lang's silent film *Frau im Mond* showed audiences in 1929 what a journey to the Moon would really look like. The technical advice of rocket theorist Hermann Oberth made *Frau im Mond*

# On the Moon in 1929

a compelling blueprint of the future, and the film left a powerful impression on young people who would one day build the real instruments of the Moon odyssey.

From moondust to acceleration couches, surprisingly accurate touches appear throughout *Frau im Mond*. Thanks to the advanced special effects from Germany's premier film studio UFA, the space travelers even find that their drinking water forms floating spherical blobs in space, just as we would later see in Apollo television transmissions.

But the most impressive part of *Frau im Mond* is the rollout and launch of the Moon rocket. The ship is vertically assembled in a giant building and rolled out ponderously through a massive doorway as the ship stands on a platform with a latticework gantry. Dramatic searchlights play upon the rocket as it creeps toward the launch pad. Every one of these elements of a

Moon launch would one day be brought to pass under the direction of Wernher von Braun and German rocketeers who had seen *Frau im Mond* as students.

The striking appearance of the *Frau im Mond* rocket is echoed in NASA's Saturn V. The *Frau im Mond* spacecraft was painted in a stark black-and-

white scheme. The students in the audience must have registered that this was the way space rockets were supposed to look: Every major rocket built under the German rocketeers' direction would have a black-and-white color scheme just like the rocket in the movie. The Russians would use drab army colors on their Vostok, Soyuz, and N-1 rockets, and the U.S. military would leave the Vanguard, Atlas, and Titan missiles in various bare-metal shades. Only the Germans painted their rockets— from the A-4 to the Saturns—black and white, and they *always* painted them black and white. The scheme was

*A model rocket ship helps sell the bold idea to backers in* Frau im Mond. *demonstrating an approach von Braun would use in America.*

justified as a visual tracking aid . . . but perhaps it just felt right, too. The thrilling countdown to launch certainly did: Invented as a dramatic device for this film, the countdown was used by the German rocketeers in all of their subsequent launches and has become a mainstay of space exploration. In some major ways, the look and feel of Apollo began with Fritz Lang and *Frau im Mond*.

*The dramatic rollout of the vertically assembled black-and-white rocket in the German film* Frau im Mond *strikingly prefigures the Apollo scenes at Cape Canaveral some 30 years in the future.*

## WONDER AND TERROR

**D**reams of space travel and Jules Verne drove the rocket pioneers, but dreams did not pay for metalwork and cryogenic fuels. As rockets grew larger, they grew exponentially more expensive until they were quickly beyond the means of their inventors. There was only one source willing to fund expensive rocket research, and that was the military, which had taken notice of the VfR rocketeers. Von Braun faced a difficult choice when the German army made him an offer in 1932. It was the end of the line or a move into the sphere of military control. With misgivings, von Braun accepted. It was a momentous step. Von Braun's work for the German army would bring about the greatest single advance in 20th-century rocketry, but it would also begin the modern era of military rocketry and open the fearful power of the new kind of rocket to destructive aims.

By 1937, von Braun found himself directing a 10,000-strong team of engineers and support personnel developing rockets at a secret facility on the Baltic Sea called Peenemünde. Launch pads, test stands, factories, and laboratories supported a group of brilliant and capable minds working with the best resources ever placed at the disposal of rocket science. Reichsminister Albert Speer recalled visiting "this circle of nonpolitical young scientists and inventors headed by Wernher von Braun . . . a man comfortably at home in the future." The work Speer saw "was like the planning of a miracle. I was impressed anew by these technicians and their fantastic visions, these mathematical romantics." Von Braun's rocketeers had developed the 46-foot-tall A-4, a giant missile that could boost a one-ton payload to supersonic speed, with a range of some 200 miles. In a very short time, rocket science had taken a quantum leap. And the reckoning came due.

After years of dismissing the work at Peenemünde, in late 1943 Adolf Hitler seized upon von Braun's rocket as a *wünder waffen*, a "wonder weapon," that could wreak vengeance upon the Allies for their wholesale bombing of German cities. The A-4 became the Third Reich's second Vengeance Weapon, the V-2. Over 4,000 V-2 missiles were launched against Belgium, France, and Britain. Hoping that the war would end before his rocket was completed, von Braun was heartbroken when he learned his creations would be launched against civilians.

The distinguished Hermann Oberth was invited to visit the V-2 facilities at one point and was astonished to see the progress that had occurred since his theoretical concepts were published in the 1920s. But it was also apparent to Oberth that the intricate and difficult V-2 design was unsuited for artillery use as compared to some refinement of a solid-fuel rocket. The liquid-fueled V-2 with its cryogenic oxygen required a cumbersome entourage of supplies and support equipment. It became evident to Oberth that von Braun had not been building an ideal artillery missile; he had been building the prototype of a space rocket. Years later, the U.S. Army's Pershing missile would be a practical solid-fuel artillery rocket of exactly the sort Oberth might have recommended during the 1940s.

At Peenemünde, von Braun and his colleagues had been for the most part thinking of space travel even as they built their missiles. Such futurist dreams, together with von Braun's reluctance to release the A-4 for military use, were eventually too much for the Nazi Gestapo. In February 1944, the Gestapo arrested von Braun for squandering national war resources on space-rocket development. The scientist was released from prison two weeks later only by the personal intervention of Albert Speer with Adolf Hitler.

The dreaded SS took control of V-2 production, turning its manufacture into a slave-labor nightmare. As the Allies advanced across Germany near the war's end, the SS ordered the Peenemünde team to destroy its records, parts, and V-2s to prevent them from falling into enemy hands. Wernher von Braun had a different idea. Determined not to be captured by the Russians, von Braun arranged for 300 boxcar

loads of V-2 materials, along with the core group of scientists and engineers, to be secretly taken south and delivered into American possession. This voluntary surrender kept the team and all the precious benefits of their experience together. The U.S. Army had already been looking for the rocket men, so their surrender was welcomed. In a move called Operation Paperclip, dozens of German rocket scientists were brought to America to supervise the testing of the captured V-2s for the U.S. Army.

For the core group of rocketeers closest to von Braun, the migration to America was a chance to put all the deplorable aspects of their recent past behind them. Out of the ruins of the Third Reich, and from the stains of its inhuman deeds, escaped refugees who crossed like so many immigrants before them to a land where there might be a fresh start and a new beginning. Here, there was hope for a renaissance of rocket development on new soil and for a better cause. In America, the land of dreams, there would yet be a chance to reach for the stars.

## THE PLAN FOR SPACE

Based at the White Sands Proving Grounds in New Mexico during the postwar 1940s, von Braun and his team were allowed to do little more than launch the captured and reassembled V-2s as "sounding rockets," fitted now with atmospheric sampling devices. It was frustrating. As von Braun would later observe with disdain, during this time "the United States had no ballistic missile program worth mentioning." The nation was basking in affluence, the economic afterglow of victory. New appliances, stylish cars, and comfort were the national priorities, not rockets.

The outbreak of the Korean War in 1950 gave the rocket team a new assignment. Caught somewhat unprepared by the combat in Korea, the U.S. Army moved von Braun's group to the Redstone Arsenal at Huntsville, Alabama, where they were finally allowed to design the rocket that the V-2 might have been if its development had not been interrupted by war. It took three years. The perfected U.S. V-2 was dubbed the Redstone, a missile with a 200-mile range like the V-2 but with improved guidance and the ability to carry a four-ton payload. The rocket came to be known as "Old Reliable" for its excellent performance record. This was the way a German rocket was supposed to work.

As the German rocket scientists settled in and adjusted to their new life in the United States, von Braun came to a realization. He was following along with a colleague's work when suddenly he looked up and said, "You know what? Even if we continued our calculations until Hell freezes over, we will not touch or move anybody. You may continue your theoretical studies, but I will talk to the people!" Von Braun had seen the path to the future, and he rededicated himself. "We are living in a democracy," he told his friends, "where the will and the mood of the people count.

# A Plan for Space

From 1952 to 1954, *Collier's* magazine introduced the American public to the realistic possibilities ahead for space exploration with a series of articles that inspired many future engineers and rocket scientists. *Collier's* presented von Braun's vision of America's future in space as rendered into dramatic images by some of the country's best illustrators, including Chesley Bonestell.

*Cutaway of von Braun's three-stage ferry rocket concept painted by Rolf Klep. Von Braun envisioned a small fleet of these space shuttles as the cornerstone of a long-term space-exploration program.*

In bringing his vision to the American public through detailed models, paintings, and a painstakingly conceived scenario, von Braun was following a path dramatized in cinema's *Frau im Mond*, where the rocket scientist makes his ideas accessible to backers by some of the same means. Von Braun worked closely with astronomical artist Bonestell and technical illustrators Rolf Klep and Fred Freeman to ensure accuracy in the paintings, and the combined portfolio was so impressive that three books were published collecting and expanding on the series. Many of the features seen in the these paintings later appeared in real space missions.

Von Braun planned a step-by-step approach to the conquest of space, with each step building expertise and hardware for a lasting space exploration infrastructure. Such a scenario might have been a more prudent and constructive investment than the dash to the Moon that von Braun was eventually called upon to support. Von Braun's plan for space still serves today as an instructive example of how to plan for the future with both hard engineering and bold imagination.

Chesley Bonestell painted this dazzling image of von Braun's space shuttle leaving its second-stage booster behind as it heads into the sunrise of a new era. In von Braun's plan, the entire rocket was reusable, and the second stage is deploying a mesh parachute ring to ease its fall into the ocean.

*Orbiting high above Central America, the ferry shuttle delivers cargo to a "space taxi" from the nearby rotating space station, while another space taxi crew services a space telescope, the forerunner of the Hubble.*

## SHUTTLE AND STATION

In the book *Across the Space Frontier* (1952), von Braun detailed his plans for a space shuttle and a permanent space station that would serve as an observation post and a staging point for further exploration. Once satellite rockets had been perfected, von Braun imagined, a manned rocket plane would be developed to carry astronauts and cargo into orbit. Mindful of Verne's observation that low latitudes assist orbit-bound rockets, von Braun placed his launch complex not in Florida but on the even more southern U.S. possession Johnston Island in the South Pacific. From this base a small fleet of canard-winged, shuttle-like "ferry rockets" would operate as the heart of the manned space program. Their huge wings would give the shuttles a low landing speed, slower than jet airliners, allowing the spacecraft to land at conventional airports if necessary. Overcoming the heat of reentry was a problem for which von Braun had no ready solution. The eventual NASA space shuttle's use of ceramic tiles was a brilliant innovation that von Braun never envisioned, though he was confident that experimentation would solve the problem one way or another.

Blasting into space aboard the ferry rockets, astronauts would reach the altitude of 1,075 miles, a two-hour orbit, where they would construct a space-operations platform. Von Braun's space station would be a ring 250 feet in diameter, spinning slowly to produce artificial gravity. The ring station concept had been conceived by Hermann Noordung back in 1927. In the form envisioned by von Braun, it became a staple of futurist visions for the entire second half of the 20th century. Housing three decks and a crew of about 80 in a shirt-sleeve environment, the station would

*A crawler convoy explores the Moon on a 500-mile expedition. The shadows are lit by blue-green earthlight.*

provide an outstanding vantage point for weather observation and Earth survey imaging (including military surveillance). Power would be generated by a parabolic reflector system, which focused sunlight to boil mercury, the space-future incarnation of a coal-fired steam engine. A docking port at the center of the station would counter-rotate at the same speed as the station itself, holding the port stationary relative to other spacecraft for ease of docking. Two-man

*Three Moon landers fire braking thrust en route to the first landing. Built for the airless vacuum of space, the ships are non-streamlined, foreshadowing the Apollo lunar module.*

"space taxis" would transfer astronauts from arriving ferry rockets or carry maintenance crews out to the nearby space telescope, which would peer into the depths of the universe unimpeded by the Earth's atmosphere. With the space station complete, wrote von Braun's friend and coauthor Willy Ley, "the gate to the solar system will have been opened."

## MOON LANDERS

*Conquest of the Moon* (1953) presents von Braun's ambitious vision for pressing outward from Earth orbit. The space station, while serving scientific and experimental purposes, would also serve as a staging point for the construction of a Moon landing mission. Ferry-rocket shuttles would transport the components into orbit, where three 160-foot Moon landers would be constructed: a cargo ship and two crew vessels carrying a total of 50 astronauts. The huge expedition would land in the Moon's Sinus Roris, a flat *mare* plain, and settle in like Antarctic explorers, setting up a sheltered base and preparing an overland

expedition before the onset of 14-day lunar night. Toward the end of the dark period, a special 10-man team would set out in treaded tractor-trailers for the large crater Harpalus 250 miles away, carrying out an extensive scientific survey through a range of lunar landscapes. After six weeks of exploration, only one lander would need to make the return trip, carrying the entire crew back to the space station and into history.

## MARS

**M**ars had early captured von Braun's imagination, and his book *The Mars Project* (1952) not only detailed his engineering analysis of how to reach this distant world but (like Verne

*Von Braun's Mars glider is assembled in orbit near the space station. Huge fuel tanks will be disengaged before the landing.*

*The Mars landing expedition erects the nose section of their glider as a return rocket and sets up camp for over a year of exploration.*

before him) framed his scenario in a work of realistic fiction. *The Exploration of Mars* (1956), written again with Willy Ley, updated the plan and detailed the architecture of a 12-man expedition and its unique lander. Assembled in orbit like the Moon landers, the Mars mission would center around a huge glider with a 450-foot wingspan. This vast glider-lander would carry nine explorers in a dramatic descent to the Martian surface for a grueling land expedition lasting over a year. The round trip would carry its astronauts on an epic voyage of 2 years and 239 days. Mars was still an object of great mystery when the book was written, and the mysterious

Martian "canals" had not yet been detected as optical illusions. New information about Mars would dramatically change our picture of the Red Planet, but when that happened, von Braun would have a new plan ready.

**W**orking out the technical details of all these scenarios made von Braun an engineering expert on space exploration well before any of it had occurred. His visions, brought grandly to life by Bonestell, stirred the American imagination. They also made von Braun the man who could design the real rockets and space stations to carry real astronauts across the space frontier. And the time for assaulting that frontier was coming, sooner than he thought.

If you want to accomplish something as big as travel into space, you must win the people for your idea." Von Braun was determined to do exactly that. "Being diplomatic is necessary, but it is not enough," he decided. "You have to be filled with a burning desire to bring your idea to life. You must have absolute faith in the righteousness of your cause, and in your final success. In short, you must be a kind of a crusader!"

"Luck," read a card he later kept on his desk, "is what happens when preparedness meets opportunity." In 1951 von Braun's old VfR friend Willy Ley organized a private symposium on the future of space and rocketry at New York's Hayden Planetarium. Von Braun delivered an inspiring presentation of his vision, which led to a series of articles in the widely read *Collier's* magazine. From 1952 to 1954, eight *Collier's* articles by von Braun and other experts presented a fascinating and beautifully realized outline for America's future in space. Von Braun offered no casual sketch of possibilities but instead a tightly coherent, well-conceived plan that would stretch over decades, building upon itself to create a complete space infrastructure. The plan's detailed realism, like Verne's fiction, made it especially compelling.

So popular were the *Collier's* articles that Walt Disney approached von Braun to collaborate on television programs that would dramatize the vision of America's future in space. Von Braun rose to the occasion again, and with the designs slightly revised, his plan was presented on Disney's television series. The first episode, entitled *Man in Space,*

*Von Braun's space shuttle as seen on the cover of* Collier's, *1952.*

# Disney's *Man in Space*

Walt Disney teamed with Wernher von Braun to bring von Braun's plan for space to a television audience, preparing the American imagination for the challenges of the space frontier. In three episodes of *Disneyland* broadcast in 1955 and 1957, Disney made the concepts of space travel accessible and fired enthusiasm for the adventure that awaited mankind in space.

Walt Disney and Wernher von Braun collaborated to stir American enthusiasm for space exploration.

**W**alt Disney loved optimistic futurism and had built "Tomorrowland" in his Disneyland theme park to share his enthusiasm for what the future could bring. To promote Tomorrowland, Disney's longtime collaborator and lead animator, Ward Kimball, had the idea of bringing the *Collier's* space exploration scenario to television on the Disney series.

Disney and Kimball wanted their films to be technically accurate, educational entertainment, so they went right to the sources. Joining von Braun for interviews and consultation would be his old friend Willy Ley, now a well-known popular space writer and authority, and Heinz Haber, a space medicine specialist and contributor to the *Collier's* space series.

Three television films were produced as a result of this collaboration of great minds. The first, entitled *Man in Space*, explained the challenges that would face humans traveling into space and detailed von Braun's concepts for a reusable space shuttle, dramatizing one of its missions and ending with a spectacular night landing. *Man and the Moon* continued the scenario with the construction of a great ring space station and the first manned mission around the Moon. This journey (a preview of what would become the real Apollo 8) was portrayed realistically with actors and included a mysterious sighting of unexplained lights on the surface of the Moon, strangely prefiguring events that would occur during the Apollo missions. A final episode in the series, *Mars and Beyond*, was

Von Braun poses with a rocket model in Man in Space.

more fanciful than technical.

Some of von Braun's colleagues regarded the television programs and the *Collier's* articles as self-aggrandizing and a superficial waste of time for a rocket scientist. These academics failed to grasp the importance of popular communication to the advancement of space travel. History has shown that von Braun was right. President Eisenhower had been unsympathetic to von Braun's official requests to launch the first satellite, but *Man in Space* made such a splash that the president himself finally took an interest.

As von Braun had seen in the film Frau im Mond, models could help sell people on new ideas, and he used them constantly, as here in Man in Space.

aired on March 9, 1955, and was watched by an audience of 100 million. *Man in Space* was so popular and so provocative across the nation that president Eisenhower personally called Disney to order a copy for review by his staff and the Pentagon. It felt to many like a new age was just around the corner.

By this time von Braun and his team had almost completed a stretch version of the Redstone, which had an added solid-fuel stage on top. The solid rockets, acting on the staging principle advocated by Tsiolkovsky back in 1903, would ignite when the booster stage had run out of fuel, shooting the upper stage to an even greater height. This "Redstone Plus" configuration was called the Jupiter-C, and in late 1956, von Braun launched one called Missile 27 from the military test range at Cape Canaveral in Florida. The rocket soared up to the incredible height of 680 miles. It was finally within his grasp: This rocket had the power to carry a satellite into space. But von Braun had been ordered to ballast the nose cone with sand. Eisenhower directly forbade the team to put anything into orbit. Missile 29, a backup (the Germans always built backups), could have been fitted with boost-to-orbit capability, but it was mothballed. And then word came that the air force had been given responsibility for all long-range missiles. The army, including von Braun's team at Huntsville, was ordered henceforth to limit itself to short-range "artillery missiles."

Von Braun had done all he could to foster American space progress, but only the White House could provide the leadership to move ahead. Von Braun had succeeded in reaching both a wide range of the American public and the highest levels of U.S. government. And, with his team, he had built the rocket that could take the first steps into space. Von Braun knew that it was all possible, but he also knew that the crucial element was, as he later observed, "the will to do it." He and those of like mind had prepared the American imagination, but it would take outside events to overcome the president's lack of interest.

President and former General Dwight D. Eisenhower had no interest in space exploration. And he specifically did not want such efforts distracting anyone from the important development of military missile capability. The United States needed instruments to deliver atomic bombs to enemies, not scientific widgets into the wild-blue yonder. In a grudging compromise, Eisenhower approved a small U.S. satellite program for the 1957–58 International Geophysical Year, a program coordinating the efforts of hundreds of scientists around the world in geophysical studies. Under the name of Project Vanguard, the United States would try to loft several miniature balls into orbit to aid in the measurement of the Earth's exact shape and size. Vanguard would not be given to the impatient von Braun group but instead to the Naval Research Institute. Eisenhower was determined not to dilute the military missile program with science. Moreover, it was felt that it would not do to have the first U.S. satellite be an accomplishment of a group of Germans. Besides, there wasn't any particular hurry. What did a little satellite really matter?

## THE BATTLE FOR THE HEAVENS

On October 4, 1957, everyone found out what a little satellite really mattered. The news swept America, as it did the entire globe. Millions rushed to their radios and tuned in on the *beep . . . beep . . .* coming from the sky: a sound of the future, a portent. Its source was the first man-made satellite, a Russian device called Sputnik. Americans looked up in dumb astonishment as the moving Russian object traveled over their backyards. It was a stunning victory for the Soviet Union, and the world reeled with the news.

As alarming as the satellite was, the rocket that launched it cast the colder shadow. On October 7, Soviet premier Nikita Khrushchev coolly informed a *New York Times* interviewer that his Soviet Union possessed "every kind of missile necessary for modern war." The home of communism could no longer be dismissed by Americans as a bombastic, backward nation of peasants with an occasionally amusing inferiority complex. Technological superiority equaled military superiority in the postwar world of atom bombs. The implications were apparent to everyone: The world had changed. The Space Age had begun, and the Americans were spectators.

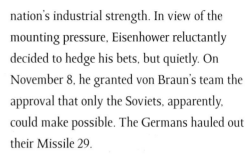

**SPUTNIK**

*Soviet schoolchildren, like people around the world, learned to listen for the first satellite's broadcast signal in October 1957.*

Washington filled with pandemonium and self-recrimination at America's commercial excesses. Loud voices decried the failure of leadership to maintain national pride and national security. Embarrassment flirted with fear at the formidable demonstration of Soviet technological power.

Eisenhower remained nonplussed. "Our satellite program has never been conducted as a race with other nations," he explained at a news conference. While alarmed Americans sputtered and pointed fingers, the Soviets sent another thunderclap rolling across the nation less than a month later. On November 3, they launched *Sputnik II*—six times heavier than the first satellite, and this time carrying a dog named Laika. With redoubled volume and astonishment roiling up from the heartland to Capitol Hill, the Eisenhower administration stuck to its guns, insisting that there was no "space race."

The headlines and popular sentiment of the country shouted otherwise, however, amid a spasm of national self-doubt regarding everything from education to the

*American headlines were filled with the stunning news of the Soviet achievement.*

nation's industrial strength. In view of the mounting pressure, Eisenhower reluctantly decided to hedge his bets, but quietly. On November 8, he granted von Braun's team the approval that only the Soviets, apparently, could make possible. The Germans hauled out their Missile 29.

Meanwhile, the "official" U.S. satellite project at the Naval Research Institute prepared for a first launch test. Vanguard's liftoff would take place in time to make the von Braun project redundant. Under the intense media scrutiny of an America waiting desperately for something to salve the national pride, the Vanguard rocket was prepared for launch at Cape Canaveral. On December 6, 1957, the slender, delicate instrument was fired, began to rise, and then sank back down on itself, crushing its engines and erupting into a huge fireball. The pathetic collapse was carried live on television, right in front of the world. *This* was what we were capable of, while the Russians rode the heavens. Grown men felt nausea.

Out of its garage, von Braun's Redstone Plus emerged into floodlights and hope. The rocket bore the same kind of black-and-white color scheme that von Braun had seen as a boy on Hermann Oberth's Moon rocket from *Frau im Mond*. Now it wasn't a model or a cinematic illusion. It was an eight-story machine filling with liquid oxygen and kerosene, carrying a small satellite in its nose. Von Braun knew every rivet in the rocket's structure and could feel the entire assembly in his bones. It was no longer a youthful dream or a Chesley Bonestell painting so realistic that it made you ache for it to be true. Now it was a hissing, fuming metal reality, surrounded by the gantries and colleagues and people who made it all work, in the nation where it could lead the way to so much more. It was fulfillment and beginning.

On January 31, 1958, the Jupiter-C was cleared for its launch attempt, and at the end of a countdown that sounded just like the one in *Frau im Mond*, the black-and-white rocket ignited. It rose on a jet of flame and lifted into the sky. After a tense interval, Goldstone tracking

## VANGUARD

*In full view of the world, America's first attempt at a satellite launch explodes into a sickening fireball at Cape Canaveral on December 6, 1957. The psychological impact of this failure served to underscore the frightening achievement of the Soviet Sputnik satellite. The Naval Research Institute Vanguard rocket held a tiny satellite weighing only 3.25 pounds, but the engineers did not have the experience of the U.S. Army's von Braun rocket team. It would be up to von Braun to rescue American pride after the Vanguard disaster.*

**EXPLORER** *I*

*Jet Propulsion*
*Laboratory director*
*William H. Pickering,*
*scientist James Van*
*Allen, and Wernher*
*von Braun hold a*
*replica of the first*
*successful American*
*satellite in celebration.*

station in California detected the little satellite, which had come all the way around the Earth. The team had done it. The first American satellite was in orbit. Sailing around the Earth in the realm of space, it was given a name: Explorer. And the headlines loved it.

After further failures, a Vanguard finally made it into orbit, followed by a second Explorer. One can only imagine what the Soviets thought of these little projects as they blasted *Sputnik III* into orbit in May. You could hold Explorer in your hands, and you could almost put the 3.25-pound chrome grapefruit that was Vanguard in your coat pocket, but

*Man of the hour, von Braun saved the*
*day for America with* Explorer I.

monstrous *Sputnik III* weighed 3,000 pounds, the equivalent of a significant bomb. The headlines trumpeted American pride, but anyone who was paying attention knew that the Soviets were far ahead.

## THE ULTIMATE CHALLENGE

It would take time for America to commit itself fully to this technological race with the Soviets, perhaps in part because the competition took a new form. It was oddly indirect—an arms race waged in the name of exploration and science. The two superpowers had become like Irish Elk, competing with antlers that were seen as expressions of inner strength. Eisenhower understood real arms races but not this symbolic contest. Most Americans felt the alarm of the Space Race at a gut level. And in such a time, the president needed not just to respond to the challenge but to lead the nation through it. The situation was not

# Soviet Moon Probes

The Soviet Union had sent up three Sputniks by 1958 and had the first man in orbit by 1961, largely owing to the genius and drive of one man, Soviet rocket mastermind Sergei Korolev. Korolev's rockets gave his nation a strong opening lead, threw down the gauntlet of the Space Race, and would become the first engines reaching for the Moon.

*The U.S.S.R.'s unknown "chief designer" of rockets, Sergei Korolev*

**W**hile America was still struggling to get anything larger than a baseball bat into orbit, the Soviets dispatched a series of probes beyond Earth orbit. Korolev's rugged heavy-lift R-7 rocket had boosted the Sputniks into space; next it would hurl probes called Luna at the Moon.

Even the Russians had had difficulty with the new higher goal. The first Luna missed the Moon by 3,000 miles and went flying off into deep space, never to be seen again. *Pravda* cleverly touted it as the first probe in orbit around the Sun. The second Luna successfully smashed into the Moon, making it the first man-made object ever to land in the heavens.

The Soviets put a camera into *Luna 3* and got it to circle around the Moon in late 1959. While traveling through space, *Luna 3* developed its own film, scanned it, and sent signals back to Earth, producing the first interplanetary fax. The images were crude, but they were mankind's first glimpse at the far side of the Moon.

The next milestone would be to land a camera. The Soviets spent three years developing a Luna that could ease in for a landing and then spent three more years trying to get the blasted things onto the Moon. Engine malfunctions from 1963 to 1965 sent Lunas all over the solar system or whacked them into the Moon at fatal velocities, aggravating their Soviet masters. It was February 3, 1966, before *Luna 9* finally achieved the first lunar soft landing on the Moon's Ocean of Storms. The lander opened its petals like a mechanical flower and looked around to transmit home the first picture of the lunar surface.

The Soviet achievements were impressive, but the greatest challenges of the space race lay ahead. Known for many years only as the "chief designer," Korolev died unexpectedly in 1966, and the Soviets would find that their early lead could not be sustained without him.

*The Soviet Luna 9 probe transmitted the first pictures from the surface of the Moon in 1966.*

a simple one that could be solved with prosaic measures; the arena was global, the prize intangible yet crucial. The challenge demanded vision.

Eisenhower responded to the Sputnik problem by creating the National Aeronautics and Space Administration, or NASA, on October 1, 1958. This civilian agency would keep space exploration and science separate from the military missile programs. NASA was assembled from a group of existing laboratories that had been loosely allied as the National Advisory Council on Aviation, an aeronautical research organization and a rich reservoir of creative talent. Eventually, NASA incorporated both von Braun's army team from Huntsville and the Vanguard group from the Naval Research Institute. NASA was given the task of putting an American man in space, and in light of the sense of urgency, the project was called Mercury, for the fleet-footed classical god.

While the engineers began to design the rockets and spacecraft, NASA planners began to design the space pilots. These men would be the first to bear the title *astronaut*. In view of the challenge of flying a new kind of craft, they would be chosen from among military test pilots. The astronauts would also be college graduates between the ages of 25 and 40, no taller than 5 feet 11 inches. And in the time-honored military tradition for extraordinarily dangerous missions, they would be volunteers. From the air force, navy, and marines, over 100 qualified pilots stepped forward and were put through an unprecedented screening process of thorough and elaborate physical tests and medical analyses until the group was winnowed down to just seven. The call had been for six, but this group defied further refinement by any criteria the doctors and specialists could devise. NASA accepted all seven men.

The astronauts personified America's response to the Soviet challenge in space. On April 9, 1959, they were introduced to the American public,

## CHALLENGERS

Above, *the superb NASA emblem designed for the space agency's inception in 1958 by the army's Institute of Heraldry. The original Mercury Seven astronauts,* right, *personified America's response to the Soviet space challenge.* Top row, from left: *Alan Shepard, Gus Grissom, and Gordon Cooper.* Front row, from left: *Wally Schirra, Deke Slayton, John Glenn, and Scott Carpenter.*

which received them, in the apt metaphor of Tom Wolfe, as single-combat warriors, representing the entire nation in the new and desperate battle of technology in space. The astronauts became known as the Mercury Seven—the Original Seven—and they became powerful symbols. Having come through such rugged testing and headed for such tremendous unknowns at the apex of our national capabilities, they were regarded with a kind of awe. They symbolized the entire national space effort, which was easier for the public to grasp in the form of seven brave individuals. So the nation vested its hopes in them, as the Soviets ruled the skies.

**D**uring the presidential elections of 1960 there was much talk about the American-Soviet "missile gap" and the faltering of American leadership. The Democratic opponent ran on a campaign pledge to "get the country moving again," and America elected as its new president a young visionary named John F. Kennedy. "Let the word go forth," Kennedy said boldly at his inauguration, "that the torch has been passed to a new generation of Americans."

The Soviets meanwhile maintained an unrelenting pace. What they had accomplished with the Sputniks was the first sign of a full-fledged space program, conducted in earnest. Kennedy had plenty of other things on his mind in the early months of his administration when the latest Soviet space victory hit the newspapers. On April 12, 1961, the Russians rocketed their first man into space. Yuri Gagarin was not only in space, he had orbited the Earth in a spacecraft called *Vostok,* Russian for "East." The same R-7 rocket that had lofted the Sputniks had been equipped with an added stage, giving the assembly enough power to orbit a manned spacecraft. Upon recovery, cosmonaut Gagarin exulted, "Now let the other countries try to catch us." Soviet Premier Nikita Khrushchev added, "Let the capitalist countries catch up with our country, which has blazed the trail into outer space." It

## GAGARIN

*Yuri Gagarin beat America's astronauts into space, blasting all the way into orbit on April 12, 1961. This major Soviet "first" prompted U.S. President Kennedy to examine his options for a space objective that America could win.*

could not be clearer that space had become a global battleground of ideologies, and up there, the Soviets ruled.

Five days later, just over four months into the new president's term, the United States suffered the humiliating defeat of CIA-sponsored forces in an attempted invasion of Cuba at the Bay of Pigs. American prestige was at an all-time low. On April 19, the last of the demolished forces were withdrawn from the Bay of Pigs. The president sought desperately for something that could rebuild the American image, and on April 20, Kennedy gave Vice President Lyndon Johnson a memorandum. "I would like," the president wrote, "for you as Chairman of the Space Council to be in charge of making an overall survey of where we stand in space. Do we have a chance of beating the Soviets by putting a laboratory in space, or by a trip around the Moon, or by a rocket to land on the Moon, or by a rocket to go to the Moon and back with a man? Is there any other space program which promises dramatic results in which we could win?" This memo set in motion the first stirrings of a tremendous mobilization.

## KENNEDY'S MEMO

*Less than two weeks after Gagarin's orbital flight, Kennedy drafted this memo to Vice President Lyndon Johnson that would set America on the course for the Moon.*

**M**eanwhile, NASA had prepared a different kind of payload for the "Old Reliable" Redstone. Contractor McDonnell Aircraft in Saint Louis had created the Mercury capsule, a stubby cone packed with equipment and a seat. The capsule sat on top of the Redstone, giving the assembly a height of 93 feet. This was a missile stretched with a nose cone that a man could, just barely, cram into. And we were going to ignite almost 30 tons of liquid oxygen and kerosene underneath him and hope that it all stayed under control.

On May 5, 1961, 37-year-old navy commander Alan Shepard was strapped and bolted into the capsule he had named *Freedom 7*. After a suspenseful, delayed countdown, Shepard blasted into the sky. At the peak of his flight, he reached 115 miles above the Atlantic Ocean, weightless like a diver who has just taken a tremendous leap from a diving board, hanging in that place between up and down where gravity has released the body and weight is nothing. Shepard arced through that moment for five full minutes before his capsule began to decelerate, buffeted by the thickening atmosphere as he dropped. Parachutes deployed, and he splashed down as planned, 304 miles off the Florida coast. The first manned Mercury flight was a success.

**FIRST OF THE SEVEN**

*Alan Shepard is wished a safe flight by his fellow astronaut Gus Grissom just before Shepard boards the* Freedom 7 *spacecraft capsule for America's first manned rocket launch.*

**S**eventeen days later, on May 25, Kennedy stood in the U.S. Capitol before a joint session of Congress. He had received Lyndon Johnson's reply to the space memo and had made his decision. There was a major goal that we had a chance of winning—one that hung higher than an orbiting laboratory might, one that offered a real destination, the only one within our possible reach, and one that the entire world could see: the Moon.

"These are extraordinary times. And we face an extraordinary challenge. Our strength as well as our convictions have imposed upon this nation the role of leader in freedom's cause. . . .

"If we are to win the battle that is going on around the world between freedom and tyranny, if we are to win the battle for men's minds, the dramatic achievements in space which occurred in recent weeks should have made clear to us all, as did the Sputnik in 1957, the impact of this adventure on the minds of men everywhere who are attempting to make a determination of which road they should take.

"Now it is time to take longer strides—time for a great new American enterprise—time for this nation to take a clearly leading role in space achievement, which in many ways may hold the key to our future on earth.

"I believe we possess all the resources and talents necessary. But the facts of the matter are that we have never made the national decision or marshaled the national resources required for such leadership. We have never specified the long-range goals on an urgent time schedule, or managed our resources and our time so as to insure their fulfillment.

"Recognizing the head start obtained by the Soviets with their large rocket engines . . . and recognizing the likelihood that they will exploit this lead for some time to come in still more impressive successes, we nevertheless are required to make new efforts on our own. For while we cannot guarantee that we shall one day be first, we can guarantee that any failure to make this effort will make us last. We take an additional risk by making it in full view of the world, but as shown by the feat of astronaut Shepard, this very risk enhances our stature when we are successful. . . .

"I believe this nation should commit itself to achieving the goal, before the decade is out, of landing a man on the Moon and returning him safely to the Earth. No single space project in this period will be more impressive to mankind, or more important for the long-range exploration of space, and none will be so difficult or expensive to accomplish."

The speech was candid and inspiring. The battle was for global stature, the object to win people's minds to the path of democracy and freedom. Failure in this battle would leave the world in the hands of tyranny. Like dominance combat between bull animals, the cost of the

**FREEDOM 7**

*America's first manned
rocket launch, May 1961:
The Mercury-Redstone
carrying Alan Shepard
lifts off from a small but
historic launch pad at
Cape Canaveral.
Cryogenic liquid oxygen
in the lower half of the
rocket makes the hull
cold and shrouds it in
condensed water vapor.
The Redstone was
designed by von Braun
and his German
rocketeers and painted
black and white to aid in
visual tracking. The color
scheme also echoed the
look of the visionary
spaceship of the film
Frau im Mond.*

effort would prove out the victor. And as in so many other great ventures, there was little suspicion at the beginning of where it was really leading, of what it would really mean.

As the young president spoke his words in a calm, clear voice, America hung in the moment that Alan Shepard had just experienced. The richest and most powerful nation the world had ever known committed itself to a goal that would leave its mark on history for all time.

## MERCURY

**W**e had just launched our first man into space, a five-minute visit only 115 miles high, and we were still calculating with slide rules. Our abilities were absolutely primitive, yet Kennedy had committed us to reaching the Moon by 1970. It was a tremendous statement of faith in all that the nation could bring to the challenge.

The president was not unaware of the magnitude of what he had done. In fact, it was exactly the magnitude of the massive undertaking that made the Moon commitment the only move in the geopolitical chess game with the Soviets that could give America a chance to recover. In a speech at Rice University in 1962, the visionary president spelled it out:

*"We choose to go to the Moon in this decade—and do the other things—not because they are easy but because they are hard.*

*"We set sail on this new sea because there is new knowledge to be gained and new rights to be won. And they must be won and used for the progress of all mankind.*

*"We shall send to the Moon, 240,000 miles away from the control station in Houston, a giant rocket more than 300 feet tall, made of new metal alloys, some of which have not yet been invented, capable of standing heat and stresses several times more than have ever been experienced, fitted together with a precision better than the finest watch, carrying all the equipment needed for propulsion, guidance, control, communications, food, and survival . . . on an untried mission to an*

*unknown celestial body. And therefore, as we set sail, we ask God's blessing on the most hazardous and dangerous and greatest adventure on which man has ever embarked."*

Kennedy's words, delivered with passion and charisma, forged the inspiration and commitment that the nation needed to go to the Moon. Accomplishing this goal would require superhuman abilities; it was not a task that America's engineers and scientists could simply carry out at the executive order. No mere policy could specify that thousands upon thousands of workers and managers stretch themselves to their mental and physical limits for years to accomplish this impossible goal within a decade. The necessary commitment to endless late hours and intense sustained effort across such a broad group of people would have to come from a genuine shared belief in the magnitude and significance of the great undertaking. Kennedy's leadership stirred the emotion that made this united national commitment possible.

### VISIONARIES

*Kennedy committed America to reaching the Moon before anyone was certain how it might be possible. The man who had the expertise to design a Moon rocket was von Braun, seen here with Kennedy and (as ever) a model of his latest rocket proposal— a prototype Saturn.*

**W**e would have to take increasingly bold steps. Indiana astronaut Gus Grissom rode a second Redstone up to that 115-mile point before curving back to a splashdown in the Bahamas. Now, could we get a man to circle the Earth? The Redstone couldn't do it; it was no equal to the heavy-duty Soviet R-7. An astronaut in a capsule was just too heavy. So for the second phase of Project Mercury, NASA adapted the nation's first intercontinental ballistic missile, the air force's Atlas rocket, only recently developed, to carry a Mercury capsule rather than a nuclear bomb.

The Atlas rocket did not have the reliable Redstone performance record, but it was the

only tool available to do the job in 1962. Its walls were so thin that the vehicle would collapse under its own weight without pressurization inside its tanks. But the Atlas had the strength to hurl a one-man capsule to orbital velocity.

Astronaut Col. John Glenn would be that man. On February 20, 1962, piloting the third manned Mercury space capsule, he circled the Earth three times. With Glenn in orbit, America went berserk. John Glenn came back from the realm of the heavens, and New York erupted in praise and celebration for his return.

Subsequent Mercury flights tested astronauts' ability to carry out scientific experiments in orbit and extended the mission duration to prove out the limits of both man and machine. The sixth and last Mercury flight carried Gordon Cooper around the Earth over 30 times in May 1963. Cooper orbited his home planet in a corrugated can that would leak if left in water for too long. He flew in the lethal vacuum of space at a speed of 17,000 mph, at an altitude of 190 miles, entirely out of reach of any material assistance if things went wrong. And this flight was designed to test the endurance of the machine, to see when things *would* go wrong.

On the 19th orbit, the first fault in the electrical system was noticed. The problems were compounded during subsequent orbits, the electrical power surging and shorting out systems until the spacecraft was barely functioning. John Glenn, serving as communications link to the astronaut in orbit, had to relay line-by-line instructions from Mission Control to Cooper, instructing him on how to bring his ship home without the automatic control system. If it had not been piloted by a human astronaut, the mission would certainly have been lost. We were still just learning how things worked in space. And one thing we learned was that the Mercury capsule couldn't take it indefinitely. With his systems malfunctioning and controllers wondering whether they could even get him down alive, Cooper reentered the atmosphere on manual control. In a hypersonic fireball born of friction with the air, Cooper returned to blue skies, to make a successful Pacific splashdown in the aptly named *Faith 7*. We had learned all we could from the Mercury program and taken it to its limits.

## GEMINI: TRAINING FOR THE MOON

To reach the Moon, NASA had defined a project called Apollo. But as planners looked ahead, they realized that there was a great deal more to learn before Apollo could be conducted with any confidence. Even as the Apollo hardware was being designed and prototyped, NASA initiated a separate project that would train and test every part of the system—controllers, astronauts, designs, and techniques—for the tremendously complex Apollo missions ahead. This interim program would be called Gemini. McDonnell Douglas Astronautics built a two-seater version of the corrugated space capsule as the planners set out their goals. Very specific questions needed to be answered.

To carry out the Moon mission, we would have to link up two ships in orbit. Could we actually achieve space rendezvous, or would it be impossible to dock two ships shooting around the planet? No one knew. Further, it would take over a week to get to the Moon and back. Cooper's Mercury ship had seemed as if it wouldn't last another five minutes. Could we keep man and machine in space safely for long enough to accomplish the landing and return? Apollo crews would need to operate outside the spacecraft. Could an astronaut leave his ship and safely move around without its protection? Could he accomplish work while weightless? Mercury had given us the basics. Gemini would be our training ground for lunar operations.

As Project Gemini moved into gear, the American Moon effort took on a mighty scale, with huge increases in NASA's budget powering a massive mobilization unheard of in peacetime. NASA directly employed 33,200 people, and space contracts were scattered through some 20,000 companies across the nation, employing a vast labor force to solve the problems and build the devices that would take America to the Moon. Kennedy's vision had forged the national commitment, and the vast Apollo team's work ethic was extraordinary, displaying the commitment and the sense of common duty and higher purpose that only war had ever been able to muster before.

All this was possible only because it felt like a war, at least at first. Sputnik and Yuri Gagarin's orbital flight had so powerfully stricken the nation with fear and alarm that Kennedy's impossibly grand vision had drawn strong support in Congress for the necessary funding. By the days of Gemini, the "Sputnik effect" had lost some of its edge. Reassured by our own space efforts, we no longer felt quite so far behind. But the Russians kept up their lead with one spectacular feat after another, maintaining a residual Sputnik effect that was enough to hold off a complete return to American complacency.

In June 1963, the Soviets sent up *Vostok VI,* which carried Valentina Tereshkova, the first female cosmonaut. Tereshkova was not even a pilot, and the flight was no more than a stunt, but it made the history books with a first. Firsts won prestige, and prestige was the goal of the space race. In the fall of 1964, while NASA was still struggling to ready its two-man Gemini capsule, the Soviets astonished our engineers by sending up *Voskhod I,* a ship crewed by *three* men. Our

spacecraft designers could only shake their heads.

A spectacular achievement that would amaze the world was unveiled six months later. In the spring of 1965, cosmonaut Alexei Leonov stepped out of his Voskhod into space. While his pilot flew the ship, Leonov emerged from an inflatable airlock and spent 10 pioneering minutes "spacewalking." Photos showed Leonov on this incredible high-ground frontier wearing the Cyrillic letters CCCP, the brand and blazon of the enemy. The Soviets were still far ahead of the United States. The rocket that sent Leonov's Voskhod into orbit was *three times* as powerful as the Titan II of the Gemini program.

**L**eonov's space walk had raised the bar, and the United States had to respond. After two unmanned Gemini flights and then a shakedown voyage piloted by Mercury astronaut Gus Grissom, we would send Gemini 4 up to match Leonov's feat. And with superior Kodak film, we would try to make ours look better.

On June 3, 1965, astronaut Ed White opened the hatch of the Gemini 4 capsule while his command pilot Jim McDivitt flew the ship. The Gemini had no air lock, so the two astronauts had bled their cabin atmosphere off to space before opening the hatch. Ed White breathed air supplied by a golden umbilical cable and unstrapped himself from his seat. He stood up, and then drifted away, weightless, slowly tumbling above the dazzling sight of the entire planet Earth moving below him.

**FRIENDSHIP 7**

*John Glenn's spacecraft lifts off atop an air force Atlas, a silvery intercontinental missile more powerful than the Redstone. The Atlas would boost the Mercury capsule not just a short hop into space but into orbit around the Earth.*

## STARS AND STRIPES IN SPACE

*The United States was still striving to catch up to Soviet space "firsts" with Gemini 4, which in June 1965 sent James McDivitt and Ed White,* shown at right, *into orbit for the first American space walk. Until Gemini 4, U.S. astronauts had worn only the NASA seal on their spacesuits. White and McDivitt bought their own large American flag patches and had them sewn to their uniforms as a statement of patriotism. U.S. astronauts would always wear the flag after this flight.*

A vibrant, intense blue shone up from the oceans. A million scintillating white clouds glittered like fresh snow in bright sunlight. The colors of the land below were subtle and infinite. Beholding all this, White felt the sensation that you feel when a roller coaster plunges down a hill. He was falling endlessly around the world. He was exhilarated, captivated by the experience that only one other man had ever felt, being out here suspended in nothingness. And he felt no fear at all. On the ground, they could not see the wonderment in Ed White's face.

The astronaut caught the sun as he turned. A golden, mirrored visor shielded his eyes, making him an enigmatic figure in the photos that would come back to Earth. Against the unknown factors of the realm he soared through, he had the thin layers of his $28,000 space suit. What of meteoroids hurtling through the abyss? What of cosmic rays or as-yet-undiscovered hazards? His nation had prepared him as well as it could, and now he was on the front line. What he really wore was a suit of Space-Age armor, for a symbolic battle that took place amid real dangers. On White's shoulder was the pennant of the cause: a big American flag, its red, white, and blue colors radiant in the unfiltered sunlight.

All too soon, flight control radioed up that it was time to return. Gus Grissom was the Capsule Communicator, or Capcom, the one man who relayed Mission Control's message to his fellow astronaut in orbit. "Get back in," Grissom directed White.

"Back in?" White said, wanting more time.

"Back in," confirmed McDivitt.

"This is fun," White said. "I don't want to come back in, but I'm coming."

The idyll's time was over. "Let's get you back in here before it gets dark," McDivitt urged his shipmate.

It turned out to be a bit tricky to do that. Without handholds, tumbling with nothing to grip or push against, White had a slow time returning to his seat. But soon enough he was settled. It was over. White turned to his pilot.

"It's the saddest moment of my life," he said with a smile.

The photos McDivitt had taken revealed this space walk to the world in all its glorious color, and an amazed America shared in the space knight's heroism. A beautiful U.S. postage stamp was quickly commissioned, a two-parter showing Gemini 4 on one side and spacewalker Ed White on the other. What an age of marvels this was.

There was wonder, and there was hard work. Every single Gemini flight advanced the state of the art toward the goal of mastering the skills needed to accomplish the Moon mission. To practice the rendezvous of the spacecraft and its lander, Wally Schirra's Gemini 6 was supposed to hunt down and catch up to an unmanned Agena rocket stage, but the Agena malfunctioned and exploded shortly after launch. Flight controllers came up with a somewhat daring alternative: Schirra could chase Gemini 7. Commander Frank Borman and his copilot Jim Lovell would launch first and stay in space for a record-setting two-week endurance test, along the way serving as the rendezvous target for Schirra and his copilot, Tom Stafford.

Borman's Gemini 7 blasted into orbit on December 4, 1965, leaving behind the usual destruction to launch pad 19, the only one rated for Gemini launches. Titan rockets packed a punch that the Redstones hadn't. The crews, who usually had two months to repair everything, did the work in a day. Schirra and Stafford were atop a Titan missile in their Gemini space capsule in record time. And it was about to get interesting.

**NEW GEAR**

*During Ed White's adventure in open space, a golden umbilical cord connected him with his Gemini spacecraft and provided the spacewalker with oxygen. To maneuver, White carried a gas jet gun that could pull him forward with triggered bursts.*

**KODAK MOMENT**
*Ed White's first U.S.
space walk on Gemini 4
was one of the shortest in
American space history,
but none has ever been
photographed more
beautifully. Mission
commander Jim
McDivitt captured the
images, which inspired a
U.S. postage stamp.*

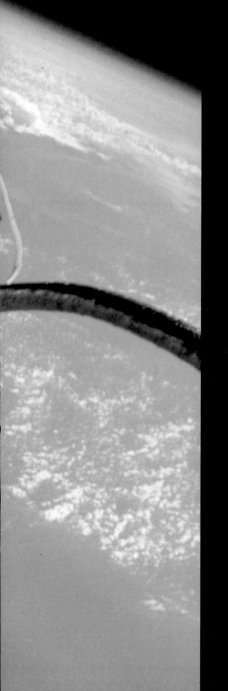

Richard Gordon sits
astride his spacecraft
advancing NASA's
knowledge and expertise
in extravehicular activity,
or E.V.A. Spacewalking
would be an important
capability on the Apollo
lunar missions.

## THE RIGHT TOUCH

Buzz Aldrin developed
an effective approach to
spacewalking that used
technique rather than
force to deal with the
weightless environment.
Aldrin is seen here
during the second
day of the four-day
Gemini 12 mission.

Borman and Lovell were orbiting 203 miles above, waiting for their compatriots to join them. The Gemini 6 countdown hit zero, and the Titan's dual engines bellowed flame, building thrust. The astronauts braced themselves for the rising acceleration of launch, and then felt the roar suddenly stop, an ominous silent gulf like a jet-engine flameout. Nothing like this had ever happened. In that stunned instant, time stood still, so much hanging on the suspended moment. If the rocket had left the pad, if it were hanging even a foot above the surface, it would settle back down and then burst into a horrible explosion like Vanguard had done. The event nearly stopped hearts.

**MISFIRE**

*Mission commander
Wally Schirra coolly
averted disaster during
the Gemini 6 aborted
launch. For moments no
one knew whether the
rocket would explode.
Asked by radio if he and
his crewman Tom Stafford
were all right after the
harrowing near miss,
Schirra quipped, "We're
just sitting here bleeding."*

A hundred feet above the engines, inside the two-seater capsule, Schirra's hand was on a D-ring that would eject him and Stafford from the Gemini. This spacecraft had no escape tower, only dangerous, jet-fighter-style ejection seats. At low altitude, ejection could kill the astronauts instead of saving their lives. As one of the original Mercury Seven, Schirra had been chosen from the best of the best, and he didn't pull the ring. An explosion seemed imminent, but it hadn't happened yet, and until it did, he wasn't pulling. Launch controllers quickly determined that an automated system had detected an anomaly and shut down the engines before liftoff; the situation was not critical, and there would be no explosion. If Schirra had followed the rule book, the mission would have been lost. As it was, "cool hand" Schirra was back in the same capsule a few days later, and this time, Gemini 6 roared skyward.

Entering orbit, Schirra and Stafford followed flight-plan directives from Mission Control, which was carefully tracking both ships. Once within visual range, Schirra

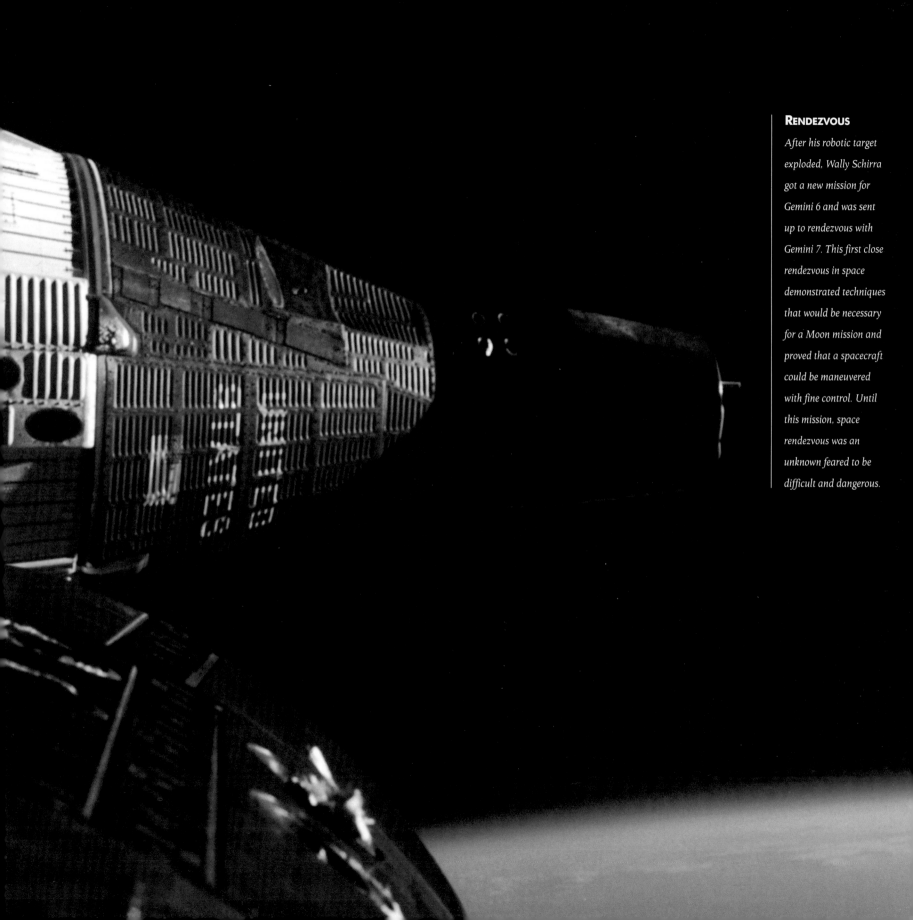

## RENDEZVOUS

*After his robotic target exploded, Wally Schirra got a new mission for Gemini 6 and was sent up to rendezvous with Gemini 7. This first close rendezvous in space demonstrated techniques that would be necessary for a Moon mission and proved that a spacecraft could be maneuvered with fine control. Until this mission, space rendezvous was an unknown feared to be difficult and dangerous.*

jockeyed his capsule to race down Frank Borman's drifting Gemini 7. After 13 days cramped in the tiny capsule with shipmate Lovell, the stern, professional Borman was glad of something new to do. Schirra moved in closer and closer until the two capsules were only a few feet apart, racing over the continents and oceans at about Mach 25, or 25 times the speed of sound.

They had achieved close rendezvous, proving that the Gemini rocket thruster systems could control fine maneuvering. Now NASA needed to prove that two spacecraft could make a "hard dock" in space, actually linking the two craft. This would take outstanding piloting skill, but on Gemini 8 there would be an outstanding pilot at the controls. Gemini 8 would test him, but he had already been through plenty. He had flown the X-15.

The X-15 test vehicle had put its pilots in the nose of a big, black rocket engine with small geometric bits of fins stuck on it. The "plane" could scream up to altitudes of 40 miles, at the edge of space, and could hit record-breaking speeds of over 4,000 mph. The searing velocities ripped the paint off the ship, and the hypersonic atmosphere buffeting the cockpit wanted to shatter the small windows, which NASA accordingly made smaller and then even half armor-covered. There was practically no air at the X-15's operational ceiling, so they had to equip the vehicle with rocket maneuvering thrusters like the Gemini capsules had. One of the X-15 pilots had become a full-time astronaut in the group of nine who followed the Mercury Seven, and his name was Neil Armstrong. He would be commanding Gemini 8, going up with David Scott to make the first hard dock in space.

Quiet, serious, and cool under pressure, Armstrong was a consummate professional. At his hands, Gemini 8 tracked down an Agena target and made the first successful hard dock in space. But then a faulty thruster misfired, sending the joined spacecraft tumbling wildly. Armstrong stabilized them and jettisoned the Agena target, but the continuing misfire was on their own ship, and it spun them again, faster and faster. The two pilots fought against mounting g forces as they tried to get control of their spinning ship before they blacked out. Armstrong made an emergency decision to use their reentry fuel system. Counter-firing thrust bursts with extraordinary skill, Armstrong got the ship stabilized. They were brought down for an emergency landing in the Pacific. It would not be the last time that Neil Armstrong had to take over manual control in an emergency.

After Ed White's dreamlike space walk on Gemini 4, NASA needed to know whether an astronaut could effectively work out there. Gene Cernan, copilot of Gemini 9, took on this challenge and found out, in space, that it was not easy. In fact, in weightlessness, with nothing to hold onto, he found that his task was nearly impossible. Wheeling around in space, Cernan struggled to get control. He was as strong as any of the astronauts, but his strength was doing him no good in this environment. As his heart rate rose to 180, his helmet faceplate began fogging up. Soon he would be blind. The more he struggled, the less control he had. Cernan sweated furiously as alarm crept up. They would later find that he had lost *10 pounds* from the effort, spending over two hours outside the spacecraft. Even with careful direction from his shipmate, Cernan was barely able to get back into his capsule. Any further delay might have made the outcome much worse.

# Military Space?

Space exploration developed as a peaceful pursuit, but history could have been very different. The U.S. Army developed extensive plans for a 12-man moonbase called Project Horizon, which might have been operational in 1966 if the program had gained approval. Lunar outpost Horizon never made it off the drawing board, but other military space programs did.

In 1933, German rocket scientist Eugen Sänger designed the infamous Silverbird, an intercontinental rocket bomber that could have reached New York. Ignored by the Third Reich, Sänger's military spaceplane concept was picked up in 1956 by the U.S. Air Force, which began developing the X-20, a one-man orbital bomber called Dyna-Soar for "dynamic soaring," since the rocket-launched plane would glide back to Earth. A prototype was test-flown over the Atlantic, pilots were selected, and the first manned launch was planned for 1966. But in December 1963

Dyna-Soar was canceled, just six months before the first spacecraft would be ready for tests.

Secretary of Defense Robert McNamara had chosen to divert the X-20's funds into a new program called Manned Orbiting Laboratory, or M.O.L. The M.O.L. would be a small military space station whose missions included defense reconnaissance, satellite interception, and the development of military space capability. NASA Gemini capsules would ferry the crews. M.O.L. was, in the words of Journal and

Register space editor James Haggerty, "an ominous harbinger" of a change in direction from the civilian to the military conquest of space and a sign that "the military services may play a more prominent role in future space exploration at NASA's expense." A M.O.L. "boilerplate" dummy was test-launched in 1966, and a full prototype of the station was completed in 1968. The first manned launch was set for 1972, but M.O.L. was canceled in 1969.

Under President Nixon, the air force was directed to exploit NASA's space shuttle rather than develop space capabilities of its own. Haggerty's 1964 prediction came true as the military made heavy classified use of the space

shuttle in the 1980s. On these secret missions soldier-astronauts manned the shuttle. The air force even constructed its own shuttle launch complex at Edwards Air Force Base in California. The explosion of the *Challenger* in 1986 abruptly ended military interest in the NASA shuttle, which had become a descendant of the X-20 Dyna-Soar and Eugen Sänger's German Silverbird.

*The air force actually launched a dummy version of its military space station M.O.L. on November 3, 1966.*

*The U.S. Air Force Dyna-Soar shuttle would have been launched on a Titan III rocket, shown here as a model.*

This was bad: Apollo would require space-walk capability in case a docking tunnel hatch jammed and the astronauts had to transfer from one ship to another by working their way outside from one main entry hatch to the other. Extravehicular activity, NASA called it, or E.V.A. If it turned out to be impractical, Apollo would lose a key safety measure.

The problem was solved by Buzz Aldrin, or "Dr. Rendezvous" as he came to be called. The only Ph.D. in the early astronaut corps, Aldrin had written his doctoral thesis on orbital mechanics. As an intellectual, he took a different approach to the space-walk problem from the test pilots'. Aldrin took advantage of training underwater, where neutral buoyancy could be achieved and the effects of weightlessness simulated. When Aldrin went up on Gemini 12, he proved out his ideas and accomplished his tasks without even breaking a sweat. It was all a matter of technique. We had E.V.A. down. And Gemini had accomplished its goals.

**SPACE BARNSTORMER**

*Gemini astronauts pushed the edge of the envelope on every flight. On Gemini 12, Buzz Aldrin demonstrated his mastery of difficult spacewalking techniques like a biplane wing-walker, paving the way for successful U.S. space walks in the future.*

**T**he Apollo launch complex was under construction; the Apollo spacecraft and the rockets were in intense development. But the Moon remained, in Victor Hugo's words, "the kingdom of dream, the province of illusion." We didn't even know whether it was possible to land on it. Were there bottomless pools of dust? Were there unstable chemicals that would erupt in flame at the touch of a boot? No one knew. But there was a new way to find out. The development of the computer had created a new kind of scout. Robot probes would explore the Moon before men did and transform our understanding of the world we had watched for so long. Struggling through a series of explosions, misfires, and crashes, NASA built its experience

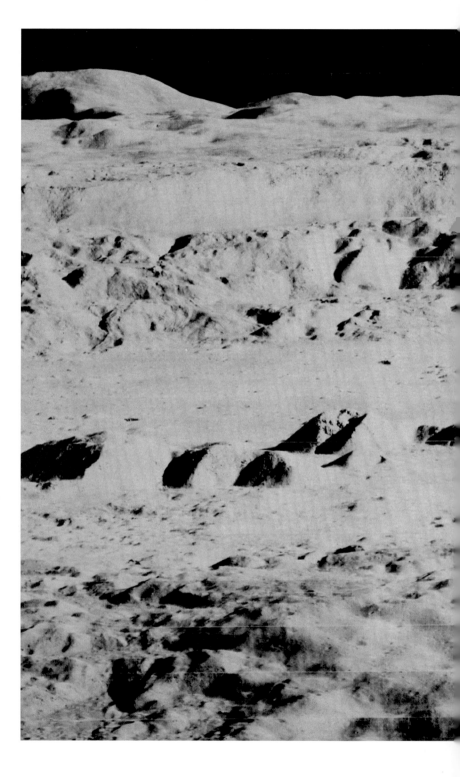

and resolutely assaulted the compelling silvery orb with three series of probes. Primitive Rangers televised images up until the last second as they deliberately smashed into the Moon; Surveyors soft-landed in five locations to examine the surface; and five sophisticated Lunar Orbiters circled the cratered world with high-resolution camera eyes, scouting for Apollo landing sites.

The most famous of the Lunar Orbiter images thrilled the public with the promise of a new kind of experience ahead. *Lunar Orbiter 2* transmitted an oblique shot of the great crater Copernicus from just over 28 miles above the lunar surface, showing 2,700-foot mountains, rugged terrain, and flat valleys. The photo made the front pages of newspapers all over the world. In this image people could see the Moon not from overhead, as if through a telescope, but as a wide landscape with a horizon, as if they were flying above it. This was how a *pilot* would see the Moon. The papers called it "the Picture of the Century," though there were greater wonders to come. But to reach those wonders, we had to prepare new vehicles and the pilots who would see that lunar horizon with their own eyes.

**A NEW WORLD**

*With his telescope Galileo had transformed the Moon from a celestial abstraction to a location with terrain. The American Lunar Orbiter probes, above, circled the Moon with advanced Kodak cameras and transformed our perception once again, revealing the Moon's landscapes from a new perspective. When* Lunar Orbiter 2 *sent back this image, left, in 1966, it was like nothing anyone had ever seen before, and an amazed U.S. press dubbed this glimpse of the future "the Picture of the Century."*

# America's Moon Scouts

NASA scouted the Moon with three series of increasingly sophisticated robot probes. "Crash camera" Rangers, soft-lander Surveyors, and "sky eye" Lunar Orbiters gave us our first close-up looks at the Moon, tested its surface, and sent back high-quality mapping photographs. Together, these automated advance scouts blazed the trail for American astronauts to follow.

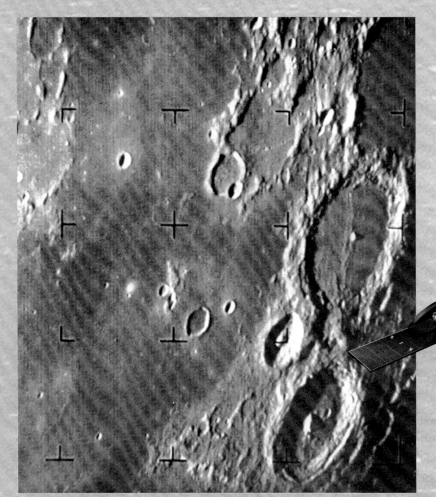

*The unmanned Ranger probes televised images from "suicide missions" on their way to crashing into the Moon. These images gave us an early close look at the Moon before complex maneuvering control was developed for robot probes.*

## RANGER

**T**he first U.S. Moon probes were the Rangers, built to torpedo straight into the Moon, televising pictures furiously up to the very last second. The expendable cameras were a good solution to getting close-up photographs quickly until more sophisticated probes could be developed. In the beginning, just getting the probe to the Moon was going to be challenging enough.

The Rangers were mounted on top of Atlas missiles as John Glenn's Mercury capsule had been, with a small added stage to boost the probe to the Moon. Launch after launch, failures of every kind occurred. NASA lost, exploded, or crashed five Rangers before it actually got Ranger 6 to its proper target, the Sea of Tranquility. Unfortunately, electrical problems at launch had fried the camera system. *Ranger 6* smashed blindly into the moondust to make an even half-dozen failed probes, much to the chagrin of the program engineers.

So it astonished everyone from space workers to the general public when, on July 31, 1964, *Ranger 7* actually began transmitting images during its approach. National television excitedly carried the broadcast with the words "LIVE FROM THE MOON." Two more successful Rangers followed, completing the program's mission.

## SURVEYOR

The second series of American Moon probes were sophisticated soft-landers called Surveyors. The Russian *Luna 9* beat *Surveyor 1* to the Moon, but when the NASA probe landed four months later on June 2, 1966, it soon began transmitting images of much better quality than *Luna 9* had delivered. *Surveyor 2* crashed, and *Surveyor 4* lost communication just as it began braking for its landing, leaving it to an unknown fate. But four other Surveyors made successful touchdowns in locations scattered across the near side of the Moon. Their automatic cameras gave us the first clear views of the lunar surface, which turned out to be no exotic realm of spectral dust pools but an airless desert. Their robot arms scooped up soil to probe its consistency, and the flight engi-

neers even tried refiring the landing rocket to "hop" some of the Surveyors around on the lunar surface to prove that nothing drastic would happen to a rocket lifting off from the Moon. The Surveyors demonstrated that a landing was possible and that the surface of the Moon could be explored by man.

## LUNAR ORBITER

To determine the best locations for Apollo landings, NASA needed high-resolution photographs, and the only way to get them was to send a robot "eye" to orbit the Moon. To meet this need, NASA developed the Lunar Orbiters. Our space engi-

*Soft-landing Surveyor probes proved that the Moon's surface was safe to land on and used robotic arms to test the nature of the moondust. (The* Surveyor 3 *probe is pictured on p. 152.)*

neering skills had improved since the Rangers, and every Lunar Orbiter mission was successful.

American photography industry leader Eastman Kodak designed a 150-pound twin-lensed camera for the Lunar Orbiter probes. To prevent blurring of the images as the Orbiter sped around the Moon at thousands of miles per hour, Kodak

devised a complex system which sensed the altitude and velocity of the probe, advancing the film itself during the exposure in a precise increment to cancel out the motion of the camera.

Five Lunar Orbiters peered down at the Moon from close range between August 1966 and August 1967, each taking about 200 pictures. The Kodak imaging system worked beautifully, returning sharp and detailed lunar photos of a quality never before seen, showing details as small as three feet wide. Through its powerful telephoto eye, *Lunar Orbiter 3* was even able to spot *Surveyor 1* sitting on the Moon below it. With the Lunar Orbiter data, NASA flight planners were able to finalize the landing-site selection for the early Apollo missions.

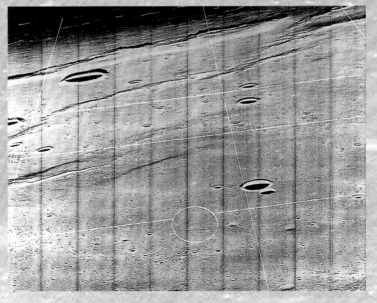

*Lunar Orbiter 3 sent back this image of "site 5," a prospective early Apollo landing site on the Ocean of Storms. Lunar Orbiters focused on scouting the "Apollo Zone," a broad band along either side of the lunar equator, since orbital mechanics made this zone easier to reach.*

## BACK FROM THE NEW OCEAN

*Astronaut Pete Conrad is hauled from the sea by a U.S. Navy helicopter winch after splashdown of the Gemini 5 mission. After orbiting the Earth, NASA space capsules would fire a powerful retro-rocket to slow their speed and drop them back into the Earth's atmosphere, through which they would rip like hot meteorites. When they had slowed sufficiently, the capsules released parachutes and dropped into the ocean near waiting navy recovery teams. Early recovery operations such as Conrad is undergoing here were based on navy rescue procedures for pilots downed at sea.*

JOHN F. Kennedy had pledged America to reaching the Moon "before this decade is out," skillfully finessing the nation's short-term prestige losses in space by redefining the ultimate contest as one that America had a chance of winning. In spite of our embarrassing failures and almost pitiful space capabilities in 1961, Kennedy had made his bold move and expressed unflinching confidence in the face of demonstrated Soviet superiority. Now it was up to the entire nation to deliver on his promise. The power of such a grandiose declaration might have waned if not for a sniper's bullet in Dallas, Texas. In 1963, John Kennedy's assassination turned the political pledge into a deadline graven on a national headstone and lit by an eternal flame. There could be no compromise now, no reconsideration that would dishonor Kennedy's memory and belie his visionary faith in America's ability. The looming deadline would drive all our efforts as we struggled to make manifest the instruments and abilities that would accomplish the Moon odyssey.

# Aiming for the Moon

## THE PRICE OF "GO FEVER"

**T**he Apollo project was taking every ounce of effort that NASA and its industry allies could muster, and it still did not seem to be enough. By 1965, the time to the deadline was half gone, and the Apollo program had not yet launched a single ship. Urgency nipped at everyone's heels, and intensity permeated the Apollo effort throughout the major contractors across the nation. They called it "Go Fever."

There were problems with the Apollo capsule. The new prime spacecraft contractor was not McDonnell Douglas, but North American Aviation, which did not have the same experience with this kind of huge and complex project. Actually, no one had experience with *this* kind of project because the new Apollo ship was more than an order of magnitude more complex than McDonnell's Gemini two-seater had been, making it by far the most complex vehicle ever built. The capsule's design and manufacture were falling behind schedule.

The new Apollo command module, or C.M., was a squat gumdrop that could seat three astronauts. Led by fabled spacecraft mastermind Max Faget, armies of engineers were involved in the Apollo C.M.'s design. This was a long-range spacecraft with much more complicated navigation, guidance, and communications gear than Gemini. The Apollo was built to operate not 850 miles up like Gemini but 250,000

### BLOCK I

*The prototype version of the Apollo command module, below, was called Block I. The advanced Block II, with improved functions, would not be ready in time for the early Apollo missions.*

miles away and around the far side of the Moon, entirely out of contact with Mission Control. Earlier capsules had been short-range vehicles. Apollo would be a vessel

for the deep void, an oceangoing ship compared to the orbital river-boats of Mercury and Gemini that rode just above the blue skies. The Gemini astronauts had always been able to look out their windows and see the Earth spread out below them. Apollo would leave the home planet behind. A small universe of technology, the Apollo spacecraft would present a new level of challenge to the astronauts as well as to the engineers.

Most of the Mercury Seven pilots were out of commission when the Apollo mission command lineup began taking shape. Alan Shepard, America's first man in space, was off flight status due to inner-ear equilibrium problems. John Glenn, the first of the astronauts to make orbit, was retired as a national hero, considered too valuable a symbol to risk any further. Two others, Scott Carpenter and Gordon Cooper, had been moved out of prime rotation, Carpenter after his subpar Mercury performance and Cooper during Gemini. One astronaut, Deke Slayton, had been grounded by an insignificant heart murmur, much to his chagrin. Slayton's fellow Mercury astronauts unanimously requested that he be made the head of a new astronaut office in compensation for his misfortune, and now he was making the crew assignments for missions he could never fly himself. The job was a bitter irony for a grounded pilot, but Slayton undertook the responsibility with the same gruff dedication that had won him a place among the Original Seven. Reviewing his personnel to select the commander for the first Apollo mission, Slayton had only two of the Mercury Seven available. One was Wally Schirra, the precision "textbook" pilot. The other was the most senior astronaut, America's second in space, a man of few words named Gus Grissom.

Grissom had nearly drowned on July 21, 1961, when his hatch blew open and his Mercury capsule *Liberty Bell 7* sank after splashdown. When it came time to break in the new Gemini ship, it was Grissom at the helm on the first manned launch. Stung by inaccurate criticism

**APOLLO 1 CREW**

*Three generations of astronauts comprised the Apollo 1 crew. Gus Grissom* (far left) *was one of Project Mercury's Original Seven. Pioneering Gemini 4 spacewalker Ed White* (center) *was one of the so-called New Nine. Roger Chaffee* (right) *was a rookie from the third group of astronauts, recruited for Apollo in anticipation of America's space adventures to come.*

suggesting that the Mercury accident might have been his fault, he called his Gemini spacecraft *The Unsinkable Molly Brown* and turned in an outstanding shakedown mission for the Gemini program. Now he would be called upon to prove out another brand-new spacecraft. A taciturn, no-nonsense professional, Grissom was solid test-pilot material, and it was to this man that Slayton handed the challenge and responsibility of Apollo 1.

In the Apollo 1 capsule, Grissom would be backed up by well-chosen teammates. Slayton had selected as Grissom's command module pilot Gemini 4 hero Ed White, the first American to walk in space. Together Grissom and White were a pair of veterans in a nascent field. If anyone could handle Apollo, it would be these two men. Joining them was newcomer Roger Chaffee, who represented the new group of astronauts brought in by NASA to fill out the ranks for the many anticipated missions ahead.

The team was good. But their Apollo spacecraft was having serious technical problems. North American was having trouble meeting deadlines and getting everything in the capsule to function according to specifications. Grissom, normally the last person to say much of anything, openly criticized the capsule's failings. To show his disgust, he hung a large lemon on it while visiting the Downey, California, plant where it was being built. In order to meet deadlines, the manufacturer was even shipping unfinished assemblies to the Cape, where more work would need to be done. North American was a new contractor, without the experience that McDonnell Douglas had built over the two previous programs, but it was also revealing weaknesses in its management structure and project oversight abilities. Compounding the difficulty, the Apollo spacecraft

was simply a much bigger beast than its predecessors. The magnitude of it was taxing everyone, even the NASA management team working with North American. Resources were not the issue, since Congress had provided a sufficient budget to accomplish the project's goal. But time and personnel could only stretch so far, and all were driven by the deadline and by the Russians into "Go Fever," determined to make progress no matter what.

In spite of the constant frustrations with the new equipment, NASA prepared for a "plugs out" countdown demonstration test on January 27, 1967. This test would require the spacecraft to operate on its own, without power and direct hookup lines to ground control, simulating the spacecraft's operational independence just before launch. With the trouble-plagued system, this was asking a lot, but the test proceeded as planned anyway. The Apollo capsule sat atop its new rocket on pad 34. The astronauts were loaded and locked in as if for a real launch. And the radios were barely working. Static kept interrupting the efforts of the control team to communicate with the crew. Grissom even had to repeat himself in exasperation: "I said, Jesus Christ, if we can't communicate across three miles, how the hell are we going to communicate when we're on the Moon?" An astronaut's work was hard enough when the equipment worked perfectly. This kind of systems failure and the stakes of spaceflight did not mix well, and Grissom didn't like it. Management was pushing ahead anyway.

The capsule was over-pressurized with 100 percent oxygen for the first time during this problem-plagued test. For over five hours the men lay strapped in, repeatedly holding the count while the communications problems were tested. Now they were waiting through what they hoped would be the final hold before the last ten minutes of the countdown,

scheduled to start again at 6:31 P.M. There was only one minute left to go when a piece of exposed, uninsulated wiring underneath Grissom's couch produced a tiny electrical arc. Flight controllers saw a burst of bright orange light through the window on their TV monitors.

There were shouts. "We've got a fire in the spacecraft," came Roger Chaffee's urgent voice. In the pure oxygen of the capsule, the flames were fed by five times as much oxygen as occurs in normal air. The fire erupted and burned with unnatural fury. The flammable Velcro everywhere burst into flames that quickly surrounded the three astronauts in their claustrophobic metal compartment. In high-pressure pure oxygen even aluminum will burn fiercely. Grissom and White struggled with the hatch. Burly Ed White was one of the strongest men in the astronaut corps, but he and Grissom were fighting a devilishly complex hatch design that took a full minute and a half to open under normal circumstances. Bolts had to be unscrewed. And, built to open inward, the door could not possibly budge now. The fire swelled, raising the pressure inside the capsule and sealing the hatch against the hull. The capsule grew so hot that the pressure burst a hole in the ship, spewing flame out the side and giving the fire a path across all three men. They were trapped in a furnace.

Twenty-seven crew outside—every man on the gantry—rushed to

assist, choking on the poisonous fumes, fighting to open the hatch, which had already become too hot to hold. The awful firelight blazed behind the crystal windows. Mission control heard just a few terse snatches of voice over the pickup, as the astronauts tried to describe their situation and open the hatch. There was a cry of pain.

Five minutes and 20 seconds after the fire began, the hatch was wrenched open. Inside was charred incineration. Apollo 1 was over. The first Apollo crew had been killed without even leaving the launch pad.

Apollo 1 was NASA's darkest hour. A full investigation was mounted by NASA itself, led in part by astronaut Frank Borman, and reports were made before a congressional hearing. The messy story of the Apollo spacecraft was painstakingly unraveled and held up to intense scrutiny. The design, with its exposed wiring, highly flammable environment, and overly complex hatch, had been inadequately conceived, and the fire should not have happened. The inquiry concluded that both North American and the space agency had been negligent, compromising too much, rushing attempts to fix previously identified problems, failing to stabilize the ship's design and proceeding with a fundamental disregard for the astronauts' safety. It was heartrending and sobering for the people involved. With so many trying so hard, it was deeply painful to be confronted with such terrible proof of their own human failings—and all the more bitter because those who had paid the price were not those who were responsible.

Apollo 1 forced a major internal reassessment of NASA and the

Moon program in 1967. It was Kennedy who had trusted the people who claimed they could take America to the Moon, but he was gone. Could they find the faith now to go on? President Johnson, a strong NASA supporter as Kennedy's vice president, focused on other

# Command Module

The most sophisticated component of a Saturn rocket was the command module, or C.M., with some two million parts and dozens of separate systems. Cockpit, observatory, galley, cargo hold, and sleeping quarters all in one, the C.M. served as the control center of the rocket and also had to function as a completely self-contained spaceship for the fiery trial of reentry.

Three acceleration couches lay at the Apollo capsule's center, with a huge dashboard of main controls and instrumentation ranged above them. In the peak of the capsule was a tunnel to the ship's upper hatch, where the ship would dock with the lunar module on missions that included the lander. Below the couches was the aft compartment, consisting of the confined space between the seats and the floor. In zero gravity, the space became adequate for sleeping. Beta-cloth storage compartments were tucked in throughout the complex environment, holding everything from toothbrushes and breakfast food to a medical kit and star maps. A sextant station beyond the feet of the couches allowed astronauts to take navigation sightings on key stars through scopes that looked out of the back of the capsule. Next to the sextant station was the Apollo computer display/keyboard, or DSKY (pronounced 'dis-key'), advanced and compact for its day but less powerful than today's calculator watches. It had just 4K of memory.

The C.M. was ruggedly built to protect its astronauts. The ship's armored main hull was an inch and a half thick at its base, where the epoxy resin honeycomb heat shield layer was 2.7 inches thick. At the peak of the capsule was a ring compartment containing the tightly packed mortar-launched parachutes of the recovery system. Overall this protective capsule weighed more than six tons, a ton and a half heavier than the entire unfueled lunar module.

Until the very end of the mission, the command capsule would be joined to the 16-foot-tall service module, which held fuel and oxygen tanks and fuel cell batteries—a "utilities in the basement" approach pioneered in a rudimentary form on the Gemini capsules. Combined, the two elements were properly known as the command and service module, or C.S.M., but the term *command module* commonly applied to the capsule with or without its service module. For reentry the capsule would separate from the service module, becoming the only part of the entire space vehicle to return to Earth.

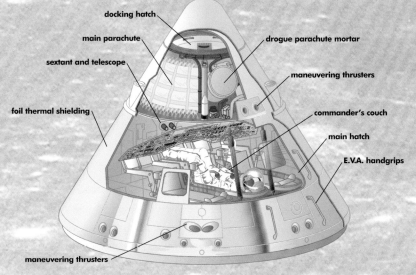

docking hatch
main parachute
sextant and telescope
foil thermal shielding
drogue parachute mortar
maneuvering thrusters
commander's couch
main hatch
E.V.A. handgrips
maneuvering thrusters

*The command module pilot flew the spacecraft from the center couch. On his left was the mission commander's couch, and on the right was the lunar-module copilot's couch.*

concerns now that he was chief executive himself. The conflict in Vietnam was occupying an increasing amount of his attention, and NASA could not look to him for leadership. Critics of the space program filled the air with condemnation and finger-pointing, claiming everything from incompetence to irrelevance. The Moon program was a waste of money and now of lives, they said. It had to end.

The pyre on the pad could have ended America's reach for the Moon. Instead, somehow, in spite of this hour of crisis and failure, the compelling force of Apollo overcame the voices of doubt. The nation had changed

in the six turbulent years since it had cast its eyes upward to the Moon and now found itself faced with a nightmarish overseas jungle war and troubling social unrest at home; in such a time it could never have pledged itself to achieving an impossible, visionary dream. But Apollo defied the enervating decay around it as if sustained by some intangible force. The commitment to doing what could not be done came from an earlier and stronger time, and it remained as if graven

in stone, flickering in the light of an eternal flame. Apollo's special origin now protected it.

The entire Apollo team—and they felt like a team, every one of the hundreds of thousands who worked on Apollo at its height— remained steadfast and had not lost heart. By and large, these people believed in the vision of Apollo and felt the power of its extraordinary aim even if they could not precisely explain its effect on them. The loss of the astronauts was painful, much more so than when test pilots had died previously during routine flight accidents. But pilots understood the risks of their profession, and none better than the crew of Apollo 1. Just one week before the fire, Gus Grissom had spoken with the eloquence of a man of few words: "If we die, we want people to accept it. We are in a risky business, and we hope that if anything happens to us, it will not delay the program. The conquest of space is worth the risk of life."

Haunted and emboldened by these words, the Apollo team members across the country undertook to rebuild the future from the charred remains of the lost mission. The astronauts' sacrifice would not be in vain. Apollo would go on.

**A**fter the intense reassessment that followed the Apollo 1 fire, the problems with North American's command module were identified, faced, and solved. Engineers dismantled Apollo 2's capsule in parallel with the wreckage of Apollo 1 as the legion of investigators went through every aspect of the design to root out flaws. Apollo 3 was scrapped. The Apollo capsule plan underwent 1,300 changes, and the ship emerged in a new incarnation called Block II. Fireproof materials were used throughout the capsule, every component was carefully finished and insulated, the hatch was completely reworked to open outward, easily, and these were only the beginnings of the redesign. The Block II Apollo capsule was engineered to be the safest spacecraft ever flown.

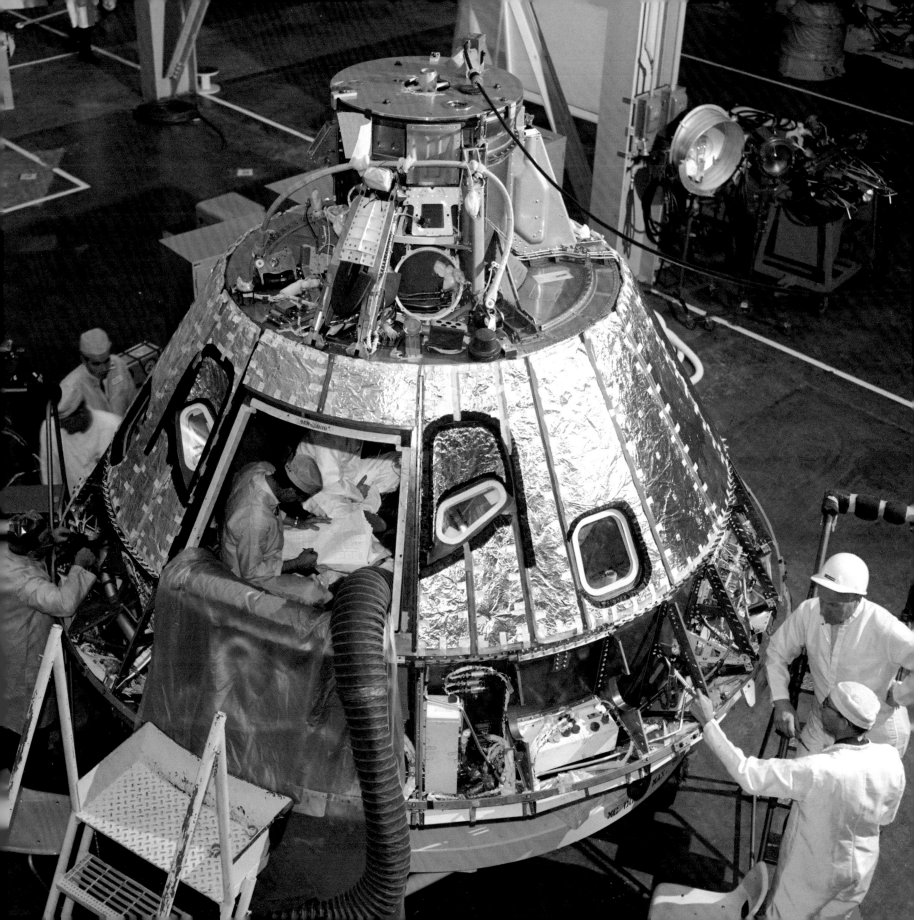

An irony of the Apollo 1 fire is that it almost certainly saved NASA from a much greater disaster. No one had realized how much more work the Block I capsule design needed, and if Apollo 1 had gone as planned, we might have learned its shortcomings in space. A catastrophic, fatal failure in flight could have done far worse damage to the Moon program as a whole and changed the way we regarded space. It could have been seen as a realm of failure, as proof of the limits of mankind's abilities. As it was, the terrible fire on the ground gave designers the time and knowledge they needed to build a good, new ship.

In addition to the lesson it taught the engineers, Apollo 1 also made mission planners more cautious. Three unmanned test flights—Apollos 4, 5, and 6—followed Apollo 1, proving out the equipment before NASA would risk men in space again.

Apollo 1 had cost us almost two years. By late 1968, we were less than 15 months away from the deadline, and of the major hardware elements required for the Moon mission—the Saturn V, the Apollo command module, and the lunar lander—not one had yet been tested in manned flight. We might make it—if absolutely everything went right. Two extra years of redoubled effort since the fire, and the hopes and prayers of the extended Apollo team: All of it was building up to the return of the astronauts to space. All of it was building up to Apollo 7.

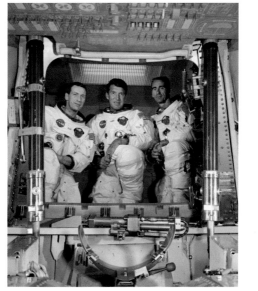

## APOLLO 7: PHOENIX FROM THE ASHES

**T**remendous pressure faced the crew of Apollo 7, the first manned flight of the new Block II capsule. Apollo 7 would also be the first manned flight of the Saturn IB rocket, von Braun's improvised predecessor to the Moon rocket, which was built partly from a bundle of Redstone missiles strapped together. NASA needed an astronaut commander who could fly an absolutely textbook mission and prove out the new ship and all the concepts embodied in it. They had the perfect man for the job, a man who was also now the senior astronaut, a 45-year-old veteran of both Mercury and Gemini flights who had a reputation for flawless, by-the-book spaceflight. NASA would give Apollo 7 to Wally Schirra.

Expansive, good company if you were an insider, and fond of a good joke, Schirra was a perfectionist when it came to his command. Schirra took a very close and personal interest in the development of the Apollo 7 command module. He and his crew practically lived with the spacecraft during its preflight checkouts in Downey, California. The builders at North American took to calling it "Wally's Ship." Access to the new ship was tightly controlled, with every object going in or out logged so that there would be no surprises.

Schirra and his crew were to take Apollo 7 on the longest first piloted flight of any vehicle ever built. Their 11-day mission was to orbit the Earth, keeping their ship in space for the full length of time that it would later take to travel to the Moon, to demonstrate the command module's endurance. Along the way they would conduct complete performance tests of the equipment in the fabulously intricate spacecraft.

The Apollo was so much more complex and difficult than any previous spacecraft that even the hard-working astronauts were nearly taxed to their limits. Twelve hundred hours were added over and above the normal mission training schedule. The astronauts even traveled to Griffith Observatory Planetarium in Los Angeles to practice identifying the 37 navigational stars that would be used by the Apollo guidance computer. Schirra and his crew prepared with intense dedication, knowing that complete mastery of their vessel was vital in case anything went wrong.

*Wally Schirra's crew rode
Apollo 7 atop Wernher
von Braun's improvised
Saturn IB rocket. With
its first stage built of
"Old Reliable" Redstone
missile tanks strapped
together, the Saturn IB
boosted an advanced
cryogenic S-IVB stage
(marked USA) that
would see service on the
Moon missions.*

Launch Complex 34 was the site where Schirra's friend Gus Grissom had died with his fellow astronauts in the Apollo 1 capsule a year and a half earlier. Now, in the small hours of a cool October night in 1968, floodlights at Complex 34 illuminated a 20-story metal framework cocoon enveloping the steel-plated concrete pad. Ten minutes after 4:00 A.M., with a light breeze ghosting across the site, the great cocoon began to pull back along heavy tracks to reveal the shining white creation it had been protecting: Apollo 7, Wally's Ship, the Phoenix.

The launch preparations for Apollo 7 filled the Cape community with emotion. No astronauts had lifted off from the Cape for over two years, and the cloud of the fire still hung invisibly in the air. If Apollo 7 had problems, the Moon might recede so far out of reach that Kennedy's deadline would be lost. If, on the other hand, Apollo 7 succeeded in proving out the new spacecraft and the team behind it, the whole operation might find in it a cleansing catharsis from the terrible effects of the Apollo 1 disaster. The ground operations team was at maximum alert. The crew had been loaded in. And up in the spacecraft, the mission rested with "cool hand" Wally Schirra.

Pad 34 released its last rocket as Apollo 7 lifted into the skies on October 11, 1968. Hurtling smoothly around the Earth at altitudes of over 142 miles, Apollo 7 played precision cat-and-mouse with its discarded S-IVB second stage, demonstrating rendezvous techniques just as Schirra had first done with Gemini 6.

But mission commander Schirra would find a new challenge in orbit this time: He soon felt the bizarre effects of developing a cold in weightlessness, and his crew were quick to follow. Extremely physically fit, all three of the Apollo 7 astronauts had nonetheless caught colds from the relentless pace of their training. A cold in space was a new phenomenon and no joke: Without gravity, the sinuses did not drain, and the astronauts' heads became badly clogged. Schirra became an appreciative supporter of the decongestant Actifed, packed in the mission medical kit. Without the medication to relieve the cold symptoms, the mission would have been recalled early.

### COLD IN SPACE

*On Apollo 7 Wally Schirra dealt with a common cold in the uncommon environment of space. The cold symptoms became very uncomfortable in weightlessness, but Schirra maintained his reputation for flawless mission performance.*

In addition to managing a cold while he commanded the Apollo spacecraft, Schirra soon learned that he would have other nuisances to deal with: unscheduled requests from Mission Control for additional experiments and observations that had not been listed in the painstakingly prepared flight plan. Schirra grew impatient with the added duties, insisting that flying the spacecraft successfully was more important. The Apollo 7 crew eventually obliged NASA's Public Affairs Office with no fewer than seven good-natured TV broadcasts from "the lovely Apollo Room, high above everything," but when Mission Control first asked, Schirra replied that they had work to do running the spacecraft, and he flatly refused. "We have a new vehicle up here," he said. "I'm saying at this point, television will be delayed, without further discussion, until after the rendezvous. . . . I refuse to foul up our timeline at this point." No astronaut had *ever* refused directives from Mission Control before. Schirra's independence did not sit well with director of flight operations Chris Kraft. Schirra continued to be intransigent, ridiculing the added duties and experiments that continued to be radioed up to him and raising ire and frustration among the flight controllers.

The "Schirra effect" had earned the Apollo 7 commander a reputation for some difficult egotism back during the Mercury days. When discussing any design issue with engineers, Schirra would take the last word whether he was right or wrong by loftily declaring,

*The Apollo medical kit was made of fireproof Beta cloth like the spacesuits. A kit like this one provided Wally Schirra's crew with Actifed decongestant for cold relief.*

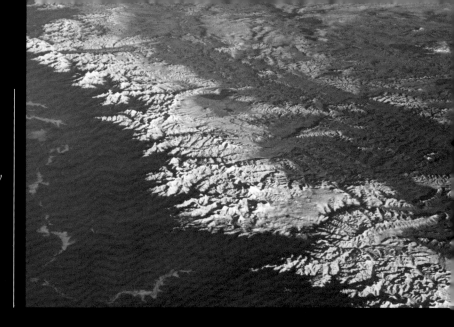

### HIGH ABOVE THE HIGHEST

*On their 10-day orbital mission, Schirra and his crew photographed many landmarks, including this view of the world's 12 tallest mountain peaks in the Himalayas. Mount Everest can be seen at lower center.*

### LONG WATCH

*Walt Cunningham maintains his vigil during Apollo 7's extended journey around the Earth.*

## Live from orbit

Apollo 7 presented the world with the first television broadcasts from space. During these light-hearted transmissions, Schirra's crew spoofed old radio traditions with preprinted messages.

## Orbital glory

Wally Schirra's Apollo 7 mission captured some of the most beautiful images ever taken of the Earth, including this sunrise over Florida and the Gulf of Mexico.

## Space tag

Apollo 7 practices orbital rendezvous with its spent S-IVB stage. The open panels expose an empty garage that would have contained a lunar module on a Moon mission. Cape Canaveral, including the Moon launch complex with its long crawlerway and twin pads, can be seen below and to the left of the S-IVB. Schirra had carefully prepared in the simulator to take this photograph in orbit.

"Well, if you'd been *up there.* . . ." Astronauts got a fair amount of leeway, but lead flight director Gene Kranz could not believe he was seeing this kind of behavior during a mission, and he silently steamed at Schirra.

What the people on the ground perhaps took too little into account was that the previous manned Apollo capsule had incinerated three of these astronauts' friends. Schirra's mission was to prove out the new Block II Apollo in space, and he was not about to jeopardize it with "Mickey Mouse" experimental add-ons and "tests that were ill prepared and hastily conceived by an idiot." After all those infinite hours of training, now they had a few extra things to add? Where the hell were their priorities? "We have a feeling that some of these experimenters are holier than God down there," Schirra commented. "We are a heck of a lot closer to Him right now." Walt Cunningham, lying in the seat next to Schirra and swamped by the additional procedures, agreed with his commander's sentiments. "We'll go on record here," Cunningham clipped, "as saying people that dream up procedures like this after liftoff have somehow or other been dropping the ball for the last three years." The irritation mounted to the breaking point, and Schirra made a command decision. "I have had it up to here today, and from now on I'm going to be an onboard flight director for these updates, revised schedules. We are not going to accept any new games . . . or going to do some crazy tests we never heard of before."

Arguments between ground and Apollo 7 continued even to the point of reentry. The commander wanted permission for his crew to keep their bubble helmets off during reentry so they could clear their cold-clogged ears during pressure changes. Mission Control didn't want the helmets off since they protected the astronauts against the danger of explosive

decompression in the event that the ship was compromised during the incendiary return through the atmosphere. Exactly this kind of decompression would later kill three cosmonauts in 1971, and Mission Control ordered the helmets on. Schirra retorted that, as commander, he was making the final decision, and they stayed off.

Kraft vowed that neither Schirra nor either of his crewmen would ever fly again, but Schirra was retiring anyway, and he had delivered exactly what he'd been chosen for: a perfect textbook flight. Schirra was a consummate astronaut professional in his performance, no matter what his manner was. Apollo program director Gen. Sam Phillips delightedly pronounced the mission a "101 percent success," thanks to the accomplishment of a couple of those added procedures. The spacecraft was proven, the astronauts had gone up and back safely, the community could move on with renewed confidence, and Apollo could reach for the Moon. And on Earth, in recognition of those exciting first live television broadcasts from a space capsule, astronaut Comdr. Walter M. Schirra Jr. took home an Emmy. And that wasn't the end of his television experience: He later did heartfelt commercials for Actifed.

## HOW TO SHOOT FOR THE MOON?

In the early days, planners had envisioned landing on the Moon with a large, tall spacecraft called the Apollo tailsitter. Launching the tailsitter on a "direct ascent" would take an absolutely titanic rocket called the Nova.

After considerable study, engineers concluded that only a Saturn-series rocket could be developed in time to meet Kennedy's deadline. So they envisioned sending the tailsitter into Earth orbit empty, then launching a second rocket carrying all its fuel. With the load thus divided into two smaller parts, the Nova would not be needed and two Saturn rockets could do the job. This mission mode was called Earth Orbit Rendezvous, and it was the favorite at NASA.

the idea seriously, Houbolt wrote an impassioned letter directly to NASA associate administrator Robert C. Seamans Jr., bypassing all the approved channels of bureaucracy and explaining that he was writing "somewhat as a voice in the wilderness." Instead of getting him fired, the letter won L.O.R. serious review, though it still faced great opposition. Houbolt made presentations over and over again, building up to one major showdown in which critical superiors "crucified" him over the dangers of his plan, as one attendee admitted.

However, if rendezvous were safe enough to attempt over the Moon, L.O.R. *would* save a tremendous amount of effort and resources. Designing the smaller spaceships involved would be easier as well, because they would be specialized and engineering teams could focus on very specific problems. Apollo was often criticized by outsiders as wildly profligate in its spending, but the truth was that every aspect of the program was carefully calculated to spend only what was absolutely necessary. L.O.R. offered by far the most conservative use of resources, and on this ground its opponents eventually yielded. The obscure technician's dogged obsession became NASA's plan for reaching the Moon.

With these decisions, the grand concepts of space exploration had begun taking specific form in the real world. The orbiting capsule became the Apollo command module, and the lander became the lunar module. Stripped down to minimum weight, they could both be carried by one rocket, but that rocket would still have to be incredibly powerful. It would in fact represent the greatest controlled power that any nation in the world could design, something more powerful than anything Chesley Bonestell had painted for von Braun, something more powerful than even the rocketeer himself had dared to describe. This would be the instrument of imagination, the realization of dreams and determination, the multi-ton statement of American ability, the Saturn V Moon rocket.

But there was a third, very different option that would split the tailsitter idea into two spaceships, an orbiting capsule and a specialized small lander. In this scenario, the lander could be made lightweight for the light lunar gravity, reducing the overall weight so much that both ships could be carried up by just one Saturn V. The trick was that the two ships would have to rendezvous over the Moon when the men in the lander came back up from the surface. Rendezvous was considered difficult and dangerous, and requiring that maneuver over the Moon gave planners dry throats and nervous sweats. But Lunar Orbit Rendezvous, or L.O.R., refused to go away quietly.

The basic idea of L.O.R. had been conceived in 1916 by a Russian, obscure and self-educated like Tsiolkovsky, a mechanic named Yuri Vasilievich Kondratyuk. Now a lower-echelon engineer at NASA named John Houbolt was pushing for L.O.R., but neither it nor he was popular. In November 1961, irritated that no one was taking

## THE SATURN V

**T**he Saturn V was the heart of the Moon odyssey. For all the brilliant theory, science, engineering, and design, for all the planning and precision spacecraft construction that might take place, no one could reach the Moon without the almost inconceivable power of the Saturn V to hurl the spacecraft to that celestial destination. The Saturn V would be gargantuan in every respect. New vehicles would have to be designed just to carry its parts. Buildings 40 stories tall would have to be constructed just to test it. And its engines would roar with deafening, literally tectonic force unlike anything mankind had ever built before. The completed space vehicle would be nearly alive, pulsing with exotic cryogenic fluids, electrified with advanced computer components, and calculating with its own 30-foot-diameter, ring-shaped internal brain. The rocket's tanks would be pressurized to tremendous levels, holding within their precision-crafted walls, stretching 363 feet into the air, the power to destroy a small city.

**ROCKET SHIPYARD**

*After von Braun's team built the first few Saturn V S-IC first stages in Huntsville, Alabama, Boeing took over and manufactured further S-ICs at Michoud, near New Orleans, Louisiana.*

The Saturn V would become the greatest pinnacle of rocket design ever achieved and an achievement ranking among the wonders of time, along with Stonehenge and the Egyptian pyramids. When the Greek historian Herodotus visited the Great Pyramid in 430 B.C., he asked the locals how many people it had taken to build the legendary structure.

"Four hundred thousand," they told him, working over 10 years, an almost inconceivable labor force to be organized toward one construction goal. When NASA took a count of the Americans working on the Moon program during the decade of the 1960s, they discovered a startling coincidence. Almost five millennia after the Great Pyramid was brought to pass, a new wonder would be formed by the same number of hands.

Five huge F-1 engines would constitute the business end of the Saturn V, and they would have to develop the volcanic thrust of 7.6 million pounds. This was almost 40 times as powerful as the Redstone engine that had shot Alan Shepard into space. New engineering solutions and new alloys had to be developed to make the F-1 strong enough to withstand its own power.

The first stage of the Saturn V would carry the rocket 42 miles high in two and a half minutes. This "S-IC" first stage contained two gigantic tanks of kerosene and liquid oxygen, enough to feed the raging F-1s at the incredible rate of three tons per second. Wernher von Braun personally oversaw the development of the first stage at Marshall Space Flight Center.

To test the colossal first stages under "live" conditions, the Marshall team built mighty test stands that tower above the green trees of Alabama. The finished stages were hauled into the huge, reinforced test chambers to be strapped down and fired. In Huntsville, the early F-1 tests were known to break windows and knock dishes off the walls for miles around until the chastened engineers realized the power of their creations. During overcast days, the sonic energy of testing five F-1 engines simultaneously on a completed first stage reverberated so badly off the cloud ceiling that minor earthquakes were felt 40 miles away. NASA constructed a dedicated test facility farther away from settled areas in a godforsaken swamp in Mississippi, to which the finished stages from Marshall or Michoud were floated upriver on special barges.

By the time the first stage was spent, the Moon rocket would be 42 miles up and powering through the sky at almost Mach 9. The second stage would then ignite and build on this lead, accelerating the Saturn V to 15,000 mph to reach Mach 22 and an altitude of 117 miles. This "S-II" second stage burned high-energy liquid hydrogen through five J-2 engines, smaller than the F-1s. Its size and cryogenic fuel made

**FULL POWER**

*Smoke and flame blast from the S-IC test stand as a first-stage booster of the Saturn V space vehicle is static fired at NASA's Mississippi Test Facility. The 138-foot rocket stage held five giant F-1 engines, which developed a thrust of 7.5 million pounds. This power would carry the 363-foot-tall Saturn V to an altitude of some 40 miles and a speed of over 6,000 mph.*

the S-II the most problematic element of the entire Saturn space vehicle, with delays, failures, and finally one of the stages rupturing at the Mississippi Test Facility before von Braun had had enough with the manufacturer and NASA stepped in to reorganize the contractor's management.

After the first two stages carried the Saturn V into the upper atmosphere, the third and final stage would take over and power the Apollo spacecraft into a parking orbit some 115 miles high, pausing while the astronauts checked out their craft for the push to the Moon. This third stage, curiously called S-IVB because of its design history, also burned liquid hydrogen and had already been test-flown on Wally Schirra's Apollo 7. After three orbits, the S-IVB third stage would reignite and accelerate the Apollo spacecraft beyond the Earth's orbit. After this final burn, the stage would be discarded, leaving the Apollo capsule and lander to hurtle to the Moon on their own at over 24,000 mph.

Topping the third stage was a black ring of instrumentation and high-speed computers called the Instrument Unit, or I.U., created by IBM. This, the Saturn V's massive brain, would monitor and control the rocket in flight, executing preprogrammed flight plan commands, throttling fuel and oxidizer lines in an ever-shifting ratio for perfect efficiency, and gimballing the roaring engines to steer the rocket. The giant rocket's every motion would register in the fantastically sensitive internal guidance system, an intricate, basketball-sized device called the ST-124 mounted within the Saturn's brain. Five seconds before launch, the I.U. was given independence by Launch Control, and the titanic machine would begin thinking for itself. As it monitored the throttle up to the full 7.5 million pounds of thrust in the F-1 engines, the I.U. would signal the hold-down arms restraining the Saturn to

release, and the rocket would separate from the Earth.

At the top of the rocket vehicle sat the Apollo spacecraft, the rocket's payload. A conical adapter would garage and protect the delicate lunar module below, and the astronauts would sit in the Apollo command module above. A needle tip on the Saturn V was the escape-tower rocket, which could pull the crew capsule to safety in a disaster.

## THE CAPE

The Moon rocket was so powerful that even a successful launch would annihilate any of the existing launch pads and blow them to rubble. No building on earth was large enough to assemble the Saturn V, and nothing in the world was strong enough to carry it once assembled. NASA needed a major new launch infrastructure to handle the behemoth rocket and its gargantuan components. So while the Gemini missions orbited above, spectacular new launch facilities arose at the Cape. The all-new Launch Complex 39 was the carefully prepared mercy seat that would make the manifestation of the Saturn V possible.

The earliest maps of Florida, drawn from the reports of Spanish explorers, identify only two features: the Florida Keys and a promontory called Cabo de Canaveral. Jutting into the Atlantic, the Cape was a sandy spit almost cut off from the mainland by the lazy courses of two rivers. With Ponce de Leon's discovery of the nearby Bahama Channel in 1513, the route up the eastern coast of Florida became the standard exit from the Gulf of Mexico for treasure ships bound for the ports of Europe. Vessels would hug the Florida coast until they caught sight of Cabo de Canaveral, where they would wheel to starboard and strike out across the open ocean. The Cape, then as later, was the jumping-off point for journeys to another realm.

It was to this stretch of low-lying, sparsely populated territory that a federal committee turned in 1946, when it had become clear that missile development would be important for future national security. Already owned in part by the government, the Cape was activated as the Joint Long Range Proving Ground in October 1949. The Cape offered an isolated area with an ocean "downrange" where dangerous missiles and ordnance could be tested without risk to population centers.

The first rocket launched from the Cape was one of von Braun's old V-2s. Over time, the Cape became populated with a series of launch complexes for new missiles, starting in the south and marching northward. In and among the missile pads were the space launch sites. The pads grew larger and more elaborate with each new generation of boosters. Launch Complex 39 would be constructed for the Saturn V. A new area well north of the earlier pads was selected to provide sufficient room for all the components. Every part of the Saturn V complex would be gigantic. The overwhelming scale emphasized the magnitude of the effort it would take to send men to the Moon.

The first need of the Saturn launch complex was a facility in which to assemble the elements of the Moon rocket: the Vehicle Assembly Building, or V.A.B. This became a 52-story monument large enough to hold four Saturn Vs. Rising above the Florida marshlands, the distinctive block became by volume the largest building in the world, a suitably awesome setting for the Saturn V's appearance.

As the engineers and manufacturers around the country completed their handiwork, Saturn V stages and Apollo spacecraft began arriving at the Cape by barge and by special transport planes. One by one, the gigantic elements were brought into the V.A.B. Inside this building was a universe of girderwork, floodlights, gantries, giant retracting platforms, and heavy-duty, overhead cranes. This realm engulfed the giant components, moving, rearranging, and transforming them into the most powerful machine ever created, an instrument that could send men to the Moon. There was nothing else like this environment anywhere on Earth. This was where wonders were built.

Adjoining the V.A.B., NASA built a futuristic-looking Launch Control Center to house the computers and ranks of technicians needed to monitor the myriad systems of the great Saturn V and bring its preparation to the crescendo of launch. From a firing room in the Launch Control Center, the NASA team would control each rocket from first assembly until the moment it cleared the launch tower.

The launch pads lay in the distance for safety. The Saturn V, with its supercooled liquid oxygen, its thousands of gallons of RP-1 kerosene, and its ultracold explosive liquid hydrogen, would pack the detonation force of a nuclear bomb if things went wrong. The fireball alone would be 3,000 feet wide, its sphere of destruction immense. NASA had to locate the pads over three miles away from the V.A.B. and Launch Control Center, and crews would not fuel the Saturn V until it was out on the pad.

launch tower

flame trench

flame trench

flame deflector

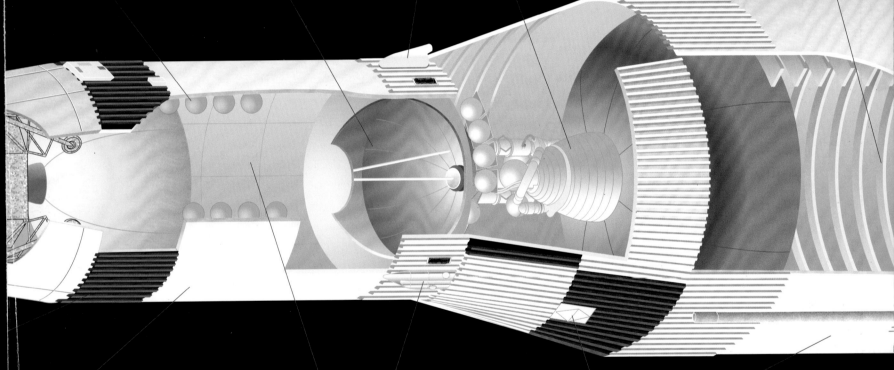

## PRESSURIZING HELIUM TANKS

The inert gas helium was used to pressurize many of the fuel and oxygen tanks in the Saturn V, driving propellant into the hungry engine turbo-pumps. Third-stage liquid helium was kept cold by placing the cryogenic spherical tanks inside the cryogenic hydrogen tank of the S-IVB stage.

## LIQUID OXYGEN TANK

Liquid hydrogen needed less than half its volume in liquid oxygen as oxidizer, so the LOX tanks in the second and third stages were much smaller than the LH2 tanks they adjoined. A common bulkhead separated the tanks in both stages to save weight.

## SLOSH ROCKETS

## J-2 ENGINE

This J-2 engine, unlike those in the second stage, made two separate burns. It boosted the rocket into Earth orbit, then shut off to allow a coasting checkout period. It was then reignited to break the rocket free of Earth's gravity and send it toward the Moon, initiating trans-lunar injection. Providing for reignition capability in space gave this stage additional design complexities.

## LIQUID HYDROGEN TANK

## S-IVB THIRD STAGE

The third stage stabilized the space vehicle in a 115-mile-high parking orbit around the Earth. After a systems-checkout period, the stage reignited to break the rocket out of Earth's gravity and send it on toward the Moon. In cislunar space, the stage would release the LM from its garage. After the spacecraft had separated from it, about four and a half hours into the mission, this booster stage was jettisoned into solar orbit or sent to crash into the Moon for the benefit of seismic readings.

## LIQUID HYDROGEN FUEL TANK

## MANEUVERING THRUSTERS

## STAGING RETRO-ROCKETS

Forward-pointing solid rockets pulled the second stage backward once it was exhausted, giving the third stage room to ignite.

## S-II SECOND STAGE

The second stage took over at 42 miles up, burned until nine minutes into the flight, and disengaged at an altitude of 117 miles. From this height the vehicle would fall a couple of miles before the third stage stabilized its orbit. Spent second stages dropped into the Atlantic Ocean southwest of the Azores.

# The Saturn V

Bold in concept, brilliant in execution, the Saturn V rocket would carry Apollo to the Moon. This most colossal yet most delicate of instruments represented the culmination of over a hundred years of imagination, research, and engineering. Under the leadership of Wernher von Braun, America's leading aerospace contractors built the most powerful and successful rocket the world had ever seen.

The Moon rocket was officially born on January 10, 1962, when NASA finalized the configuration of the advanced Saturn-series rocket and called it the Saturn V. Wernher von Braun would oversee development from Marshall Spaceflight Center in Huntsville, Alabama. Three stages would compose the huge design, using the staging principle advocated by Tsiolkovsky so long ago. Each stage would burn through its fuel and then drop off to free the ongoing rocket of deadweight. The Apollo spacecraft would sit atop the Saturn V as its payload.

The first stage of the Moon rocket would need the biggest and most powerful engines, and so von Braun decided to run them on old-fashioned kerosene rocket fuel to minimize engineering unknowns. The upper two stages could use smaller engines, lesser challenges that could be designed to burn the new high-power cryogenic fuel liquid hydrogen. Each stage would be built by a different aerospace contractor to distribute the responsibility (and funding) for Apollo across the country: Boeing, North American Aviation, and McDonnell Douglas Astronautics would build the first, second, and third stages, respectively. Rocketdyne would build the engines.

One of the greatest challenges of the Saturn V was in developing its main engines. To lift a six-million-pound vehicle, the Moon rocket's five F-1 engines would have to be incredibly powerful, generating 1.5 million pounds of thrust apiece. The air force and Rocketdyne had been working on the visionary F-1 since 1955, yet even well into their development, the mammoth engines were ripping themselves apart with their own power. The Presidential Science Advisory Committee wondered in 1961 whether an engine as large as the 18.5-foot-tall F-1 would be simply too big to

*Wernher von Braun and Kennedy Space Center director Kurt Debus with the Saturn V 500F, which served as a test article for the launch facilities before the first "live" Saturn V was assembled.*

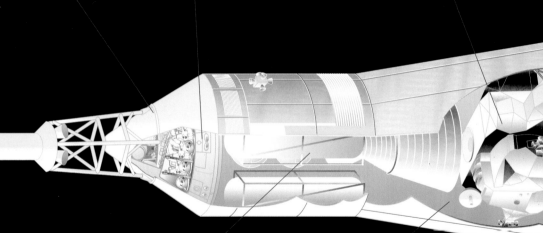

## ESCAPE TOWER
### (LAUNCH ESCAPE SYSTEM, OR L.E.S.)

During launch the astronauts were protected by the escape tower, a rocket system that could pull the command module to a safe ocean recovery even in the case of a catastrophic Saturn V explosion. The escape tower packed 147,000 pounds of thrust, more power than Alan Shepard's entire Mercury Redstone rocket. By about three minutes into the launch, when the Saturn V was 60 miles up, the command module could drop safely into the sea on its own in a launch abort, and at this point the escape tower was jettisoned.

## SERVICE MODULE

Divided into six radial sections, the service module held main engine propellants, electrical fuel cells, and oxygen supplies for the command module. One section was left empty for use in advanced future models of the spacecraft.

## LUNAR MODULE GARAGE
### (SPACECRAFT-LM ADAPTER, OR S.L.A.)

About three hours after liftoff, in space en route to the Moon, the four doors of the LM garage opened outward like petals to release the LM. The doors could be built to disengage from the garage and float off into space or to remain hinged at the base, and both configurations were flown on different Apollo missions.

## INSTRUMENT UNIT

The Saturn V's computer brain consisted of many advanced component "black boxes" and instruments, including the ST-124 inertial guidance system, bolted in place around the inside of this ring.

## LAUNCH SHIELD
### (BOOST PROTECTIVE COVER, OR B.P.C.)

To protect the command module from the friction of the supersonic slipstream during launch and then from the rocket blast of the escape tower, a fiberglass shield sheathed in cork covered the spacecraft until the escape tower was jettisoned.

## COMMAND MODULE

Sealed under the launch shield until the escape tower was jettisoned, the Apollo capsule was the only element of the space vehicle that would make the round trip. The launch shield covered all the capsule windows except the mission commander's center porthole, which provided the only view outside during launch.

## LUNAR MODULE

Suspended for transportation, the lunar module locked at the "knees" into the base of its garage, its legs folded in for tight packing. When the garage petals opened in space, the LM was triggered to release at the knee joints with springs.

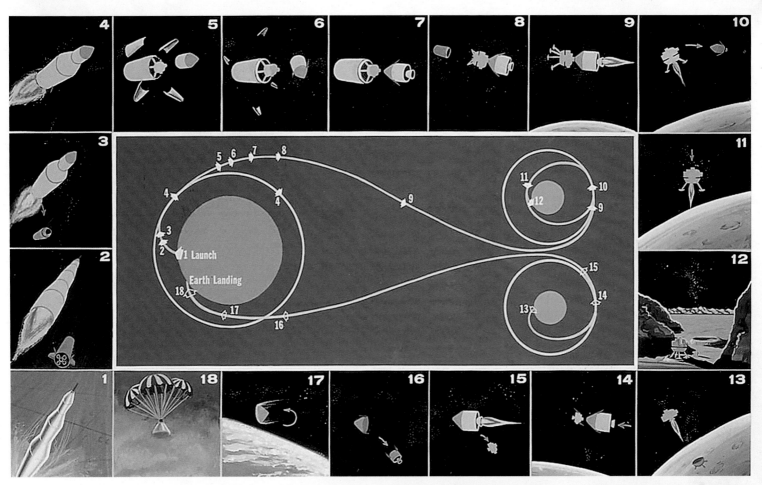

This NASA artwork painted early in the Apollo program shows the sequence of operations in a Moon landing mission. Each step is keyed to the schematic trajectory plan at center, which shows that the Moon (at right) moves in its orbit during the mission. The turnaround, docking, and pullout maneuver (steps 5–8) could not be photographed from outside the spacecraft and consequently has been the least understood.

function. But the Rocketdyne engineers kept working on the F-1, test-firing it on a 25-story Mojave Desert test stand called "The Battleship" and revising the fuel injector plate in a struggle to achieve stable combustion of the huge floods of propellant eaten by the engine.

When a successful design was finally built, the determined engineers strove to refine it still further by setting bombs inside it to disrupt combustion flow. This approach curiously recalled the ancient Greek orator Demosthenes, who practiced delivering speeches with rocks in his mouth to improve his articulation. The Rocketdyne engineers worked the F-1 injector and thrust chamber design until the injector plate bore 6,300 tiny injection holes, creating a fine mist of propellants in a pattern that achieved a mix so stable it could recover perfect combustion in just one tenth of a second after a bomb detonation inside the engine. The F-1, it appeared, was ready for anything. Such stories lay behind components throughout the Moon rocket, every piece representing the best efforts of hard-working engineers and fabricators who knew that America was counting on them.

Over one million parts composed every Saturn V. NASA had to invent scanner bar codes to keep track of all the parts, since the numbers overwhelmed any existing inventory system. In spite of all this complexity and its unprecedented size, the Saturn V was the most successful rocket ever created: In tests and in manned flight, not one Saturn V ever failed, a testament to the extraordinary dedication that the Apollo project inspired.

## LIQUID OXYGEN LINES

Liquid oxygen flowed to the main engines via five perfectly straight tubes that drilled right through the center of the fuel tank below. There could be no bends whatsoever in the tubes since they had to carry torrents of liquid oxygen at 2,000 gallons per second. Von Braun must have taken some satisfaction in seeing them built since they looked just like the dead straight fuel lines running through the propellant tanks he had conceived for his *Collier's* ferry rocket back in 1952.

## THRUST STRUCTURE BRACING

## TITANIUM FINS

## ORIENTATION MARKINGS

## STAGING RETRO-ROCKETS

Powerful solid retro-rockets, two concealed in each fin fairing, yanked the entire first stage backward when its burn was complete, pulling it safely away from the rocket before the second-stage engines ignited.

## INTERTANK CORRUGATIONS FOR STRENGTH

## RP-1 KEROSENE FUEL TANK

## REGENERATIVE COOLING

The F-1 engines burned at 4,000°F, so hot that they could quickly melt themselves. (Steel melts at 2,900°F.) Cold rocket fuel was therefore circulated through a system of fine tubes composing the upper engine bell, simultaneously cooling the engine and preheating the fuel before it hit the thrust chamber.

## F-1 ENGINES

Five F-1 engines developed the titanic thrust of 7.6 million pounds to launch the Saturn V. Any one of these engines was more powerful than the entire second stage of the Saturn V. The center engine was mounted in a fixed position, while the outer four could be steered, or "gimballed," to guide the rocket in flight.

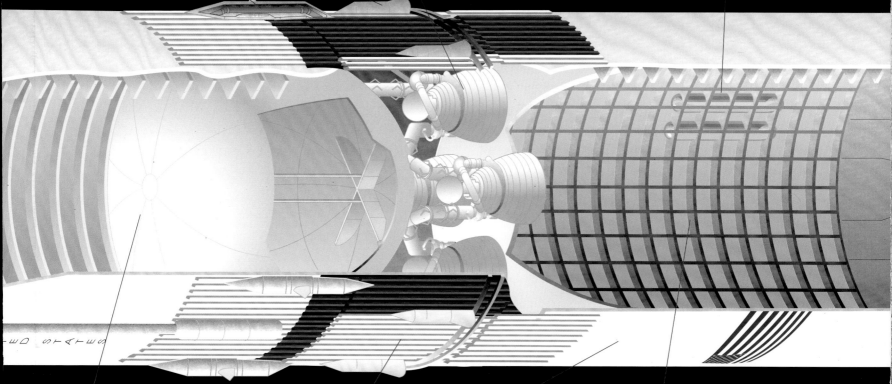

## LIQUID OXYGEN TANK

### SLOSH ROCKETS

To slosh propellants to the bottom of their tanks so that the turbo-pumps could work smoothly, solid "ullage" rockets in the interstage gave the second stage a push forward before its ignition.

### J-2 ENGINE

Five J-2 engines in the second stage burned the advanced, lightweight, cryogenic fuel liquid hydrogen, but they were far less powerful than the F-1 engines of the first stage. Each J-2 engine developed 230,000 pounds of thrust; the group of five providing a total of 1.15 million pounds, less than a single kerosene-burning F-1.

## PRESSURIZING HELIUM BOTTLES

## LIQUID HYDROGEN LINES

At -452°F, cryogenic liquid hydrogen fuel was so cold that it could freeze liquid oxygen solid. Fuel lines to the J-2 engines therefore could not run through the oxygen tank and had to be ducted outside the hull and around the lower tank, using insulated vacuum-jacketed tubes.

## INTERSTAGE

This ring, corrugated for additional strength, served as a spacer between the stage below and the stage above. It was jettisoned shortly after the first stage fell away.

## S-IC FIRST STAGE

The first stage carried the Saturn V to an altitude of 42 miles, burning for two minutes and forty seconds before shutdown and separation. Spent first stages dropped into the Atlantic halfway to Bermuda.

## LIQUID OXYGEN TANK

Moving a Saturn V and its launch umbilical tower all that way would require another of Apollo's mighty works: a crawler-transporter capable of carrying a skyscraper. Twin crawler leviathans were constructed at the Cape, square platforms two stories thick with giant treads at each corner. If the gleaming and ethereal white rocket towering into the sky looked as if it had been fashioned by Apollo himself, the crawler-transporter looked as if it had been roughly forged at the anvils of Vulcan and his cyclopes in the heart of Mount Aetna. Built like a battleship, the largest land vehicle in the world, the monster held engine rooms that could have belonged in destroyers. This was a vehicle of mythic stature to give the Saturn V good company. The crawler's road was a gravel-covered Olympian causeway 110 feet wide, with foundations seven feet deep. As the crawler crept by, it crushed the gravel stones into powder.

The road led to the launch pads—two, like the crawlers, so that there was always a backup. At the pad, the rocket would be poised over a huge inverted V called the flame deflector, which would keep the blast from rebounding into the engines and detonating the Saturn V. The deflector would split the exhaust into two opposing channels within a flame trench, and the blast would shoot out to the sides. Lining the flame trench were walls that could withstand the searing forces of 1,900°F temperatures and hypersonic flames reaching velocities of Mach 4. Lined with specially fired bricks, the flame trench was built to withstand the apocalypse.

At a maximum loaded speed of one mile per hour, a grinding crawler-transporter moved the first flight-ready Moon rocket, surrounded by a walking crew of spotters keeping watch over its every movement, out to pad 39A. The rocket was number AS-504, and it had the Germans' hearts racing. At the top of the launch pad, the crawler-transporter backed out from under its load, leaving the rocket and its tower in place, and retreated to a safe distance.

## ALL-UP

**A**S-504 was Apollo 4, and it reached its launch pad in November 1967. Equipped with a new Block II capsule, it would be flight-tested without men on board. Apollo 4 was the first fully functional realization of von Braun's monumental design, and the veteran rocketeer had badly wanted to test this prodigious machine, "his baby," one piece at a time, launching a live first stage with dummy upper stages, then adding an additional live stage at each subsequent launch. This was the most conservative approach, and it was how the Germans liked to do things. But NASA associate administrator George Mueller made one of the biggest decisions of the Apollo program and went directly against von Braun's recommendation. The Saturn V would be tested "all up," with all stages live on the very first launch. The Germans were aghast. But Mueller's approach would, if successful, make up the time lost with Apollo 1 and conserve the valuable rocket equipment for future missions.

"All-up" was a possibility only because von Braun had done such an incredible job making the Saturn V a sound and reliable instrument, but the boldness of risking the entire ship all at once was too much for its designer. Yet Mueller had confidence in the German team's work, and perhaps a purely American streak of daring in him. That together with the reliable German engineering made the ideal combination. Von Braun, as always, supported the decision of his superior in the end. On November 9, 1967, Apollo 4 was launched all-up, 100 percent live, with the launch team absolutely on pins and needles. Three million parts, and it had never flown, but on its first flight, the miracle instrument worked. In one mission, Mueller saved tens of millions of dollars in extra rocket stages and made up for our lost time at a single stroke. We were back in the race.

# The Vehicle Assembly Building

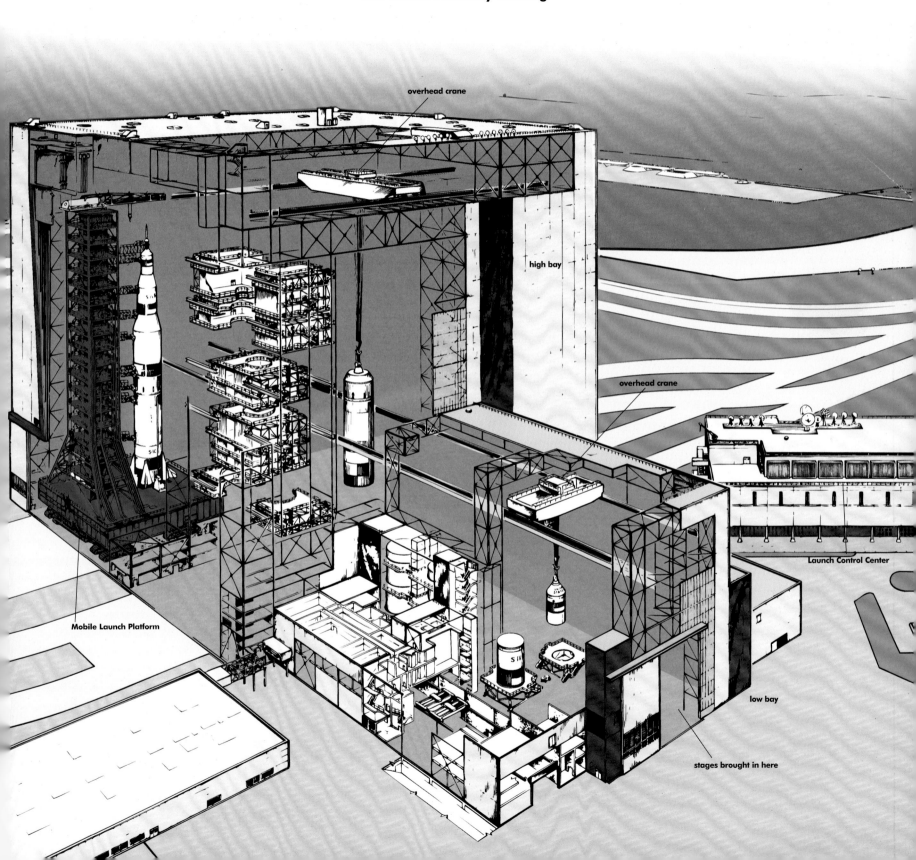

overhead crane

high bay

overhead crane

Launch Control Center

Mobile Launch Platform

low bay

stages brought in here

# The Cape

Under the direction of Wernher von Braun's trusted longtime launch supervisor Dr. Kurt Debus, Florida's Cape Canaveral grew from a primitive missile test site into the colossal Apollo spaceport facility. Here at the Cape, all the elements of the Apollo program came together as the Saturn V rocket components were assembled, prepared, loaded with astronauts, and launched for the Moon.

*Circle indicates Cape Canaveral, Florida.*

**A**pollo's Launch Complex 39 facilities were sited on Merritt Island, at the north end of the Cape's series of launch pads. The 52-story Vehicle Assembly Building, or V.A.B., was the center of Moon rocket assembly operations. The final endpoints of Launch Complex 39 were the twin launch pads A and B, three and a half miles away.

The Saturn V components were so massive that transporting them to the V.A.B. from across the United States involved major logistical efforts. The S-IC and S-II first and second stages were both 36 feet in diameter. These monsters could only be transported to Florida by water. The S-ICs, built near New Orleans, were shipped along the Gulf Coast, while the S-II stages, built in California, had to make the long journey through the Panama Canal. A barge channel at the Cape brought these giant constructions to a turn basin for unloading close to the doors of the V.A.B.

The smaller S-IVB third stages had been slated for a similar long boat trip from their construction site near Los Angeles, but a visionary entrepreneur created a bizarre cargo plane called the Super Guppy, built specially to hold the oversize rocket-stage cargoes. The bulbous plane lifted the largest air-cargo volumes ever flown and saved NASA months in delivery time, flying the stages to an airstrip near the V.A.B. The redoubtable Super Guppy also ended up ferrying the delicate lunar modules and the command and service modules from their construction sites on Long Island and in Washington state. All these components were trucked the short distance from the Cape airstrip to the V.A.B.

In the early days of manned spaceflight, Mission Control had been on-site. The legendary Chris Kraft defined and created the archetypal new role of flight director beginning at Mercury Mission Control in the southern part of the Cape. By the days of Apollo, Kraft was overseeing a new generation of flight controllers at the impressive new Apollo Mission Control facilities in Houston, Texas. The launch teams at the Cape released control of each Apollo Saturn V to Houston as soon as the rocket cleared the launch tower.

*NASA shared the Cape with the U.S. Air Force, whose nuclear missile launch pads formed "Missile Row," seen in this 1964 view looking north. Beyond the missile sites lies the Apollo launch complex, with the VAB under construction.*

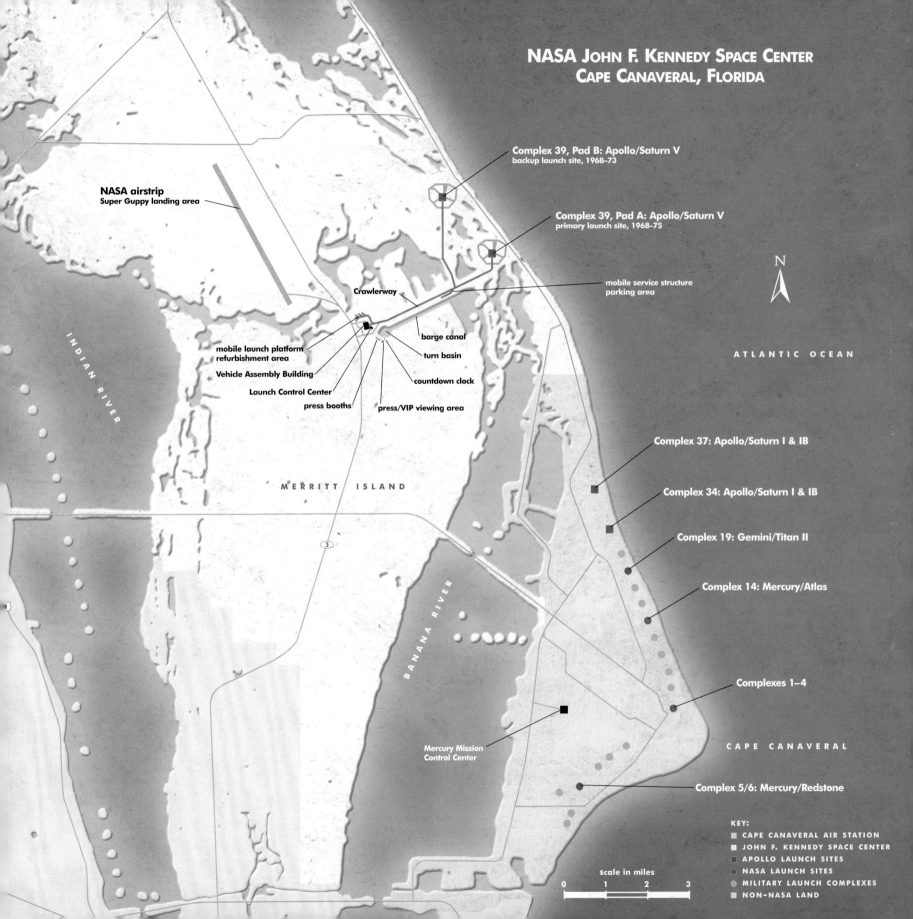

# NASA JOHN F. KENNEDY SPACE CENTER
## CAPE CANAVERAL, FLORIDA

**Complex 39, Pad B: Apollo/Saturn V**
backup launch site, 1968–73

**Complex 39, Pad A: Apollo/Saturn V**
primary launch site, 1968–75

**NASA airstrip**
Super Guppy landing area

mobile service structure
parking area

Crawlerway

ATLANTIC OCEAN

barge canal

mobile launch platform
refurbishment area

turn basin

Vehicle Assembly Building

countdown clock

Launch Control Center

press booths

press/VIP viewing area

INDIAN RIVER

N

MERRITT  ISLAND

Complex 37: Apollo/Saturn I & IB

Complex 34: Apollo/Saturn I & IB

Complex 19: Gemini/Titan II

Complex 14: Mercury/Atlas

BANANA RIVER

Complexes 1–4

Mercury Mission
Control Center

CAPE CANAVERAL

Complex 5/6: Mercury/Redstone

KEY:
- CAPE CANAVERAL AIR STATION
- JOHN F. KENNEDY SPACE CENTER
- APOLLO LAUNCH SITES
- NASA LAUNCH SITES
- MILITARY LAUNCH COMPLEXES
- NON-NASA LAND

scale in miles
0   1   2   3

b

a

## STACKING

*Rocket stages are brought into the Vehicle Assembly Building, or V.A.B. (a), to be "stacked" into a complete Moon rocket. Larger stages arrive by canal at a nearby turn basin (k). Movable platforms inside the V.A.B., above, allow close inspection of every phase of operations.*

## ROLLOUT

*Each Saturn V stacked in the V.A.B. is monitored from first assembly through launch from one of the four firing rooms in the adjacent Launch Control Center (c), which serves as "Mission Control" for launch operations. Each Saturn V is stacked on one of three mobile launch platforms (f), which carry a built-in launch umbilical tower (e) equipped with fueling connections. When the rocket assembly is complete, the Saturn V is rolled out of the V.A.B. to begin its journey to the launch pad. The mobile launch platforms are brought back to an outdoor parking area near the V.A.B., above (right), for refurbishment after the violence of a launch.*

## TRANSPORT

*The treaded crawler-transporter (d) carries the Saturn V and its mobile launch platform 3.5 miles from the VAB to the launch pad. Four million-watt generators driven by two 2,750-horsepower diesel engines give the crawler-transporter its motive power. At up to a maximum loaded speed of one mile per hour, the crawler moves its colossal load along a special 110-foot-wide roadway (g) covered with gravel. The crawler traveled 3.5 miles to reach pad A, or 4.2 miles to reach pad B, the journey taking about six hours since the crawler was not always run at maximum speed. A twin crawler waits on standby near the VAB as a backup.*

## SERVICE

*The crawler-transporter places the Saturn V and its platform and tower on the launch pad, then withdraws to pick up the mobile service structure (i), above (right), which provides final servicing to the Moon rocket. Just before launch, the mobile service structure and crawler retreat to a parking area (j) away from the blast zone.*

## LAUNCH PAD

*The Saturn V and its mobile launch platform stand in readiness over the heavily reinforced cellular concrete launch pad 39 A (h), right, as the crawler makes its way back down the ramp. A backup flame deflector can be seen to the right of the pad. Around the perimeter of the pad are storage facilities for Saturn V propellants: White spherical tanks hold cryogenic liquid oxygen and liquid hydrogen, and square ponds contain any spilled RP-1 kerosene. At the pad the Saturn V is fueled and boarded for launch. An identical pad 39 B (b) lies nearby as a backup.*

*The first men headed for the Moon walk through the Manned Spacecraft Operations Building at Kennedy Space Center on the way to the transfer van that will take them to launch pad 39A. Apollo 8 mission commander Frank Borman is followed by Jim Lovell and Bill Anders, each carrying portable pre-launch cooling units for their spacesuits.*

## APOLLO 8

The reliability of the Saturn V became the crux of the greatest gamble ever taken in the American space program when CIA intelligence reported that the Soviets appeared to be on the brink of sending two cosmonauts on a mission looping around the back of the Moon. Still in the dark about the true capabilities of the U.S.S.R., NASA believed that America was on track to make the first Moon landing before the end of 1969. But if the Soviets put the first man around the Moon earlier, the Russians could claim to have "reached the Moon" first, and the race would be over, an American landing positioned as merely a follow-up. It would be a brilliant coup for the U.S.S.R. And it was a contingency that had not been considered until now, when the impending possibility drenched those facing it

with reality. The high-stakes game that made all this worth $24 billion and the federal DX rating of highest national priority was for victory alone. As Kennedy had observed, in this race, "Second place is last." It was 1968, and we were looking at having the rug pulled out from under all our massive efforts at the Cape and around the nation. The situation was crisis.

NASA planners coolly considered their options. The lunar module was still not ready. What we did have to work with was the Apollo command module and the Saturn V. The second unmanned Saturn V launch, Apollo 6, had revealed some serious problems with vibration, but von Braun and his engineers thought they had it figured out. What if we put the Apollo 8 crew in a Saturn V and sent them around the Moon now? The sprint of the moment was to orbit the Moon, and the Apollo command module could accomplish that mission.

BORMAN LOVELL ANDERS

*Jim Lovell designed the Apollo 8 mission patch, sketching it while flying to Houston with Frank Borman the evening after he learned he was going to the Moon.*

It was the most daring proposal NASA had ever seriously considered. No one had ever flown on a Saturn V, and we were proposing to send the first manned titan all the way to the Moon. Deke Slayton offered the mission, with all its risks and unknowns, to astronaut Frank Borman. Would Borman be willing to try it? A dedicated man who lived for his missions, Borman said "absolutely." In that moment Borman committed himself and his crewmen, Jim Lovell and Bill Anders, to one of the greatest journeys of all time.

In 1865, Jules Verne had imagined that his bullet-shaped projectile would carry three men into orbit around the Moon. A century later, three men chosen to fly the bullet-shaped Apollo command module contemplated the odd coincidence that their names echoed those of Verne's heroes: in the imaginary path of Barbicane, Nicholl, and Ardan, the astronauts Borman, Lovell, and Anders would travel for real, to the Moon—the Moon, at last, in a bold national gamble to keep hold of the race.

The three astronauts stepped out of the transfer van to board their spacecraft at 6:14 in the morning of December 21, 1968. At the launch pad, their gleaming, towering, fueled, and loaded Saturn V had become an altogether different being from the monumental empty instrument that had left the V.A.B. Five hundred and twenty-five thousand gallons of liquefied gases now filled the tanks within, fighting their unnatural state, constantly boiling off, being vented out, and being replaced with more ultracold liquid gas pouring in through the launch tower's umbilical arms as the vehicle was kept ready for space. Electrical power coursed throughout the craft, running through vertical conduits on the outside of the stages, racing through 700 miles of wiring in the Apollo capsule, cascading through infinitesimal calculations and recalculations in the Instrument Unit computer brain of the Saturn V. The astronauts could feel it as they entered the launch tower elevator that would take them up the dizzying height to the top of this monster. The entire 36-story assembly, this Saturn V built by 800,000 hands, had come alive.

Rockwell technicians loaded Borman, Lovell, and Anders on board their spacecraft. The last man to see them was a favorite figure at the Cape, an ex-*Luftwaffe* mechanic named Gunter Wendt, known to the astronauts as "Der Pad Führer." Wendt smiled at the men he had come to know and sealed the hatch of Apollo 8. The Moon awaited.

Nine seconds before liftoff, the igniters fired above the cavernous engine bells of the five F-1 engines underneath the Saturn V. Fuel and cryogenic oxidizer sprayed into the injection chamber, and flame was born. Five seconds before launch, the I.U. had control of the ship and was throttling up the gouts of fire now exploding out of the engines. Seven and a half million pounds of thrust mounted and strained at the hold-down arms clamping the skyscraper to the hole in the launch platform. The I.U. took one last look at a theodolite survey marker mounted between the crawler tracks of the ramp leading up to the pad. This was the final reference to a known point on the Earth. The ST-124 inertial guidance system initialized, and the craft's awareness became completely internal. Borman, Lovell, and Anders felt the rumble originating 350 feet below them. The thrust had risen to maximum. Explosive charges fired and released all four hold-down arms within the same millisecond. The Saturn V suddenly stood on pure flame, pure force, in the air, and it rose. Fire and ice cascaded past one another as frozen condensation vibrated off the supercooled hull and rained down

**DER PAD FÜHRER**

*In the White Room atop the launch umbilical tower, Bill Anders is helped into the Apollo 8 capsule and wished farewell by Gunter Wendt. The astronauts specifically requested Wendt as the pad director because of his strict professionalism during the Mercury and Gemini programs. Wendt was the last person whom departing crews would see until their return.*

around the engines. The holocaust poured and blossomed. Hypersonic waves of flame bathed the flame deflector's surface, the searing 1,900°F torrent blasting almost an inch of ceramic surface off the device. For 12 seconds, the Saturn V lifted, its engines moving to steer it from drifting into the launch tower.

Twelve long seconds was enough time for the penetrating sound of the Saturn V to roll across the Cape. The sound shook the ground. Onlookers at the press site felt something grab their feet and beat at the air in their lungs. It was the crackling sonic impact of the gigantic missile rising above the tower. The Saturn V was fighting the Earth, defying gravity through sheer raw force, and the body could feel every ounce of that screaming will as the rocket rose on an amplified Niagara of solid, white-hot flame. And at the top of this inferno was the Saturn V. Inside a small room at its apex, the control panels shook around three astronauts, the first men to endure such an experience.

Thundering violence battered the cockpit of the rocket as it rose. The spectators were three miles away from this monstrous din; the astronauts were right above it. For them it was like being in an earthquake with the roar of a dam breaking. Bill Anders, experiencing his first rocket launch, was astonished at the magnitude of it all.

As soon as the rocket was safely clear of the tower, the I.U. started gimballing the F-1s to tilt the vehicle to the east, over the Atlantic, beginning its arc toward escape velocity. The astronauts could feel the movements below them, the center of gravity shifting as the engines moved. Gaining speed, the Saturn V drilled relentlessly through the heavy atmosphere, oblivious to every gust or patch of turbulence, every influence of the jet stream or any other force of weather. The ST-124 inside the I.U. brain noted every slight buffeting, every distortion of the intended course, and did nothing. While the F-1 dragons burned, the Saturn V would have drilled straight through a tornado. The flight path was predetermined. Only when the first stage was spent would the ST-124's data be used to steer the Saturn V to compensate for any

**APOLLO 8 LIFTOFF**

*The first manned Saturn V makes a flawless launch in December 1968 on NASA's most daring Apollo mission, a quantum leap for lunar orbit. The huge Moon rocket would trail an 800-foot flame as it rose above the launch tower.*

weather interference it had encountered. Von Braun's engineers had found that the natural harmonic frequency of the complete Saturn V stack was alarmingly close to that of the engine control system. Too much gimballing could set up feedback cycles that would quickly tear the rocket apart, especially if it were trying to compensate for every eddy in the atmosphere. So the Saturn V wore blinders for the first 42 miles of altitude, following its plan and controlling the engines. There would be time for course fine-tuning soon enough.

**B**orman's ship coasted around the Earth for three orbits as the astronauts checked out all their systems on the other side of the sky. Apollo 8 was performing perfectly.

Mission Control in Houston had smoothly taken over from Launch Control at the Cape. To keep communications with the astronauts clear, only one person was authorized to use the direct radio link to the capsule: the Capcom, who relayed all necessary information to the crew. Normally, the Capcom was a fellow astronaut. At Mission Elapsed Time 6:37, the man sitting at the fourth seat in the second row of consoles at Mission Control was Capcom Michael Collins, who had been scrubbed from this very mission due to the occurrence of a bone spur on his spine. Now fully recovered from an operation to remove it, Collins was serving as Capcom for the colleagues who were flying in his place. Collins would follow soon enough. Though he did not know it at the time, he would pilot a command module on the first lunar-landing mission. But that lay in the uncertain future. In the tense moment of the present, Flight Director Gene Kranz

### GREEN AND GO

*Several flight control teams operating under color-code names worked in shifts to provide round-the-clock support for each Apollo mission from the instant the Saturn V cleared the launch tower. Here "green team" flight director Clifford Charlesworth monitors the launch of Apollo 8 at Mission Control in Houston.*

# Saturn V Launch

Massive preparations by a team of over 5,000 people at Cape Canaveral built up to the moment when a Saturn V rocket with all its explosive power would be ignited. Four hundred and fifty people manned the firing room alone. A flawless performance by every individual made the difference between a Moon rocket and the world's tallest bomb.

Countdown began 28 hours before launch time with the words "T minus 28 hours and counting." From this point on, Apollo operations at Cape Canaveral were at their highest level of alert. A Saturn V launch was coming. It was like knowing where a tornado was going to hit.

The 402-foot, 9.8-million-pound mobile service structure contained movable platforms deployed to envelop the Moon rocket during its preparation and testing at the launch pad. At T-11 hours, the service structure was withdrawn to a parking area 7,000 feet from the pad, and the Saturn V was on its own.

Sixty television cameras monitored the rocket, transmitting information back to 15 display screens in the Launch Control Center firing room, where technicians sat at 150 consoles monitoring every aspect of the colossus on the pad during the countdown. Wernher von Braun, Kennedy Space Center Director Kurt Debus, and Launch Operations Director Rocco Petrone oversaw their men on-site.

The stages were powered up one by one and loaded with their fuels. The crew were boarded and strapped in by T-2 hours and 10 minutes, and the hatch was closed for good 30 minutes later. The launch-escape-system pyrotechnics were armed. At T-3 minutes 10 seconds, a firing command initiated the automatic launch sequencer. At 50 seconds the Saturn V was on its own internal power. Ten seconds before the moment of liftoff, water began pouring into the flame trench below. At 8.9 seconds, the F-1 engines ignited, vaporizing much of the water as it continued pouring in. By the final seconds, all five engines were thundering at full thrust, and then the Moon rocket was released by the 20-ton hold-down clamps. A million-gallon deluge flooded the deck of the launch platform to prevent its incineration as the rocket rose, and each of the withdrawn umbilical arms on the launch tower were showered as well. Within 12 seconds, the rocket cleared the tower, and at that moment Mission Control in Houston took over. The Cape had done its job, and the bird was in the air.

*The first stage disengages and falls behind as the Saturn V speeds onward. Small solid rockets, trailing thin flames, slosh fuel to the bottom of the tanks before the second stage engines ignite.*

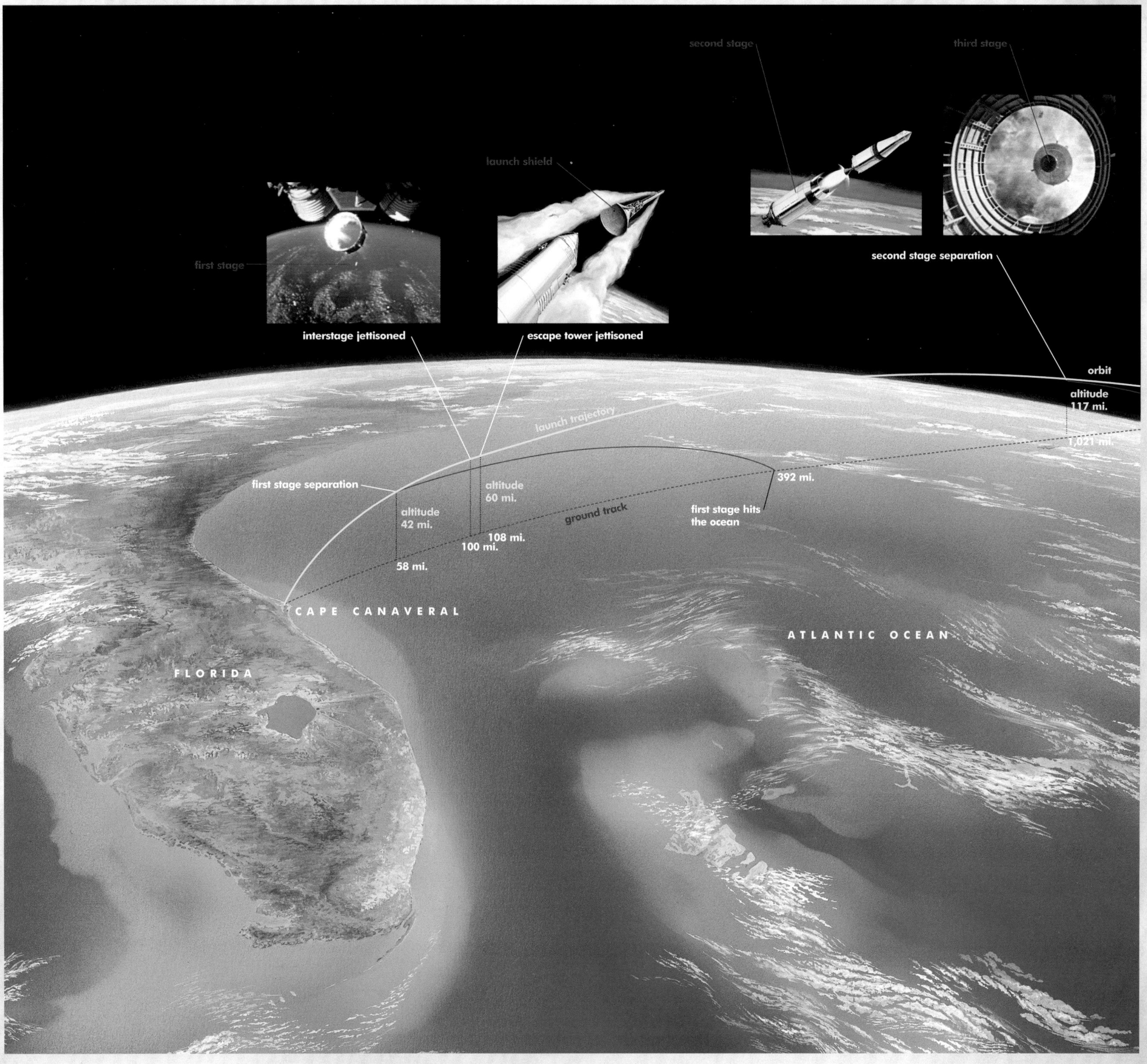

first stage

interstage jettisoned

launch shield

escape tower jettisoned

second stage

third stage

second stage separation

orbit

altitude
117 mi.

1,021 mi.

launch trajectory

first stage separation

altitude
60 mi.

altitude
42 mi.

ground track

108 mi.
100 mi.

58 mi.

392 mi.

first stage hits
the ocean

CAPE CANAVERAL

ATLANTIC OCEAN

FLORIDA

*From the launch site at Cape Canaveral, the Saturn V arced eastward, building the 17,386-mph speed that would keep it in orbit around the Earth. Orbital altitude was only 117 miles up, far lower than might be imagined. Spent Saturn V first and second stages plunged into the Atlantic, the first halfway to Bermuda and the second southwest of the Azores.*

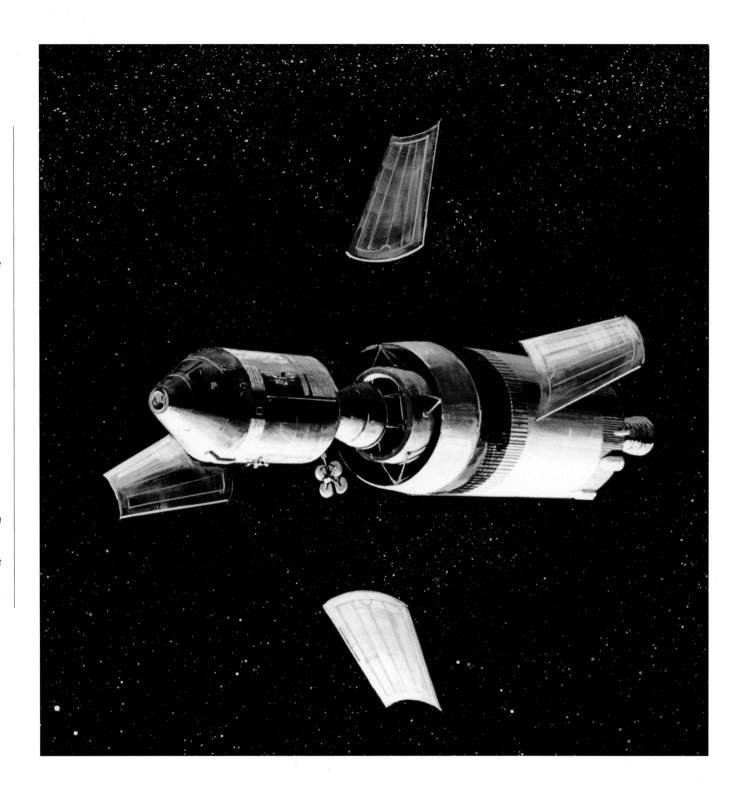

## SEPARATION

*This NASA artwork shows Frank Borman's Apollo 8 command module breaking free of the Saturn V third stage that boosted it toward the Moon. Four petal-like panels of the lunar-module garage float off into space behind the command module, revealing the deadweight strapped in place of the lunar module, which was not yet ready for Moon service. Wally Schirra had observed one of the LM garage panels jam on Apollo 7 and recommended that they be built to disengage completely on later missions.*

had polled his lead men, and all systems were Go. He gave the nod to Collins, who delivered an approval never before spoken in earnest: "Apollo 8, you are Go for T.L.I." T.L.I. meant Trans-Lunar Injection, the rocket burn that would make this mission different from all that had preceded it, American or Soviet. Never before had men fired a rocket that would send them beyond the reach of Earth's gravity. The command that Frank Borman initiated fired the single J-2 engine of the S-IVB third stage, to which his command module was still attached. This burn would accelerate Apollo 8 from 17,000 to 24,000 mph, breaking away from Earth.

The Earth shrank visibly outside their window. The world from which they had launched became a rounded horizon as they floated high above it. Now—and they could see this—they were leaving it. As they watched, it receded behind them—along with every person, every place, and every thing they had ever known. They had stepped out into the void.

**T**he Moon grew before them. Sixty-six hours they spent crossing translunar space. The silvery disc that had waxed and waned over a thousand million landscapes since before the dawn of man hung large in a world of blackness. The astronauts could not see it, as their ship hurtled silently toward it, tail-first, oriented to fire braking thrust when it was time to slow themselves. They could not see how the disc changed and began to bulge toward them. As their intricate vessel slid ever closer at inconceivable yet imperceptible speed, the infinite detail of the Moon slowly crystallized. The disc became a vast sphere. The sphere became a planet, which enveloped and captured Apollo 8 within its gravitation.

As they entered orbit, they saw a great gulf of darkness eclipse the stars. As they neared the illuminated side of the world they circled, Bill Anders became aware of something that looked to him like streaks of oil running down the capsule window. He looked closer, knowing that this would be impossible in space. They all looked. The gently moving ribbons of light were not on the window. They were faintly lit, undulating hills. "Oh my God," Anders gasped. It was the Moon.

The planet had become finally a horizon—but not horizontal, as on Earth; instead, due to their orientation, this visual limit ran vertically, to their side, as their ship cruised around the alien world's equator. It was as if they were flying along the face of a vast rocky cliff that hung above an abyss.

Apollo 8 entered orbit around the Moon, 240,000 miles away from Houston, and prepared to travel around the far side. The astronauts readied themselves for unprecedented isolation. One half of their world would be the dead Moon, its dry, craggy face hanging in the airless void, a scant 69 miles away from their capsule. The other half of their world would be infinity: the endless black that stretches beyond the stars, to galaxies and to the uttermost reaches of nothingness. And aside from each man's two comrades and the limits of their 214-cubic-foot capsule, there would be no trace of humanity anywhere in their universe. Not a radio signal, not a light, nothing.

Apollo 8 traveled silently around the far side of the Moon on December 24, 1968. Borman, Lovell, and Anders had sailed beyond the edge of the world and were traveling farther than anyone had ever been before, mankind's boldest scouts, pioneers of the heavens. Below them lay terrain never before seen by human eyes. The Moon that all the world sees in its familiar sky never turns its back to the Earth. Three men now saw this hidden side as eyewitnesses for the first time.

The eons-old craters of the Moon flowed past outside the capsule's crystal windows. Each man struggled to describe what he saw to the voices in their headphones coming from somewhere warm, somewhere very far away. "It looks like plaster of paris," Lovell commented. "Like dirty beach sand," Anders said. "The Moon is a different thing to each one of us," Borman told Mission Control.

**DESTINATION**

*For three days the Apollo 8 astronauts journeyed outward toward a goal they could not see. The Moon would fill their view once they slipped into orbit around it.*

*Apollo 8 moved farther away from Earth than anyone had ever been before, the crew marveling at their increasingly distant home radioed back their impressions. "The Earth from here," Jim Lovell said, "is a grand oasis in the big vastness of space."*

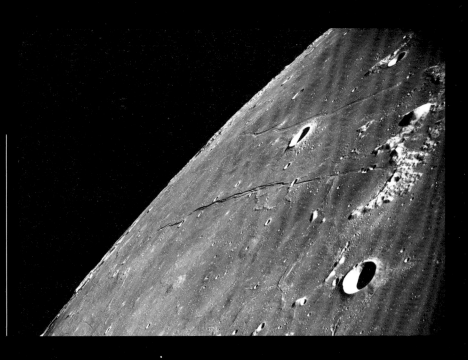

### FORBIDDING WORLD

*The Moon presented Apollo 8 with a harsh contrast to the soft and vibrant colors of the Earth. This view was captured as the spacecraft cruised over the dead landscape of the Sea of Tranquility.*

### WORLD OF ASH

*"A vastness of black and white," Bill Anders called the closest view men had ever had of the Moon. "Absolutely no color." "It certainly would not appear to be a very inviting place to live or work," commented Frank Borman.*

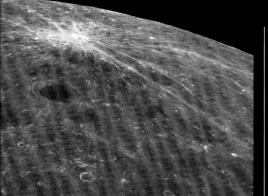

## PERSPECTIVE

Frank Borman called it a "foreboding horizon." Jim Lovell said, "The vast loneliness up here at the Moon is awe inspiring, and it makes you realize what you have back there on Earth."

## BATTLEFIELD

Ancient rille channels mark the floor of crater Geoclinus, with younger and older impact scars lying beyond it.

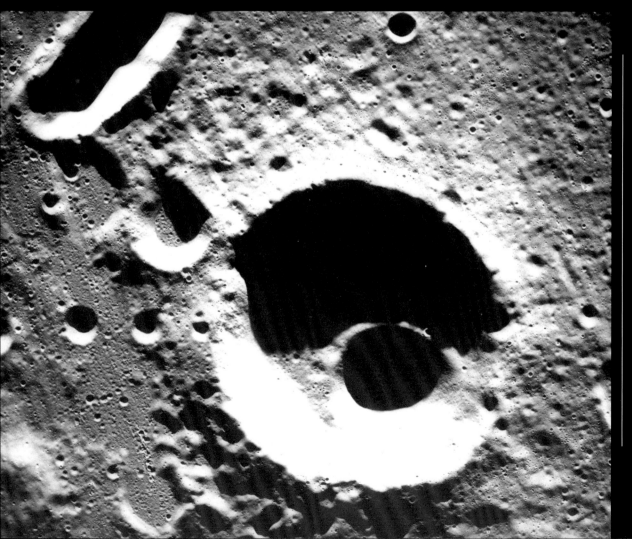

## SHADOWS

Apollo 8 was an experimental mission in which any serious malfunction could have stranded the astronauts in space. Views of the overwhelmingly barren realm below them prompted the travelers to muse on their situation. "Well," Jim Lovell said at one point, "did you guys ever think that one Christmas you'd be orbiting the Moon?" Bill Anders replied, "Just hope we're not doing it on New Year's."

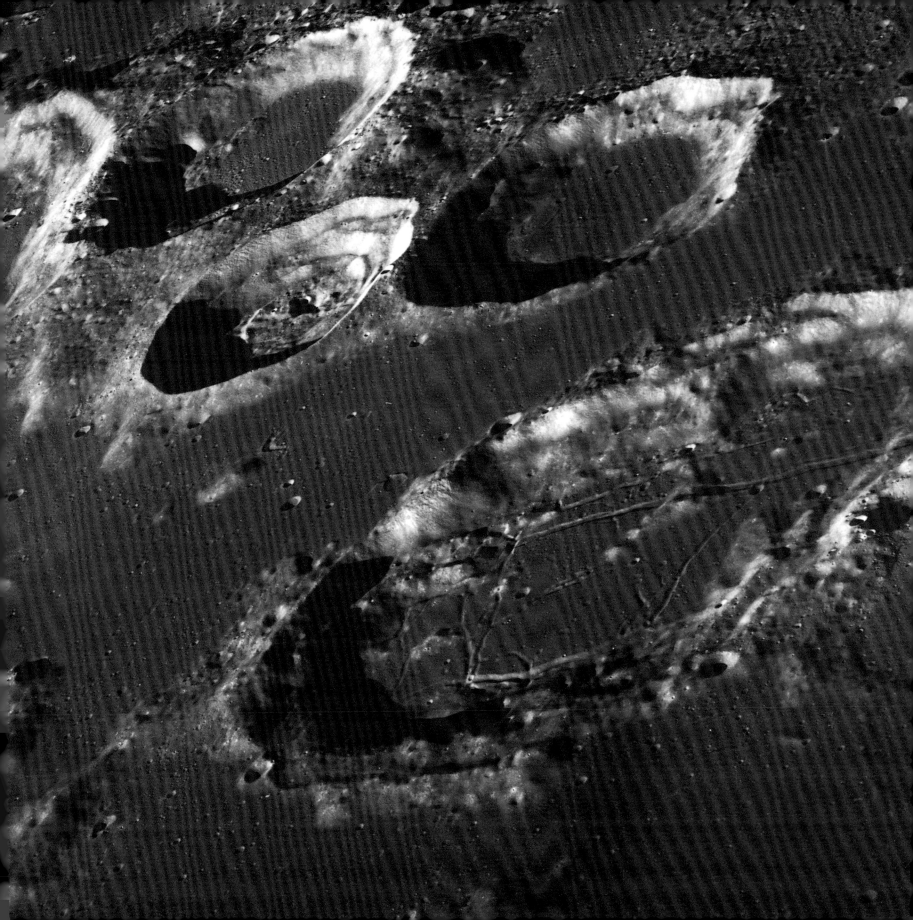

"It looks like a vast, lonely, forbidding place, an expanse of nothing. . . ." Anders watched the craters flow past their windows. "You can see that the planet has been bombarded through the eons with numerous meteorites," he reported. "Every square inch is pockmarked."

The rugged, abandoned battlefield below them rolled on as their course carried them around the world of ethereal, delicate grays. And then a blue-and-white light appeared on the horizon. It slowly rose and became a disc. For the first time, humans saw their home planet above another body: It was an earthrise. This would become the enduring image of Apollo 8, captured for their fellow humans back home by the cameras they carried on board. It was truth, light, warmth, and richness, circumscribed in a perfect circle, surrounded by an endless sea of utter blackness and shining above a dead world which had none of its luxuriance.

Apollo 8 had kept in touch with Earth, showing the world to itself as a small smudge on TV. Before they sailed once more around the far side of the Moon, they had a message. It was Christmas Eve, and the world was listening. As they approached the last moments of contact, mission commander Borman and his crewmates read a passage they had brought with them. Their words came from a quarter of a million miles away, and they could not have been more profound.

"In the beginning," Anders began, as he sailed through the void between the blue world and the gray, "God created the heaven and the Earth. And the Earth was without form, and void; and darkness was on the face of the deep. And the Spirit of God moved upon the face of the

waters. And God said, 'Let there be light.' And there was light. And God saw the light, that it was good. And God divided the light from the darkness."

Jim Lovell continued: "And God called the light Day, and the darkness he called Night. And the evening and the morning were the first day. And God said, 'Let there be a firmament in the midst of the waters, and let it divide the waters from the waters.' And God made the firmament and divided the waters which were under the firmament from the waters which were above the firmament. And it was so. And God called the firmament Heaven. And the evening and the morning were the second day."

Frank Borman now took up the text. "And God said, 'Let the waters under the heaven be gathered together unto one place, and let the dry land appear.' And it was so. And God called the dry land Earth; and the gathering together of the waters he called Seas. And God saw that it was good." Their last second of contact was coming up, on this Christmas Eve in space. "And from the crew of Apollo 8," Borman said with emotion, "we close with good night, good luck, a merry Christmas, and God bless all of you, all of you on the good Earth."

After Apollo 8, the world would never again see itself from the same perspective. We could no longer pretend that our world was without limits; we would see that we were an island paradise in the vast cold void of space. The image of the earthrise communicated this perspective in a language that transcended cultural differences. As Bill Anders later shared with the space historian Andrew Chaikin, we had come all this way to study the Moon, and what we discovered was the Earth.

## EARTHRISE

*The Apollo 8 mission plan did not include instructions to photograph this scene, but Bill Anders's earthrise would become one of the great images of the 20th century. For the astronauts, the sight of their home planet brought thoughts of their distant homes and families and of the warmth of Christmas Eve so far away on December 24, 1968. "There's a beautiful Moon out there tonight," Mission Control radioed to Apollo 8. "There's a beautiful Earth out there," Frank Borman replied softly.*

THE moment was almost upon us. On the brink of Kennedy's deadline, NASA stood poised to take the final step. The Moon lander unfurled its wings in space. A new suit of armor clothed the space warriors, making them invincible to the powerful forces of deep space and the lunar surface. Daring astronauts flew over the face of the Moon, scouting the route ahead. The years of preparation were coming down to the last test flights, the final proving missions, as piece by piece the instruments of the Olympian panoply were completed and readied for their ultimate purpose. Into the spotlight of history now stepped three men who prepared to carry out the great expedition as the zero hour drew upon them. In the final moments a nation that had begun to lose its way saw what it was about to do and caught its collective breath. The nation, and the world, watched as this monumental effort drew to its astonishing climax, and for one precious, shining moment, a single step would unite humanity.

# Landing on the Moon

## ON THE BRINK

**B**y the dawn of 1969 America seemed to have lost much of its original interest in the Space Race. With intercontinental ballistic missiles on both sides of the Iron Curtain now, the Soviet space presence no longer stirred the same dramatic fears, and problems closer to home felt like the ones in need of remedy. With the landing attempt only months away, even reporters wondered aloud if the thrill of space had gone for good.

By 1967, with most of the development for Apollo completed, NASA's annual budget had already begun to diminish, but total spending for the Apollo program was still expected to come in on target at $24 billion. Its high costs and high visibility made Apollo an easy target, and the space program found itself placed in opposition to such causes as poverty and racial harmony. Were solving the problems of hunger, discrimination, and poverty worth more of our effort than the Moon? Even Apollo's proponents tended to think so. Unfortunately, those aims involved much more difficult and

unclear goals and required a special kind of leadership that seemed in too short supply. Apollo was revealing an uncomfortable truth: America, it seemed, could do anything it chose to put its will to. It was going to the Moon. So why wasn't it choosing to foster and accomplish greater social harmony and prosperity? That question was hard to answer. And the space program had nothing to do with it. Neither, really, did the space program's budget, as our willingness to spend far greater quantities of blood and treasure on Vietnam attested. Indeed, as Lyndon Johnson observed with some bitterness, for all the decried cost of space exploration, Americans spent more each year on cigarettes, alcohol, or horse races. And it seemed lost on many that

the money spent "on the Moon" wasn't locked away in a box on the Moon—it had been injected into the U.S. economy, paying the wages of engineers and managers and circulating throughout the country.

Amid the disenchantment and tired spirits came a transformation as the Moon grew close. There was an undeniable, intangible power in this endeavor. Apollo's gleaming spire made Americans question why they had not achieved so brilliantly or invested so much in other areas, but almost a decade after the decision that put it in motion, the project also revealed that it was more than its movers had intended it to be. We had embarked upon the quest for the Moon amid a deadly serious global challenge to prove that we had the most effective political system to ourselves, to our enemies, and to the world. Since then, the goal had taken on a deeper meaning of its own.

Nearly everyone, from grandmothers to cab drivers, in America and abroad, began to feel the magnitude of what was about to be attempted. When Kennedy had made the decision to aim America at the Moon, there had been no discussion of the spirit of exploration, the mark on history that reaching the Moon would make, the impact upon the human imagination and its meaning for mankind. But here, now, on the brink of that goal, that sense grew within us, amid doubt, wonder, and an increasing awareness that an extraordinary time was really here.

## FINAL PREPARATIONS

**A**t the beginning of 1969, just after the return of Apollo 8, NASA had just twelve months remaining to accomplish its mission and land a man on the Moon. The Apollo mission profiles had code letters, and the A, B, and C missions were completed: unmanned tests of the Saturn V and the command module (A), unmanned tests of the lunar module (B), and Wally Schirra's manned test of the command module (C). Yet major preparation milestones remained: Two key hardware elements had never

**APOLLO LEADERS**

*Standing (left to right) in the Launch Control Center are Dr. George Mueller, NASA's associate administrator for manned space flight; U.S. Air Force Gen. Sam Phillips, director of the Apollo program; and Deke Slayton, director of flight crew operations. Seated at far right is Dr. Kurt Debus, director of the Kennedy Space Center. General Phillips's decisive will ensured that the Apollo program was successful.*

been tried by men in space, and crucial pathfinding still had to be done. The lunar landing craft had to be finalized and tested (the D mission), the Apollo Moon space suit had to be likewise proven, and finally, the actual approach route over the Moon for the landing had to be scouted by astronauts on the scene (the F mission). E missions, never flown, would have been further D-style spacecraft tests in high Earth orbit, if necessary. All this led up to the G mission, which would be the first lunar landing. A sense of awe and urgency mounted throughout the space agency as the goal grew closer, and the Apollo team worked intensely to overcome every remaining hurdle—ever mindful

*Grumman model of the lunar-module concept in early development. The LM shape grew increasingly utilitarian and would lose the last vestiges of the smooth cockpit hull seen here.*

that they must remain tightly focused to prevent the mistakes of haste and another Apollo 1. Looking ahead at the test flights that would precede the first landing attempt, those inside the program knew that there was a great deal of work yet to be completed.

## THE LUNAR MODULE

The only part of the entire Apollo-Saturn space vehicle that would actually land on the Moon would be the specialized lunar module. Its name had originally been lunar excursion module, or LEM, but the name got shortened to lunar module, or LM, when NASA reflected that "excursion" sounded too casual for the craft that would actually accomplish "the most hazardous and dangerous and greatest adventure on which mankind had ever embarked." So they dropped the "E," but everyone still pronounced it "LEM" anyway.

## PREPARATIONS

*Above, a one-sixth gravity simulator rig at NASA's Langley Research Center helped astronauts get the feel of moonwalking even though they had to be hung sideways. Astronauts on the Moon would report that such simulations were surprisingly realistic. Grumman's first lunar module, right, is loaded in place for Apollo 5 at Kennedy Space Center's Manned Spacecraft Operations Building.*

Grumman Aerospace won the honor of crafting the lunar-landing vehicle in January 1963, when NASA had finally made up its mind to go with Lunar Orbit Rendezvous. The principal design engineer was a likeable man named Tom Kelly, who led his team on a formidable ground-up design project with no precedents. The lunar module proved to be one of the most challenging design elements of the entire Apollo project: Built for a completely new purpose, it was the most specialized and exotic package of hardware in the system. It was a vehicle built on Earth but meant solely for the environment of space. The lunar module symbolized the farthest reach, the ultimate goal of Apollo's efforts, and Tom Kelly was determined to make Grumman's ship worthy of the honor his group had been given. But after five intense years of development at Grumman's Long Island headquarters in Bethpage, New York, Kelly's team still did not have a Moon vehicle completely ready in early 1969.

The first lunar module, LM-1, had gone into Earth orbit atop a Saturn IB rocket on its own special unmanned test flight (Apollo 5) in January 1968. The remote-controlled maneuvers had proven that the engine systems operated well under flight conditions, but Kelly's Grumman engineers were still working on getting the spidery ship light enough to make it to the Moon. LM-2, also too heavy for lunar landing, was sent to Houston for structural and vibration tests, leaving Kelly's team working fervently to get the next LM ready for real astronauts. The lunar module would be the last major piece of Apollo hardware to be qualified for the landing mission.

The LM consisted of a cockpit "head" and a lower landing stage with legs and the main engine. The landing stage would be left on the Moon, serving as a launch pad for the LM's upper half. The detachable cockpit stage held the astronauts and a smaller engine that would boost them back up into orbit for a rendezvous with their crewmate circling in the Apollo command module.

As Kelly's dismayed engineers learned when the figures came through, this landing craft was allowed to weigh just over four tons, yet it had to incorporate myriad systems—well over one million parts—and be rugged enough to carry twelve tons of propellants and land in a rocky wilderness no one had ever visited before. It had to be absolutely dependable in an alien environment completely beyond rescue, yet a miracle of lightweight "watchmaker" engineering with a hull like an eggshell. The unforgiving factor of weight-saving beat the lunar module into one of the most thorough statements of pure functionality ever to come off a drawing board. Every single expendable half-ounce had been trimmed away from the bizarre creation that emerged, one of the most otherworldly pieces of hardware ever developed.

### LM COCKPIT

*This photograph of the lunar-module trainer now at Huntsville shows the mission commander's piloting station. The lever at left (on ribbed base) throttled the main descent engine; the gray pistol-grip joystick at right controlled maneuvering thrusters.*

The astronauts had to pilot the ship while standing, since Kelly's team had removed the LM's seats to save weight. The LM cockpit offered the astronauts the space of a crowded walk-in closet, just 42 inches deep. There was just enough room to stand at each piloting station, barely enough room to wriggle in or out of a space suit, and two men had to eat and sleep in here too. Behind the cockpit stations was a small closet-like annex that held supplies and the life-support backpacks. Below the center dashboard computer was a square hatch that led out to a small platform, and from there a ladder would lead down to the Moon's surface. The original design had included a rope ladder to save weight, but tests quickly showed that this was a disastrous idea. The frustrated, dangling astronauts would have been better off just jumping from the LM. So they got a real ladder—but to save weight and to keep it from being bent by a hard landing, it ran only partway down the leg.

The outside of the lunar module looked almost as if it were its insides. The roof was festooned with antennas. Geometrical panel shapes made up the LM's exterior, everything dictated by minimalism and utility, its hull paneled in polygons of thin aluminum. Almost everyone but the Grumman engineers called the funny-looking creation "the spider" or "the bug"; the purely functionalist design had something of a face and achieved a nearly animate character. In the end it won a kind of affection. Volkswagen decided that it had found a kindred spirit and used a picture of the LM in an ad for its famous Beetle automobile, with the tag line "It's ugly, but it gets you there."

The lower stage, wrapped in lightweight gold-foil insulation, contained the LM's landing engine, the first large rocket engine in space exploration to be equipped with a workable throttle. With throttle control, the LM would fly rather like a "hot helicopter," but held up by thrust from below instead of by spinning blades above.

It took six years of hard work, but by mid-1969 Kelly and his exhausted Grumman team had hand-crafted the real lunar module that had seemed an impossible job on paper. They had made the entire design as simple as possible, to reduce the chances of malfunctions and systems failures; they had tucked 40 miles of wiring inside it; they had x-rayed and inspected every last bolt, screw, joint, and quarter-inch of weld. The fully fueled machine would collapse under its own weight if placed on the ground, but in space it would sing. And, as for the Moon, the LM was the glittering wonder, the gold-foil miracle, the only thing in the world that could get you there.

### SIMULATOR

*Detailed cockpit simulations involving projected images of lunar landmarks helped astronauts practice maneuvering and landing the lunar module. Hundreds of hours of "flying" on the ground would prepare the pilots for the brief moments over the Moon, when no mistakes could be made.*

# Lunar Module

The lunar module had to serve as Moon lander, exploration base camp, and manned rocket launch platform, and it had to be built out of just 4.3 tons of material. Nothing like a LM had ever been built before. Tom Kelly and his team labored through six years of overtime, difficulties, and schedule delays to create the superb machine uniquely capable of accomplishing the Moon landing.

The lunar module stood 22 feet tall and 31 feet across, and every ounce had been trimmed from its final design to make it light enough for the Saturn V to send it to the Moon. Grumman used advanced chemical milling techniques to etch away all but the structurally critical parts of each metal component, creating shapes impossible to achieve by conventional machine milling. The crew cabin hull ended up as thick as three sheets of aluminum foil. Miles of cockpit connections were made in fragile, fine 26-gauge wiring to save cumulative weight. And instead of heavy, pneumatic shock absorbers, the landing legs held struts of lightweight, crushable aluminum honeycomb to absorb the one-time impact of lunar landing. If the astronauts had been allowed to bring toothbrushes, the Grumman engineers would have cut the handles short to make them lighter. But even toothbrushes and soap got cut from the weight-saving list.

The LM cockpit, or ascent stage, protected its astronauts inside a triple-layered shell. The aluminum inner hull was swathed in multilayered foil insulation blankets, then covered over with thin outer plates that formed a "bumper" to dissipate the power of tiny meteoroids before they could puncture the inner hull. The blanket and bumper layers were held apart by hundreds of delicate plastic straws.

With no air in space or on the Moon, the LM had no need of aerodynamic streamlining,

lunar contact probe

*LM-5, Neil Armstrong's Eagle, was in preparation for Apollo 11 when Grumman created this artwork. Constantly being refined, each lunar module had its own idiosyncratic details. This view shows four lunar contact probes, but the one on the front leg would be removed before Eagle actually flew, so that when bent by landing it would not get in the way of the astronauts' first steps.*

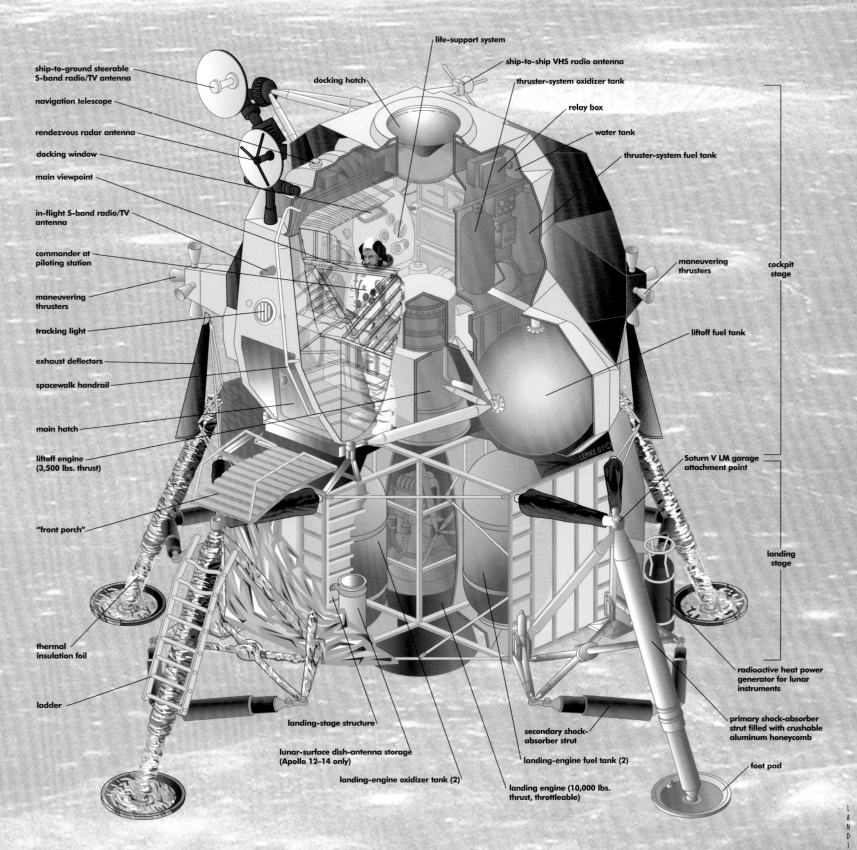

ship-to-ground steerable
S-band radio/TV antenna

navigation telescope

rendezvous radar antenna

docking window

main viewpoint

in-flight S-band radio/TV
antenna

commander at
piloting station

maneuvering
thrusters

tracking light

exhaust deflectors

spacewalk handrail

main hatch

liftoff engine
(3,500 lbs. thrust)

"front porch"

thermal
insulation foil

ladder

life-support system

docking hatch

ship-to-ship VHS radio antenna

thruster-system oxidizer tank

relay box

water tank

thruster-system fuel tank

maneuvering
thrusters

cockpit
stage

liftoff fuel tank

Saturn V LM garage
attachment point

landing
stage

radioactive heat power
generator for lunar
instruments

primary shock-absorber
strut filled with crushable
aluminum honeycomb

foot pad

landing-stage structure

lunar-surface dish-antenna storage
(Apollo 12–14 only)

landing-engine oxidizer tank (2)

secondary shock-
absorber strut

landing-engine fuel tank (2)

landing engine (10,000 lbs.
thrust, throttleable)

*Weight-saving dictated almost every aspect of the lunar module's unique appearance. Windows were very heavy compared to the lander's thin hull, so they were minimized to triangle shapes, efficiently angled forward so the pilot could look out and down at the landing site ahead. A tiny rendezvous window above the pilot's head let him look up to sight on the command module for docking.*

and Grumman's initial smooth-hulled concept for the LM soon became a faceted, geometrical shape in order to save weight and simplify construction. Asymmetrical bulges at the sides of the cockpit held the unequally sized fuel and oxidizer tanks for the cockpit's ascent engine.

The lunar exploration hatch in the LM's "face" had originally been a round backup for the docking hatch on top of the ship, but astronaut Roger Chaffee had shown the Grumman engineers that the hatch needed to be rectangular to accommodate the blocky life-support backpack that Moon explorers would wear. Grumman's adoption of the rectangular hatch thus preserved a legacy of one of the lost Apollo 1 crew members in the shape of the spaceship that made it to the Moon.

*NASA's Langley Research Center developed early concepts for the lunar excursion module (seen here with Buzz Aldrin), which eventually became the LM.*

The lower stage of the LM lacked the outermost meteoroid bumper plates, leaving its foil blanket protection visible. The foil, developed specially for the LM project, was hand-crinkled to reduce points of contact for heat transmission through the layers.

Safety dictated maximum simplicity in the LM designs, with redundant systems so that no single failure would compromise the well-being of the crew. The simplified ascent engine had no pumps, no igniters, no gimbals, no complex regenerative cooling system for the "disposable" engine bell, and plumbing throughout was minimized. There were at least two ways or two sets of equipment to accomplish virtually every important task that the LM had to support. As a result of the countless hours of design work on the LM, just two astronauts would be able to launch their LM cockpit rocket off the Moon, whereas it took 5,000 support people at the Cape to launch their Saturn V.

The LM could keep in touch directly with Houston, carried its own radar for docking and landing tracking, and gave its

*At Kennedy Space Center's Manned Spacecraft Operations Building, LM-6, destined for Apollo 12, is hoisted to a work stand where it will be loaded into its garage for launch.*

astronauts a comfortable, 75°F home even in the tortured extremes of space and the lunar surface. It even carried enough extra oxygen, water, and power to serve as a "lifeboat" in case the command module suffered damage—a frightening scenario that would be put to the test on Apollo 13. Thanks to the lunar module's conservative design, it could have withstood a slide down an incline into a boulder or a landing with some legs in pothole craters or hung up on two-foot-tall rocks—much more rugged terrain than it ever encountered at the Apollo landing sites.

Apollo's fleet of seven Moon-ready lunar modules cost more than $1.4 billion to develop and build. Chief engineer Tom Kelly's team had initially numbered in the dozens but had grown to three thousand by the completion of the LM design. After all of Grumman's work, the astronauts got to pilot a completely unique vehicle in space. Following the LM's first space trials during Apollo 9, pilots Jim McDivitt and Rusty Schweickart enthused that the LM

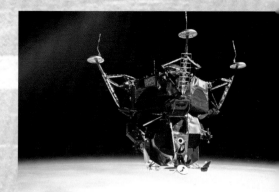

*Apollo 9 LM on its flight trials in Earth orbit. In zero gravity with no up or down, the pilots stood weightlessly at their stations, held to the cockpit floor by cables clipped on at their waists.*

was "a great flying machine. And when it's just the ascent stage alone, it's very quick. It snaps to the controls like a fighter plane, or a sports car. It was super to fly!" The later Apollo missions would stretch the LM's abilities further as astronauts flew the capable craft through steeper approaches into more difficult terrain. On every mission the lunar module would prove to be a dependable spacecraft for another world, worth all the effort it had taken to create.

## APOLLO 9

**N**ow it was time for astronauts to fly this incredibly complex lunar landing vehicle, the symbol of the coming ultimate reach. Apollo 9 would fly a D mission and prove out the lunar module, readying it for the coming dress rehearsal around the Moon and for the landing to follow. The elaborate maneuvers of Lunar Orbit Rendezvous had never been flown before, and on this mission the crew would fly the Apollo command module and lunar module through a complete sequence of docking, separation, flight maneuvers, and rendezvous. These were among the final preparations. On March 3, 1969, Apollo 9 lifted into the sky and pierced the cloud ceiling like a lit needle disappearing into cotton.

**LM** GARAGE

*Moon-bound missions would unpack the LM in cislunar space, but here Apollo 9's Earth-orbital, flight-test LM floats above the clouds as it awaits extraction from its garage atop the spent third stage of the Saturn V.*

Orbiting 119 miles above the Earth, the S-IVB third stage of the Saturn V carried the LM sealed in its conical adapter, its "garage," the whole assembly topped by the Apollo C.S.M. with the astronauts on board. Inside the nose of the space vehicle, command module pilot David Scott prepared to carry out the complex ballet that would extract the lunar lander from its garage. Scott was a precision pilot, like most of his astronaut brethren, and Apollo 9 was a test pilot's dream. It was the absolute edge of the envelope: new machines, high flying, and difficult maneuvers. L.O.R. required the tricky maneuver he was about to perform to accomplish the Moon landing: It was called transposition, docking, and extraction. The economical L.O.R. mission mode NASA had chosen for the Apollo project depended heavily on expert piloting and expressed great faith in the astronauts. It was time to justify the plans and the faith.

Explosive strip charges ripped through the seal that connected the C.S.M. to the stack, and in one searing burst the stack broke apart. Scott pulled the C.S.M. gently away as the conical garage split into four petals. The petals opened out and then separated, drifting gracefully away from the garage, revealing the precious package within: the lunar module, seated in the top of the third stage.

Scott had in his hand a joystick that controlled the ship in which he and his two crewmates rode, and he would carry out this celestial dance. High above the blue and cloud-dappled Earth, Scott slowly rotated the C.S.M. 180 degrees, positioning it directly nose-in toward the LM in its garage a few hundred feet away. Sighting the LM's docking target through his forward-looking rendezvous window, Scott brought them in and smoothly seated the docking probe on the capsule's nose into the docking port on the roof of the LM. "We have capture," Apollo 9 radioed to Houston. Twelve automatic docking latches fired in a jackhammer bang, sealing the two ships together. "We have hard dock," Scott confirmed.

The next move was to get the LM out of its garage. Scott triggered releases in the third stage, and springs ejected the pair of docked spacecraft gently. Scott pulled them away in reverse with the maneuvering thrusters, completing the transposition, docking, and extraction. The third stage was now just a collision and explosion hazard, so its thrusters were fired to send it sailing out into the void, well away from the two docked Apollo spacecraft. When it was over 2,000 feet away, it fired its main engine to burn off its remaining fuel. "It's just like a bright star disappearing in the distance," Scott said, watching it recede. Like several other S-IVB stages, Apollo 9's would be left to sail away from the Earth and circle the Sun in interplanetary space—still out there, somewhere, today.

**M**ission commander Jim McDivitt put the LM through an exhausting series of maneuvers as the two spacecraft orbited the Earth. Responding to his work at the controls, the LM traced huge loops in space, finally flying over a hundred miles away from

### APOLLO 9

*Command module pilot David Scott emerges from the hatch of the Apollo capsule, photographed from the porch of the docked LM by Rusty Schweickart while he was testing the Apollo Moon suit.*

**RECOVERY**

*The Apollo 9 command module floats in the Pacific after splashdown. U.S. Navy recovery frogmen have detached the capsule parachutes that deployed from the exposed area around the peak of the ship. Reentry has torn the capsule's thermal insulation foil covering to shreds.*

## LM LOADING

*At Kennedy Space Center, Apollo 10's LM is moved into position over the base of its garage, the Spacecraft Lunar Module Adapter, or S.L.A., which will protect it on its journey into space.*

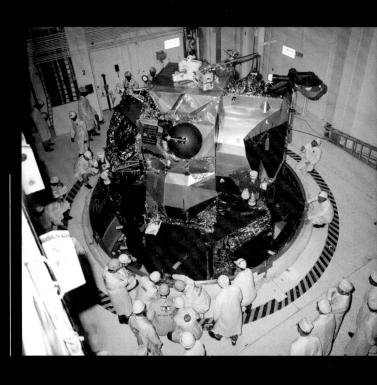

## THREE TO MAKE READY

*Technicians help Apollo 10 mission commander Tom Stafford (front) and his crewmen John Young (middle) and Gene Cernan (rear) suit up for a countdown demonstration test in preparation for the Apollo 10 lunar orbital mission, a dress rehearsal of the real lunar landing.*

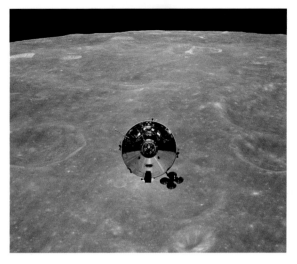

Scott in the command module and then proving that the ships could relocate each other and rejoin, just as they would do on a lunar mission. By the time the LM tests were complete, McDivitt felt as wrung out as Tom Kelly's engineers. Houston advised him that he had won the right to take a break, and he radioed back, "Man, when I take a break, I'm going to bed for three days!" But they had their verdict: The lunar module was ready for the Moon.

## APOLLO 10

In spring 1969, there was only one more preparatory mission to accomplish: the F mission, a full dress rehearsal of the lunar landing. The crew, with a fully functional LM, would go all the way to the Moon and execute the flight plan of the landing mission, following exactly the same orbital paths under the same lighting conditions. Mission commander Tom Stafford piloted his LM much closer to the Moon than Apollo 8 had reached, flying to within an altitude of 50,000 feet, not much higher than a commercial jet liner flies on Earth.

"Oh, we are low. We are close, babe," Stafford's copilot Gene Cernan radioed back to Earth. The landscape's finest details showed crystal clear in the Moon's airless atmosphere and Cernan felt practically on top of the boulders he saw below. "We is down among 'em, Charlie," the commander exulted to Charlie Duke, the Capcom in Houston. After patrolling and scouting the path the next ship would take, Stafford was to jettison his lower stage (simulating an aborted landing attempt) and return to higher orbit and dock with the command module, just as returning Moon explorers would do.

On the way back up to the C.S.M., the LM automatic guidance system sent the maneuvering thrusters firing wildly, throwing the tiny ship into a gyrating spin high above the dead landscape below. "Son of a bitch!" Cernan shouted. Moon and black space wheeled around the LM until the astronauts got manual control of the craft, bringing it back to perfect stability within a few terrifying seconds. Other than a few missed heartbeats monitored back in Mission Control, the mission was none the worse for wear. This was exactly the kind of surprise Apollo 10 was designed to turn up. The landing mission would have enough unknowns on the lunar surface. It didn't need any in space. The malfunction was traced to an incorrect switch setting owing to a confusing checklist sequence, and it wouldn't happen again.

Flying their "hot helicopter" in the airless blackness nine miles above the Sea of Tranquility, Stafford and Cernan had carefully examined the terrain of the future landing site from a closer range than anyone had ever done before. They gauged it with the fine resolution of the human eye, not limited by the film grain of a photograph. They saw that the landing crew would have their work cut out for them. Suitable landing areas lay below, but most of the terrain was strewn with boulders and craters. "It looks a lot smoother than some of the photos show," Stafford radioed back. "I estimate a 25 to 30 percent semi-clear area. So if the LM has enough hover time, it should not be a problem. However, if you come down in the wrong area and you don't have enough hover time, you're gonna have to shove off." Hover time. That would be the critical factor. And by the time it neared the lunar surface, the LM would have a very limited supply of "hover" fuel left.

## THREE FOR THE MOON

The public had come to know Neil Armstrong's name as soon as it became clear that the Apollo 11 crew was slated for the Moon landing. Armstrong would be the mission commander. A 38-year-old from a small town in Ohio, Armstrong was quiet, almost shy. He accepted his role in the media's eye dutifully but responded only as a professional, keeping his emotions very much to himself. He often paused for thought before answering reporters' questions and tended to answer directly and precisely. Unlike many of his fellow astronauts, he no longer held a military commission, which coincidentally would make the first step on the Moon free of any military overtones whatsoever. A civilian test pilot, Armstrong was the highest-paid man in the astronaut corps at an annual salary of about $30,000 in 1969. He had flown the record-setting X-15 rocket plane, he had saved Gemini 8 from destruction in space, and he was an outstanding pilot with an intense inner focus on complete control of the skills he needed to accomplish his missions. Married and the father of two boys, Armstrong was low-key in all but the most personal situations and possessed of a dry sense of humor only occasionally revealed. He could have a good time and cut loose with his buddies, but his personal life was very private. He endured the public spotlight but never sought it. His personal qualities would shape the character of Apollo 11, making this a mission that bore the mantle of history with soft-spoken honor rather than superficial humor or brash ego.

*The eloquent Apollo 11 mission patch*

Accompanying Armstrong to the surface of the Moon would be Edwin "Buzz" Aldrin, the 39-year-old Gemini veteran with a doctorate from M.I.T. Technically focused and ever analytical, Aldrin had solved the problems of spacewalking during Gemini by reasoning out the correct approach. Aldrin's early nickname, "Dr. Rendezvous," partly reflected the fact that he didn't mix easily with the test pilot crowd. He had an academic's impatience with non-intellectuals and had drawn considerable disfavor from his fellows when he openly jockeyed to be the first man out on the lunar surface; glory-seeking was not considered appropriate in such a group. For Aldrin, it was a very personal matter, and he tended to see the situation in terms of how it affected him. "We have been given a tremendous responsibility by the twists and turns of fate," he told the press before the mission. "I think it's difficult to cite previous examples of challenges that have been so tremendous for individuals to face."

Michael Collins would pilot the Apollo command module around the Moon solo while his crewmates descended to the surface. A 39-year-old air force lieutenant colonel, Collins didn't come across as a military man. Casual, likable, and prone to self-effacing wit, he was easy to talk to. As a test pilot, he was sharp and competitive, but outside the cockpit he was something of a poet. As an astronaut with an imaginative bent, he had ridden a rocket stage like a cowboy during his Gemini 10 space walk. The father of two girls and a boy, Collins enjoyed spending time with his children and working in his garden. Speaking with the press before the flight, he observed a particular irony of his position as command module pilot. "I'd like to point out," he said, "that I have no TV set on board and therefore I'm going to be one of the few Americans who is not going to be able to see the moonwalk. So, I'd like you to save the tapes for me, please. I'd like to look at them after the flight."

### APOLLO 11

Below (from left), *Neil Armstrong, Michael Collins, and Buzz Aldrin. Collins worked with Armstrong and NASA colleagues to design the mission patch. The emblem omits the astronauts' names and substitutes the Earth, representing all mankind. The American eagle holds an olive branch to express that the mission is one of peace.*

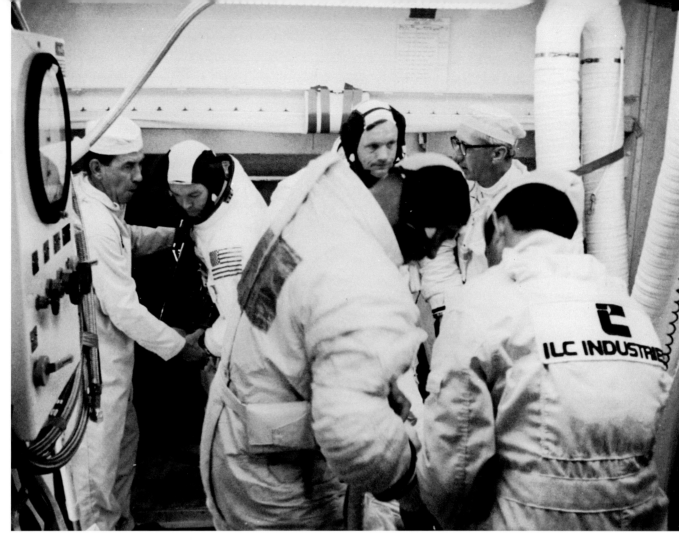

**FINAL PREPARATIONS**

*Technicians in the "White Room" atop the launch umbilical tower assist the Apollo 11 crew on the countdown demonstration test in preparation for the Moon launch. Neil Armstrong is attended by Gunter Wendt, wearing glasses. The astronauts called their cloth communications headsets seen here "Snoopy caps" for their resemblance to Charles Schulz's famous comic strip beagle.*

## APOLLO 11

**A**s Apollo 11 stood on Launch Complex 39's pad A on July 16, 1969, over a thousand VIPs from around the world filled the press stands. Foreign dignitaries mixed with 3,493 journalists speaking dozens of languages. Half a million people filled the surrounding county, packing the motels, camping in their cars, their eager eyes trained on the bulk of the V.A.B., visible miles away across the flat Florida terrain, and the white needle of the instrument of history. Through opponent and proponent alike coursed a recognition that a great moment was upon us. Sputnik had changed the world and traced in its starry path a watershed, a dividing line beyond which the world would never be the same. Now another line was about to be drawn, and this time the entire world would see it happen. Such was the American way. The four corners of the Earth were abuzz with awareness of what the Americans were about to attempt. Many countries seemed more openly thrilled with Apollo 11 than was America itself, proposing national holidays in observance of the coming moment. It was as if a power radiated from Apollo 11 that crossed borders and challenged the human spirit around the world.

**G**ood luck and Godspeed from the launch crew," said test conductor Paul Donlevy over the communication circuit. The preparations were complete.

Over the P.A., NASA announcer Jack King's voice relayed mission commander Armstrong's reply, "Thank you very much. We know it will be a good flight." There were two and a half minutes remaining to launch.

This was it. All the effort, all the leadership, the inspiration, the late hours, all the millions and billions of dollars had led up to this, the

Life *magazine followed the Apollo story closely with exclusive astronaut interviews.*

journey that began . . . now. Ignition's fire sent great white clouds billowing out to the sides of the pad. The Saturn V built to full power thrust, the inferno raging beneath it. A lighted button bearing the words "LAUNCH COM-MIT" was pressed inside the launch control center, and Apollo 11 filled the pad with light and the Cape with thunder. "We have liftoff!" Jack King called out, "We have liftoff!" All 36 stories and 3,000 tons of the rocket rose upward past the launch tower, and atop a pillar of fire it climbed into the blue sky toward destiny. Former President Johnson watched it, shading his eyes, understanding what it represented, the years of commitment, the decision made eight years earlier, and the work of hundreds of thousands of Americans. He could feel it, he said. "Half a million people were there lifting."

## JULY 20, 1969

**O**n the far side of the Moon, two linked Apollo spacecraft circled in lunar orbit, sailing soundlessly at an altitude of 69 miles and at an imperceptible velocity of some 3,700 mph. They were the command module *Columbia* and the lunar module *Eagle*. The astronaut tradition begun by Gus Grissom of adopting humorous ship names as call signs had sobered in the face of history, and at the insistence of NASA officials, who did not need to stress to the crew of Apollo 11 that their role was unique and carried special responsibilities.

The astronauts chose the name *Columbia* in honor of both Christopher Columbus and Jules Verne's visionary *Columbiad*. Such had been the reach of the author's imagination that a multibillion-dollar space program now carried his echo on the greatest mission of exploration ever mounted.

Michael Collins pressed a switch, and his spacecraft separated from the lander with a gentle push of springs. Armstrong and Aldrin were on their own now. "See you later," Collins radioed. Alone in his spacecraft, he pulsed his thrusters and moved slowly into the dark distance to give the lander room to maneuver into its descent orbit.

*Eagle* rotated so that its descent engine faced forward. With a "Go" from Houston for P.D.I., or Powered Descent Initiation, Armstrong fired the engine that would fight their hurtling speed and slow them down for landing. The main engine blasted silently as the two astronauts dropped 46,000 feet, slowing in velocity. *Eagle*'s windows looked face down at the Moon for landmark sighting, the astronauts feeling a slight sensation of weight against their feet as the rocket decelerated them. "Our position check downrange shows us to be a little long," Armstrong radioed. "You are 'Go' to continue powered descent," Houston responded. "It's looking good. Everything is looking good here."

The *Eagle* rotated faceup toward the black sky. Lower and lower the astronauts and their craft fell, until it was time to use the engine to break their fall instead of their progress. They had slowed down enough.

**COUNTDOWN**

*With just over two hours to go before the historic launch of Apollo 11, Neil Armstrong leads his crew across the gantry to board his Saturn V Moon rocket. He wears the suit that will protect him on the surface of the Moon.*

**LIFTOFF**

*Apollo 11 rises beyond the huge crawlerway leading to the pad, seen three and a half miles away from inside the Launch Control Center at Kennedy Space Center.*

**IN THE AIR**

*The launch team stands to watch Apollo 11 roar skyward. The moment the rocket cleared the tower was a tremendous relief for the Cape launch crews, and after that, they looked up in amazement like everyone else.*

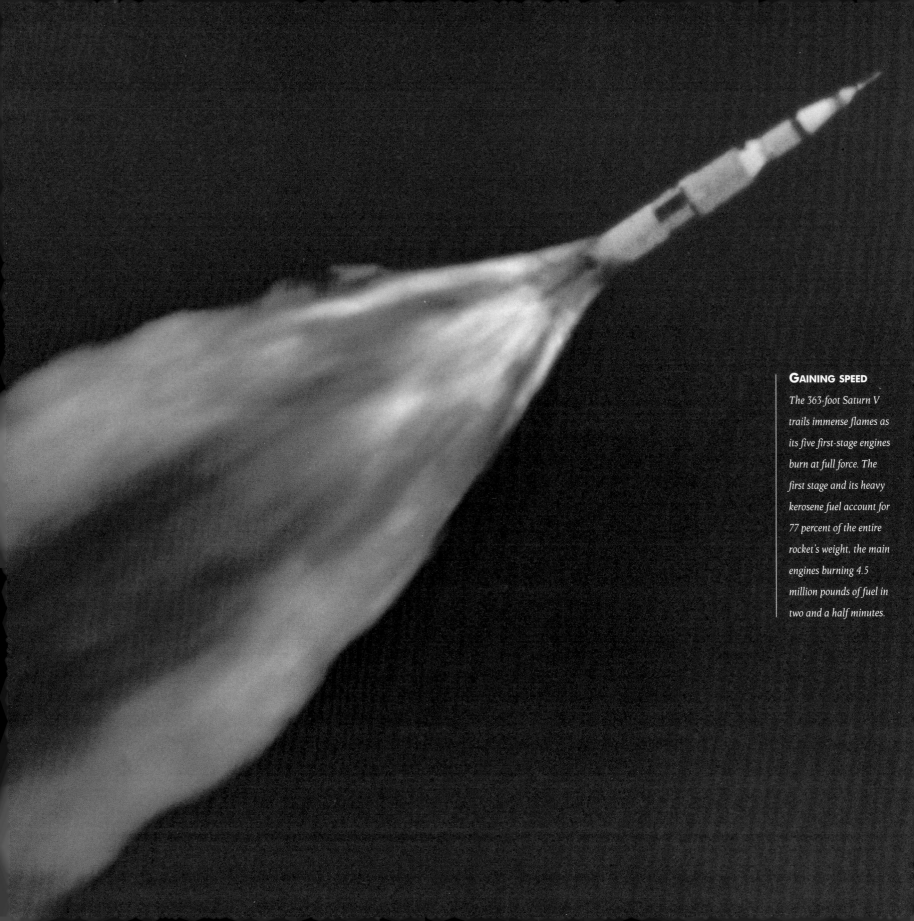

**GAINING SPEED**

*The 363-foot Saturn V trails immense flames as its five first-stage engines burn at full force. The first stage and its heavy kerosene fuel account for 77 percent of the entire rocket's weight, the main engines burning 4.5 million pounds of fuel in two and a half minutes.*

**WATCHING HISTORY**

*Over half a million people flooded into the Cape Canaveral area to watch the launch of Apollo 11, crowding every available patch of ground with a view of the launch site. The Saturn V's thunder and brilliant flame made a powerful impression on all who shared the experience.*

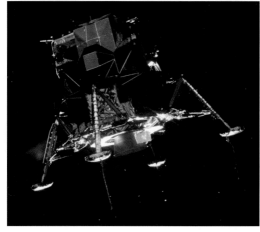

**GLITTERING WONDER**

*In lunar orbit, 69 miles high, Neil Armstrong rotates Apollo 11's* Eagle *in preparation for the descent to the Moon. The three wands projecting down from the LM legs are landing probes to indicate lunar contact.*

At 7,200 feet, about five miles from the landing site, the computer put the LM through "pitchover," bringing it face forward and ready to land. The lunar horizon rose in their triangular windows, the terrain sliding toward them until they were only 300 feet above it, traveling now at only about 30 mph.

Armstrong could now see the Sea of Tranquility better than even Gene Cernan and Tom Stafford had seen it a few months ago. As he moved in closer and closer, he could see that the computer was bringing the *Eagle* in on a boulder field beyond the intended landing zone. The rocks would wreck the lander. Armstrong switched off the computer and took over, "initiating P-66" in the jargon of the flight team. It was time for the human pilot to prove his worth.

*Eagle* diverged from the computer's path, leveling out and skimming over the boulder field. There was no time to discuss the matter with Houston, as fuel seconds were precious. He had to find a place to land, because he was burning the precious hover time. It was at this moment that the DSKY fired an alarm. "1201 alarm," the astronauts reported to Houston. Almost no one even knew what that code meant, it was so obscure. In "the trench" at the front of the control room, Steve Bales knew that it meant the computer was overloaded. "You are 'Go' on that alarm," Houston assured them. "Repeat, you are Go to land." It happened twice more. Houston insisted that they were clear to continue. The astronauts could only trust them.

The terrain of the real Moon flowed underneath Armstrong and Aldrin. Armstrong cruised over a crater named West, several miles beyond *Eagle*'s target landing zone, working his thrust controls as

Aldrin called out data. The fuel was dwindling, and they were still too high. Telemetry data curves showed that Armstrong was slightly erratic as he guided the *Eagle*, discarding one prospect after another in search of a dead-level landing site. The smooth Sea of Tranquility turned out to be rather chaotic at close inspection. Aldrin may have had time to think of Armstrong's crashes in the simulator and the training vehicle, but Armstrong kept going as the fuel level dropped toward zero. "Sixty seconds," called Capcom Charlie Duke. They waited. "Thirty seconds," Duke called.

Mission Control was hushed, absolutely silent, during these last seconds, incredulous, watching the telemetry that told them Armstrong wasn't landing. Every man at every console was riveted by this unexpected turn. Never in all the exhaustive tests had they cut it so close to running the fuel tanks absolutely dry. There was nothing any of them could do but wait. This was the moment, and each second fell with heart-thumping slowness. Neil Armstrong was the one who knew exactly what the situation really was, and his heart rate was at a record 156 beats per minute.

Finally, Armstrong saw what he wanted: a clearing, just beyond a small crater. He brought *Eagle* down at last. As the extraordinary golden lunar lander drifted in, the rocket blast began kicking up dust, shooting it away from the ship in great gray sheets like wind-driven fog, obscuring the ground and making visual navigation impossible. Armstrong set her down right through it anyway. Three of the lander's footpads had downward-pointing feelers that pierced the fog and touched the Moon. "Contact light," Buzz Aldrin called, as the blue indicator illuminated above the simple words "LUNAR CONTACT." The *Eagle* settled in, drifting slightly to the left, and all four pads touched soil. The two astronauts exchanged a rapid-fire voice checklist, powering down the engine to prevent explosive blowback and securing their systems. There was a pause, and the commander spoke for history. "Houston, Tranquility Base here. The *Eagle* has landed." Back on Earth, Mission Control erupted in cheers and applause. Some of the tough guys were nearly in tears. Capcom Charlie Duke's voice was

## THE WORLD WATCHES

*A television set at a sidewalk café in Milan gathers a crowd during the broadcast of Apollo 11. Similar scenes appeared around nearly every television on Earth as an estimated one-seventh of the entire population of the world watched Neil Armstrong's first steps on the Moon. People of every culture and nation formed the audience for this shared experience of a unique moment in history.*

*Eagle*: "Undocked." Houston: "Roger. How does it look?" *Eagle*: "The *Eagle* has wings." The lunar module had unlatched from the command module, and now Michael Collins would pull his ship away from the lander to give them room for their maneuvers. Houston: "You are looking good for separation. You are Go for separation, *Columbia*. Over."

# Apollo 11 Landing

Well clear of the *Columbia* some 60 nautical miles above the Moon, Neil Armstrong fired *Eagle*'s landing engine and dropped the LM into a descent orbit, an ellipse that would bring the lander to a low point 50,000 feet over the Moon. That low point was carefully calculated to lie 260 miles up range from Apollo Site #2, Apollo 11's chosen landing point.

Reaching the low point over lunar highlands, Armstrong initiated Powered Descent to brake their speed from orbital velocity. For over eight minutes the LM's main engine burned through Powered Descent, and as their speed dropped so did the LM, losing eight miles of altitude. The last rugged highlands slid by below as the LM reached the smoother Sea of Tranquility.

Through his triangular window looking straight down, Armstrong checked navigational landmarks and spotted the crater Maskelyne just as he had seen it so clearly on the Apollo 10 reconnaissance photos. He rotated the ship slowly around, windows up, in preparation for the approach phase. During this period, Armstrong was flying nearly blind, while a crater called Sabine E and a wrinkle in the flat sea called Last Ridge passed below. The landing site was now less than 10 miles away.

At the end of the Powered Descent braking phase was a point called High Gate, marking the beginning of the approach phase. High Gate, a mile and a half high, waited almost five miles up range of the landing target. Armstrong and Aldrin passed through High Gate, dropping at 70 mph. Closing in on the target now, *Eagle* pitched up to a more face-forward orientation that would allow Armstrong to see where he was headed. However, Armstrong and Aldrin had been so busy clearing the surprise computer-overload program alarms that it was not until the end of the approach phase that Armstrong really had a chance to look out and view the landing area he was headed into. As he closed in under 2,000 feet, the computer data told Armstrong he was headed for a spot that he could

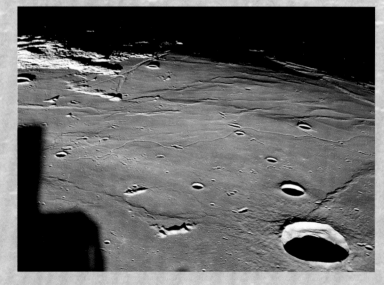

*This view from the lunar module window shows the Sea of Tranquility, key Apollo 11 landmarks, and the site of the first lunar landing in context.*

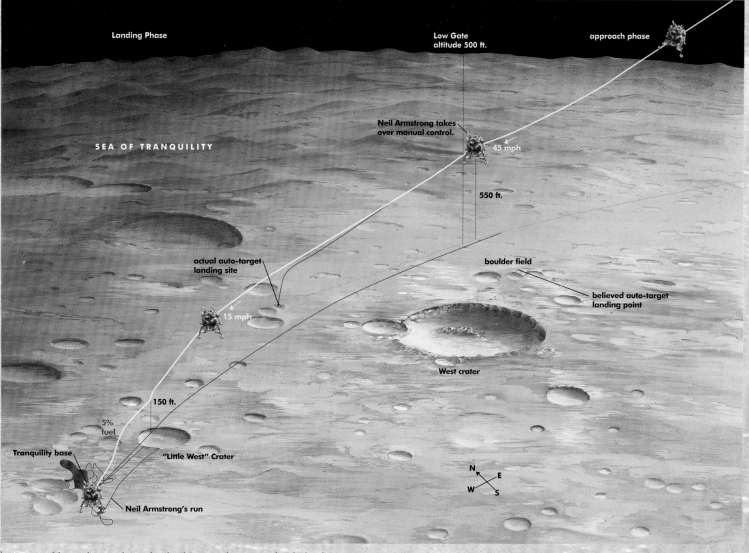

SEA OF TRANQUILITY

Neil Armstrong takes
over manual control.

45 mph

550 ft.

actual auto-target
landing site

boulder field

believed auto-target
landing point

15 mph

West crater

150 ft.

5%
fuel

Tranquility base

"Little West" Crater

N
E
W
S

Neil Armstrong's run

*Because of the way data were being relayed at the time, Neil Armstrong thought that the auto-targeting system was bringing Eagle in just short and slightly north of West crater, into its rocky halo. Post-flight analysis would reveal that Eagle was really headed for a spot more than 500 feet northwest of that point when Armstrong took over manual control and selected his own site for the historic first landing.*

see lay within the boulder field surrounding West crater.

Low Gate was a point less than half a mile from the landing site; it would mark the final landing phase. When they were descending through an altitude of about 550 feet, Armstrong took over manual control early to avoid West crater's rocky halo. He steered the lander to his left and slowed their fall to a gentle three miles per hour as he cruised in, looking for a smooth clearing. Flying beyond West crater had taken them "off the map," beyond the coverage of the high-resolution photos of the intended landing site, now almost three miles behind them. Here, a few hundred feet over the Sea of Tranquility, Armstrong was on his own. He was just 30 feet high when he committed to a safe landing site and brought *Eagle* in for its historic touchdown.

In the celebratory moments after the landing, Houston Capcom Charlie Duke radioed: "It was beautiful from here, Tranquility. . . . Be advised there's a lot of smiling faces in this room and all over the world."

"There are two of them up here," Armstrong replied. The moonwalk awaited.

shaking with emotion as he replied, "Roger, Tranquility, we copy you on the ground. You got a bunch of guys about to turn blue. We're breathing again. Thanks a lot." *The Eagle has landed. They're on the Moon.* Around the world people listened in wonder to the incredible announcement.

Twenty minutes after the landing, Armstrong radioed back a description of the place where they had come to rest. "The area out the left-hand window is a relatively level plain cratered with a fairly large number of craters of the 5- to 50-foot variety; and some ridges . . . small, 20, 30 feet high, I would guess, and literally thousands of little, 1- and 2-foot craters around the area. . . . There is a hill in view, just about on the ground track ahead of us. Difficult to estimate, but might be a half a mile or a mile."

Meanwhile, Michael Collins circled 69 miles above the Moon, solo piloting his "mini-cathedral," as he called the spaceship he now had to himself. While hundreds of millions on Earth were united around their televisions and radios, Collins was out of contact for long stretches.

Mission Control acknowledged his lonely vigil: "Not since Adam has any human known such solitude as Mike Collins is experiencing . . . when he's behind the Moon with no one to talk to except his tape recorder." Collins sailed silently on, attending to the myriad tasks of running his own world, while his comrades below prepared to walk on the surface of the Moon.

## THE APOLLO MOON EXPLORER SPACE SUIT

**T**he new Apollo space suit that Armstrong readied for the adventure of stepping outside was the finest expression of sophistication and protection that NASA's space armorers had ever conceived. The outer white covering looked deceptively soft, but inside, Armstrong was wearing a heavy pressure suit. NASA called it the Extravehicular Mobility Unit, or E.M.U., and it was no simple affair.

The entire assembly, with its life-support backpack, was a complete self-contained environment that would allow Armstrong to walk, impervious to deadly cold, blistering heat, and airless vacuum, where an ordinary man would be annihilated in seconds.

The Moon's surface temperature could range over 500 degrees, from 243°F at lunar "noon" to 279° below zero during lunar night. Apollo 11 had been planned to land during lunar morning, and Armstrong could expect moondust temperatures outside to be a cool 40° to 50°, with the shadows being some 150° below zero, conditions his suit could handle easily. But the space suit also had to protect him from other dangers. He had seen sharp-edged rocks out there, and if he fell and tore a hole in the suit, or cracked his faceplate, he could quickly die of explosive decompression, as his precious oxygen bled furiously into the airless world around him. Checking his seals and gauges, Armstrong had little concern, having come to trust the sturdy and elaborate system. In this Space-Age panoply, he could practically walk into an oven without feeling it. The Apollo space suit had first been tested during a space-walk in Earth orbit on Apollo 9, where it had performed perfectly. Now Armstrong was about to take it out into the realm for which it was designed and walk on the Moon.

## ONE SMALL STEP

**S**ix hours after the landing, the last wisps of air had been bled out of the *Eagle* cockpit. The two astronauts were sealed in their suits, their backpacks purring quietly with cool oxygen. Armstrong was on his knees, wriggling backward out of the hatch, helped by Aldrin. As the commander emerged from the lunar-module cockpit, he pulled a lanyard that dropped a black-and-white television camera out on a folding panel. A blurry, ghostly image, inverted at first, then corrected, appeared on the screens at Mission Control and around the world.

## TRANQUILITY BASE

During Apollo 11's brief moonwalk, nearly every second was accounted for in the schedule, but Neil Armstrong found a moment to run off into the wild moonscape on his own while Buzz Aldrin was setting up scientific instruments. Armstrong had flown over "Little West" crater just before landing, and he got to take a close look at it during this short interval, shooting this panorama while at Little West's rim. Armstrong's lunar-soil camera appears in the foreground, and the Eagle sits some 200 feet away.

### SECOND MAN OUT

*Buzz Aldrin emerges from the lunar module. The challenge of backing out onto the ladder with very limited visibility drew on the astronauts' experience with practice equipment back on Earth.*

### MAN ON THE MOON

*Neil Armstrong took this photograph of Buzz Aldrin, one of the best images from the entire Apollo program and one that seems to capture the extraordinary achievement of Apollo 11. Armstrong is reflected in Aldrin's visor, as are a leg of the Eagle lunar module and the few traces of mankind at Tranquility base.*

### EASEP

*Buzz Aldrin walks out onto the Sea of Tranquility carrying a moonquake detector (at left) and a range-finding laser reflector (at right), which he will unfold on the surface. These experiments comprised the Early Apollo Scientific Experiments Package, or EASEP.*

The picture recalled the earliest days of television, like something from 1948, since it was one of the first lightweight, compact television cameras. RCA had invented the first for Apollo 7.

Neil had soft-landed the *Eagle* in the confusing "ground fog" of lunar dust instead of cutting the engines at the first flash of contact light and letting the ship fall the last four feet to the ground. As a result, the leg shock absorbers were still almost fully extended, making the last step off the short ladder a three-foot jump. Standing on the footpad, Armstrong described the lunar surface and prepared to press his boot onto the Moon. "I'm going to step off the LM now," he said, as over a billion people waited, breathless. Many had asked him what he would say at this moment. He had not known himself until a few hours before, but it had come to him, and he was ready. "That's one small step for a man," Armstrong said, "one giant leap for mankind." And it was. A man had set foot on the Moon. "Impossible" would never carry quite the same finality on Earth again.

The sky above Armstrong was completely black, darker than the darkest night on Earth. Around him, like an endless sandlot, was the gray and pockmarked surface of the Moon, covered in moondust and small craters and scattered with "literally thousands" of rocks. The Sun shone brilliantly on this ashen world, casting sharp shadows and making Armstrong glad for his gold visor, which he pulled down as soon as he moved out of the LM's shadow. Standing on this brightly lit surface under a black sky was like being on a floodlit soccer field at night, but in a desert landscape. Armstrong found that he liked it. "It has a stark beauty all its own," said the Moon's first visitor. "It's different, but it's very pretty out here." The glare on the landscape drowned out the stars, making them invisible in

the black. Only the blue Earth hung in the sky, almost directly overhead. And it was smaller than a golf ball held at arm's length.

Aldrin joined his commander 19 minutes later, and the two of them began to explore the new world. Armstrong had photographed Aldrin's emergence from the hatch and had the single camera for nearly the entire E.V.A., shooting many of the most famous photographs ever taken—all of which necessarily featured Aldrin, rather than the first man on the Moon himself. Whether it was good fortune or skill, Armstrong took during his brief stay on the lunar surface the best single collection of photos ever brought back from the Moon, framing one iconic image after another and documenting the experience brilliantly. Aldrin was no less fortunate. Without trying for art at all, Aldrin took two powerfully iconic photos during the scant minutes he held the camera upon stepping onto the surface. In an effort to document the nature of the lunar soil, he intended to shoot a bootprint in untrammeled moondust. He accidentally triggered the camera as he was framing the image, snapping a photo with his boot in it—an error. The result was, however,

*Hasselblad camera built for lunar mission*

**ARMSTRONG**

*Back aboard the LM after completing his historic moonwalk, Neil Armstrong's face shows both the happiness of accomplishment and the strain of the pioneering, exhausting experience he has just been through. There would never be another landing like the first.*

so splendid and narratively effective that it became an icon no less than the isolated bootprint shot that beautifully summed up the achievement of man reaching the Moon. Not many accidental photos of a photographer's foot make it into history books, but this one worked.

"There seems to be no difficulty in moving around, as we suspected," Armstrong told Houston. "It's even perhaps easier than the simulations of one-sixth *g* that we performed in various simulations on the ground." The famously professional test-pilot Armstrong found time for joy in this moment under the weight of history, marveling at the experience. Now that he had finished speaking for history, his words were for himself and his companion, walking on the Moon. He waved his arms, and said, with quiet delight, "Isn't this fun?"

Aldrin busied himself setting up several experiments that he unpacked from the side of the LM's foil-wrapped descent stage. The LM, you might say, had a trunk. To fit in the cramped space, the experiments folded up ingeniously, snapping solar panels open like butterfly wings out of a chrysalis now that they were on the Moon. Aldrin worked to find level spots on the lightly rolling terrain, having trained to place each item at a predetermined spot, leaving nothing to chance.

Armstrong had time to go exploring, if only for a moment. He realized that he could go and take a look at the 80-foot crater he had flown over just before landing. While his crewmate worked, he loped off and took photos of the astonishingly blank landscape where he had landed his ship. It was a world of incredible absolutes, a jet-black sky, distant details deceptively crystal clear, not in the least hazed by atmosphere. The Moon's surface color seemed to vary depending on how you looked at it. If you looked "down-sun" toward your shadow, light tans and beige color could appear in the "very white, chalky gray," but the colors vanished in other directions, and the grays got darker. If you turned your head, Armstrong noted, "it's considerably darker gray, more like

ashen gray as you look out 90 degrees to the Sun."

Armstrong had placed the little black-and-white television camera on a stand a short distance from the LM. It captured the astronauts' ghostly images as they drifted back and forth in surreal motion, going about their tasks, setting up the flag. Mission Control put through to their comm link a call from the White House. "For one priceless moment in the whole history of man," said President Nixon, "all the people on this Earth are truly one." All too soon, it was time to go. The precious 2 hours and 21 minutes of this unique experience were gone, and the two men returned to their ladder. Before they left, they removed a section of gold foil on the landing leg to reveal a plaque. The stars and stripes proudly proclaimed the nation that had accomplished this wonder, but the plaque carried a picture of the entire world. "Here," it read, "men from the planet Earth first set foot on the Moon, July 1969 A.D. We came in peace for all mankind." To Neil Armstrong, these were not empty words. When the president had talked to them, Armstrong had spoken not of individual challenge or national pride. "It is a great honor and privilege," he said, "for us to be here representing not only the United States but men of all peaceable nations with an interest and a curiosity and a vision for the future." This colossal adventure had been born of an arms race and Cold War fears, but here in its climax was a transformation. There would be no victor's dance but instead a humbling, exalting experience to be shared with all mankind. Such was the way of the United States, for all its faults, and such was the character of the first man on the Moon.

Back in the LM, tired but happy, Neil Armstrong smiled.

**L.O.R.**

*Neil Armstrong pilots the* Eagle's *cockpit stage back up from the Moon to rejoin Michael Collins in the command module. This was the controversial—but very successful—Lunar Orbit Rendezvous maneuver that allowed Apollo landing missions to use just one Saturn V each.*

RETURNS

*The Apollo 11 crew came*
*back to a heroes' welcome*
*on Earth. Just a few*
*months later, Apollo 12*
*blasted off amid a*
*thunderstorm,* below, *for*
*another trip to the Moon.*

## ONE PRECIOUS, SHINING MOMENT

**T**he footsteps on the Moon really were affecting people around the world. Even *Pravda* in Moscow reported, "We rejoice at the success of the American astronauts," and carried the story at unprecedented length. The Soviet press had been short-spoken about earlier American space accomplishments, but what had just happened, for this moment, transcended even the rivalry that had set it in motion. Heads of state all over the world sent congratulation messages to the United States, praising the achievement and the Apollo 11 crew in whom were embodied the spirit of the venture. Many were moved by this event and marked it as a great milestone in the history of mankind.

Wonder of wonders: men were walking on the Moon. In such a world, who knew what the future could bring? Israel's premier Golda Meir expressed the wish that this demonstration of the possibility of the impossible would "open the way to that era of universal peace presaged by the prophets of old." Sputnik had begun the Space Race with fear. Apollo 11 ended it with hope.

### FIRST MAN OUT

**F**ate chose Apollo 11 as the first landing mission. It could as easily have been Apollo 10 or 12. If a problem had been identified that Apollo 11 would have to solve, Pete Conrad's Apollo 12 might have been given the first landing. As Deke Slayton, the ex–Mercury astronaut head of the Astronaut Office, said more than once, any of the crews were capable of taking any of the missions.

One can only imagine what other men might have made of the place in history that Armstrong stepped into. Wisecracking Pete Conrad made a joke of his first step on the Moon in Apollo 12, and his approach would have forever changed the image of what mankind's first step meant. Buzz Aldrin later suffered from very public alcoholism and depression, and some other astronauts involved themselves in unfortunate commercial stunts or scandals. Armstrong stood above it all, avoiding the spotlight, gently declining interviews after the initial publicity blaze, and steadfastly refusing over time to put his personal stamp on the position history had offered him, except through the restraint of his character.

Armstrong was in the end such a perfect person to command the first landing mission that many people later believed that some planning inside NASA must have ensured that he would take that first step. But in truth it was fate making the selection, and history is the richer for it. As Gene Cernan observed thirty years later, no one else in the astronaut corps could have risen to the occasion with the dignity that Neil Armstrong brought to the job.

### APOLLO 12

**A**mid the jubilation of the first lunar landing, plans were in motion already for the second. NASA now planned a series of "H" missions, which would use the same basic equipment as Apollo 11 but would land in new areas and explore a little farther. In November 1969, after that unforgettable July, NASA mounted the first return to the Moon and dispatched Apollo 12 into the heavens during a rainstorm.

The Saturn V on this launch battled the forces of nature. Its powerful flight into the air summoned up return violence, conjuring two lightning bolts, which seared into Apollo 12 and tripped nearly all

POISED

*Apollo 12's lunar module orbits 69 miles high, preparing to begin its descent to the Moon's Ocean of Storms. Supported by Mission Control via radio, the astronauts were nonetheless utterly on their own above this alien world.*

the circuit breakers in the command module's systems. If the entire rocket had been run from a centralized computer, the mission would have been wiped out, but von Braun's baby had its own brain (that conservative German planning), and the IBM Instrument Unit flew the rocket unharmed while the astronauts struggled with some alarm to reinitialize their cockpit systems in the spacecraft. The Saturn V seemed invincible.

Three days later, mission commander Pete Conrad flew his LM in over the Moon's Ocean of Storms, a thousand miles west of Neil Armstrong's landing site. Apollo 11 had come in "downrange," landing farther west than planned. The mission of Apollo 12 would be to make a pinpoint landing, and flight planners had selected a site with a very specific target: the soft-lander probe *Surveyor 3*, which had scouted the Ocean of Storms some three years previously. Apollo 12 would demon-

strate the ability to make a precise landing and recover pieces of the Surveyor probe so that analysis could show what effect long exposure to the Moon's environment had had on the metal and instruments. The landing site was amid several gently rolling craters, but still in one of the Moon's smooth *maria*, presenting a minimum of difficulty for the pilot. The precision landing would be enough to demonstrate on this mission. And Pete Conrad, a pilot-jock astronaut if ever there was one, loved the mission.

Precision flying on the toughest assignment possible: that was the kind of assignment these pilot types wanted most. These types didn't seem to be ideal lunar-science explorers, but during this phase of Apollo, the challenge was still flight and engineering. Once this foundation was well-established, NASA promised impatient researchers that stronger science missions would follow.

# The Moon Space Suit

The Apollo Moon space suit made an astronaut nearly impervious to the harsh forces of space and the lunar surface. Twenty-one different layers composed this 183-pound suit of Space Age armor, making it a cumbersome but powerful element of the Moon explorer's panoply. Every astronaut had to know this system inside and out, as their lives depended on it.

Three components made up the Apollo Moon suit. The first was a set of cooling long johns woven with a network of fine plastic water tubes. The circulating water maintained an even temperature throughout the suit no matter how hard an astronaut worked or what kind of solar heat he stepped into. The system was cooled by an evaporative radiator in the backpack, which used small quantities of water.

A heavy-duty pressure suit worn over the cooling garment protected the astronaut from the vacuum of space. The pressure suit felt something like a scuba wetsuit laced over a full set of football body armor. Complex joint systems and rubber bellows tubes allowed the astronaut reasonable motion while preventing his suit from ballooning out from the air pressure inside it. Rigid shoulder pads supported the weight of his backpack.

A white cover layer shrouded the whole assembly. Made up of more than a dozen layers of silvery mylar and Kapton film, the cover protected the Moon explorer from micrometeoroids and the blistering heat of the Sun. The surface of the cover garment was the futuristic Teflon-coated white fabric called Beta cloth. Completely fireproof, Beta cloth could endure temperatures of over 1,200°F. Soft and flexible, the white cover layer made the moonwalk suit look far more comfortable than it really was.

A tough gray metal cloth called Chromel-R, resistant to abrasion by Moon rocks, covered the insulated overgloves and the sides of the lunar overboots for extra protection. The moonwalkers wore as their wristwatch an off-the-shelf race-driving and test-pilot watch by Omega called the Speedmaster

*Beta cloth covered the visor shell of the early Apollo space helmet, but the cloth was omitted as unnecessary after Apollo 12. The gold visor could be lifted to provide better vision in shadows.*

*This two-piece Apollo in-flight suit is made of a heavy Teflon fabric, which is less comfortable than it looks.*

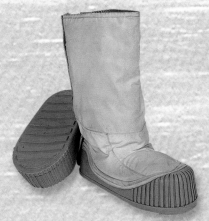

*These training boots lack the gray Chromel-R protective fabric used on Moon-rated boots.*

Professional, which proved invulnerable to anything a Moon mission could throw at it.

The Apollo backpack Portable Life Support System, or P.L.S.S., held oxygen and cooling water, pumps, and a communication system. An emergency oxygen system topped the back-pack, to be activated in case of a suit puncture or (even more frightening) a faceplate crack. A "red apple" ball on a cord was mounted over the astronaut's gut. A tug on this "panic button" would open a valve on the emergency reserve tank of oxygen on top of the backpack and flood the suit with oxygen, giving the astronaut a limited chance to sur-vive and reach the safety of the LM cockpit.

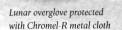

*Lunar overglove protected with Chromel-R metal cloth*

The Apollo helmet was a clear bubble, strikingly similar to the ones that pulp science-fiction magazines had been picturing on space action heroes ever since the 1930s. Gus Grissom's Plexiglas helmet faceplate on Gemini 3 had cracked, so the Apollo helmets were made of tough polycarbonate, a material 30 times stronger than Plexiglas. A pad in the back of the helmet bubble allowed the astronaut to rest his head during launch and reentry. For protection from the Sun's unfiltered glare, a reflective gold visor mounted in a shell over the bubble helmet could be rotated up or pulled down against the Sun's blistering power in the airless environment. Opaque visors over the gold one could limit glare even further. On the first two landings, a white thermal hood was worn over the helmet shell as the final covering to complete the suit. Handmade to fit each individual astronaut, the fabulously complex Apollo space suits cost in the neighborhood of $1.5 million apiece.

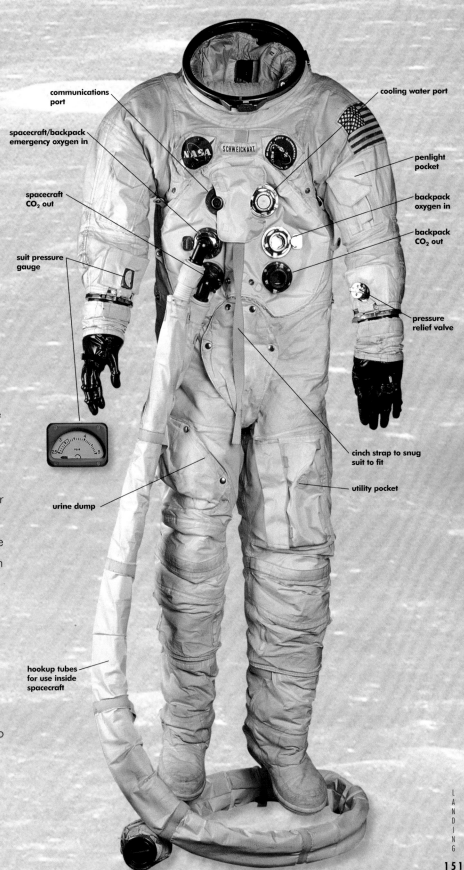

communications port

cooling water port

spacecraft/backpack emergency oxygen in

penlight pocket

spacecraft $CO_2$ out

backpack oxygen in

backpack $CO_2$ out

suit pressure gauge

pressure relief valve

cinch strap to snug suit to fit

utility pocket

urine dump

hookup tubes for use inside spacecraft

To aid the astronauts in piloting the LM to a pinpoint landing, NASA planned all the Apollo landing missions' timing such that the final descent was made with the Sun at their backs and low in the sky to cast long ground shadows. The advantageous lighting worked with the commander's detailed pre-mission study of maps and photographs to make the most of the short time he would have to orient himself at the real location for the actual landing. When Pete Conrad's LM pitched upright, he saw exactly what he expected to see: a "snowman" pattern of craters marking his landing site. Conrad eagerly skimmed in as his crewmate Alan Bean called out the data. There were no computer alarms this time. Conrad set the Apollo 12 *Intrepid* down on the Ocean of Storms no more than 600 feet from *Surveyor 3*.

In contrast to the formal operation that was Neil Armstrong's Apollo 11, Conrad and Bean ran Apollo 12 for fun. They joked, sang, and hummed as they went out onto the lunar surface. Unfortunately for the world audience, one of the first things Alan Bean did was accidentally point the television camera straight at the Sun. The camera's delicate receptor tube fried instantly, ruining it for the rest of the mission. There would be no more television, and as a result, the networks and the public lost interest in Apollo 12.

There were comparatively few following their progress when Conrad and Bean walked out to the Surveyor to examine their predecessor, which had been waiting for 31 months on the Moon. It was an extraordinary encounter with an instrument of intelligence here in this barren wilderness. They found Surveyor lightly coated with moondust stirred up by the LM's rocket blast. Oddly, the faint tinge of dust on the

**APOLLO 12 VISITOR**

*Alan Bean examines the Surveyor 3 Moon probe that served as Apollo 12's landing target. The LM and a communications antenna appear 600 feet away on the horizon.*

white probe looked light brown, but on the ground the moondust looked gray. In the sample bags, it looked black like powdered charcoal. This moondust was some weird material.

The Apollo 12 landing crew carried out two moonwalks, lasting a total of 7 hours and 45 minutes, proving that men could operate on the surface for extended periods and that future missions could be more ambitious.

Above all, Apollo 12 showed that precision landing was indeed possible. These guys were the best pilots in the world, the machines were good, and their mission support was flawless. It was an unbeatable combination. They would need a bigger challenge than this to really test them. And they would get it.

## APOLLO 13

**E**asygoing Jim Lovell had spent 14 days in space with Frank Borman on Gemini 7 and had traveled around the Moon with him on the Christmas flight of Apollo 8. On Apollo 13, Lovell was in command, and no Apollo commander would face a greater test in flight than Lovell would meet on Apollo 13.

Lovell's expedition was to be the first of the genuine science missions, an H-class "simple landing" but exploited to its fullest. The astronauts had chosen for their mission patch the motto *"Ex Luna Scientia,"* or "From the Moon, Knowledge." Lovell relished the range of roles he would be called upon to play in this mission, a commander acting as edge-of-the-envelope pilot and scientific explorer. Traveling with him would be a rookie crew of well-trained men: command module pilot Jack Swigert and lunar module pilot Fred Haise. Imaginative fiction had again provided a name for a command module, this time *Odyssey,* named in honor of Homer's poem and Stanley Kubrick's epic film *2001: A Space Odyssey.*

On April 13, 1970, the conjoined Apollo 13 spacecraft were traveling toward the Moon and were almost 200,000 miles out when Lovell and his crewmates televised a message back to Earth, showing a floating tape recorder playing the *Also sprach Zarathustra* theme from *2001*. None of the networks was carrying the transmission live, so quickly had Americans become accustomed to landing men on the Moon. But the press would take interest soon enough.

Shortly after the television transmission concluded, the astronauts heard a loud, muffled *bang*. Their ship shuddered. Then the alarm lights came on. A power failure was the first to show up. "Houston," Lovell radioed, "we've had a problem."

Flight controllers worked quickly with the confusing telemetry. Something had gone wrong on the spacecraft, but it was not yet clear what had happened. Surely some of the data were the result of bad instruments. The indicator boards made it look like a massive quadruple failure. Flight director Gene Kranz was not about to let the situation rattle his men. "Let's everybody keep cool," came his calm, even voice over the communications circuit. "Let's solve the problem, but let's not make it any worse by guessing."

The astronauts, meanwhile, looked out and saw the ghastly spectacle of their oxygen spewing out of a tank into space. There had been an explosion below in the service module. As the situation became clearer, Kranz and his controllers learned that the service module's oxygen tank number 2 was completely dead. Two of the three electrical power cells were dead, and the pressure in the remaining oxygen tank was dying before their eyes as they looked incredulously at their screens, the pressure steadily dropping. The data were all real. Other systems were failing as well, and when they completely lost power, they would lose the main engine. It dawned on them that the command module had only a short time to live.

In space Apollo 13 was surrounded by a cloud of its own blood, tiny metal fragments spinning into eternity and invisible wisps of precious oxygen lost to the vacuum. Jim Lovell and his shipmates quickly began powering down the command module systems before all their electricity was gone. In the hope that they would be able to return to Earth, the crew had to conserve the command module's small internal batteries for reentry. At present, they were hurtling toward the Moon, and no one knew exactly how bad the damage was or what their options would be. All they knew was that they were running out of air, power, and water. The prospect was extremely grim.

Flight director Gene Kranz informed his troops in the trenches and in the "backroom" of Mission Control that failure was

"not an option." In a smoky "trouble room" filled with engineers, flight controllers, and desperation, Kranz marshaled their combined expertise, the astronauts' only hope. After brief, blunt discussion and clear responsibility assignments, Kranz called for attention before he sent his "Tiger Team" out. "Okay, listen up," said Kranz, his face firm, his tight crewcut and ramrod-straight posture giving the correct impression of a man of absolute military discipline. "When you leave this room," he told the men around him, his tone like a drill sergeant's, "you must leave believing that *this crew is coming home*. I don't give a damn about the odds, and I don't give a damn that we've never done anything like this before. Flight control will *never* lose an American in space. You've got to believe, you people have got to believe, that this crew is coming home. Now let's get going!"

**NEAR-FATAL DAMAGE**
*The routine activation of an oxygen tank stirring fan triggered an electrical arc and blew out an entire side of the Apollo 13 service module.*

The LM became Apollo 13's lifeboat. The three astronauts scrambled into the lander as the command module went dark. The LM

was cramped and uncomfortable, but it would provide oxygen to keep the men alive. All nonessential systems, including life-support heaters, were shut down to conserve crucial battery power for reentry. As water froze in the command module, the temperature dropped into the 30s in the LM. The men struggled to maintain hope and conserve water, hanging in the miserable cold, dehydrating and sleepless. Mission Control decided against risking virtually all their fuel on one emergency return burn, so instead Apollo 13 looped around the Moon and back toward Earth. This necessitated making two smaller burns, using the lunar-module landing engine, and coasting for three interminable days.

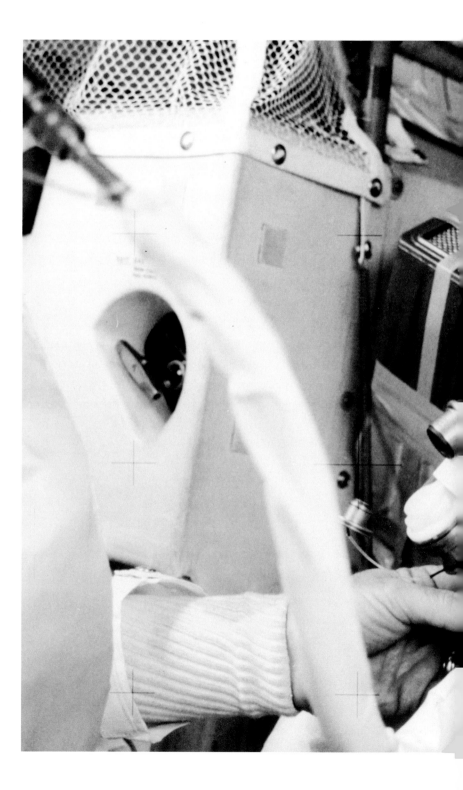

As they neared the Earth, the astronauts had to make course corrections using the LM thrusters, a difficult and unstable prospect since the fragile lander was never designed to maneuver both of the spacecraft docked together. With the guidance computer out, Jack Swigert had to time a main-engine burn with his wristwatch while Lovell and Haise struggled with the controllers to maintain their alignment, sighting on the Earth by eye.

On the ground, M.I.T. experts had furiously devised a cold-restart procedure for the command module, but no one knew whether it would work with the frozen equipment. It took Haise two hours just to write the procedure down, using the covers of manuals and every scrap of paper in both ships. Shortly before reentry, the command module came back to life on its own small batteries. This was the end of the road; there were no reserves now.

In preparation for reentry, they separated from the crippled service module and then jettisoned the lifeboat lander. What no one knew was whether the explosion had damaged the command module's heat shield. There was only one way to find out, and the moment of truth was coming.

As Navy helicopters patrolled the ocean below, millions all over the world waited in suspense through the reentry radio blackout. When Apollo 13 was a full minute and a half overdue, hearts were in agony. And when the three blossoming parachutes carrying the capsule appeared out of the clouds, there was a flood of emotion, relief, and joy around the world. Overwhelmed, the men of Mission Control burst into cheers and applause. Flight director Gene Kranz, his posture as crisp as ever, stood at his console, tears running down his face.

Intense study after the mission concluded that a damaged oxygen tank had been installed in Apollo 13's service module, its wiring built for a lower-voltage system. Higher voltage had eventually shorted out a switch inside the tank, melted off wiring insulation, and allowed for a short circuit almost 56 hours into the flight. A tiny arc detonated the

## EMERGENCY IMPROVISATION

*The Apollo 13 crew ran out of round LM air filters to remove the poisonous carbon dioxide of their own exhalations. Using a flight plan cover, a sock, a plastic bag, and duct tape, they created an adapter for the square command module air filters, buying a little more time to live.*

oxygen tank. The problem was securely identified, and not only the hardware but the procedures were improved to ensure that such a disaster would never happen again.

NASA's unwavering resolve throughout the crisis and the vast Apollo team's united ingenuity earned Apollo 13 the title "the successful failure." It really did seem that American talent could achieve the impossible, no matter what form it took.

## APOLLO 14

**T**he lunar scientists targeted Apollo 14 to the Fra Mauro highlands, on the edge of the great Mare Imbrium, hoping to find clues to the cataclysmic Imbrium Event that had made the largest visible mark on the Moon and left an entire "sea" in its wake. Fra Mauro had been Apollo 13's site, which Apollo 14 now inherited. Apollo 14's situation recalled Apollo 7, the flight that demonstrated mission capability after a disaster. And like Apollo 7, Apollo 14 would have an original Mercury Seven astronaut in command. Alan Shepard, America's first man in space, had finally been cleared for flight status again after undergoing a risky operation to correct Ménière Syndrome, a serious inner-ear equilibrium problem. He had his balance back, and in short order he had a ship: Apollo 14.

Shepard was, like Wally Schirra, a pilot's pilot. The mission was a pure flying job in his mind, and he didn't have much interest in the intellectual junk the science boys were

trying to push on him. He was enough of a professional to acknowledge that the lunar science was part of his mission checklist, and he would give it a fair shake, but he had no personal interest any more than Schirra had wanted to carry out "Mickey Mouse" experiments while proving that the Block II Apollo C.S.M. was not a lethal vehicle. Getting to the Moon after Apollo 13 had failed was exactly Shepard's kind of mission.

Apollo 14 blasted off on January 31, 1971. The service-module design flaw had been corrected, and there were no mishaps on the way to lunar orbit. Apollo 14's technical heart-stopper would occur at the very last minute. As Shepard brought his lunar module *Antares* in for a landing, a shorted switch and a resulting computer work-around blocked data from the ground-sensing radar. Shepard and his copilot, Ed Mitchell, were getting no altitude data. No landing radar at 10,000 feet would be reason to abort the mission, since the LM could misjudge the landing distance and crash. If it had been automated, it would have crashed, as many robot probes had. To them, minor malfunctions are

usually fatal. But there were top-rated human pilots on board the *Antares*, and they could implement last-minute fixes from Mission Control or override computer problems.

As Shepard and Mitchell descended, nearing 20,000 feet, the mission commander considered the fact that he could bring his ship in for a landing with or without the radar, flying by eye. And, theoretically, he could do it, regardless of what Mission Control ordered. Would Shepard break the mission rules if he had to? He was a long way from Houston up there. Fortunately, when Houston suggested that they recycle the landing radar circuit breaker, the landing radar came on line in time, and there would be no such decision. Without further computer problems, Shepard brought the *Antares* in for touchdown.

"Would you have gone ahead and landed anyway?" Mitchell asked him later. Shepard looked at him. "You'll never know," he smirked.

Having landed on the Moon, Shepard had some lunar science to carry out. His mission was to reach the edge of nearby Cone Crater, taking samples along the way. The rim of Cone Crater might contain rocks blasted out of the crust by the Imbrium Event. And the view from the edge of the crater would give them a good survey of the local landscape. Toting a substantial kit of tools, Shepard and Mitchell had more than they could carry, so NASA had designed for Apollo 14 a two-wheeled hand cart, the "lunar rickshaw." In official parlance it was the Mobile Equipment Transporter, or M.E.T. In practice, it became an accursed burden. The M.E.T. tended to get bogged down in the lunar dust, which had a habit of clinging to anything. They were more often dragging or carrying the M.E.T. than rolling it.

As the astronauts struggled along through the gray dust, Shepard was beginning to realize that none of the landmarks around him looked familiar. He had not paid very much attention to the geology briefings, assuring the scientists

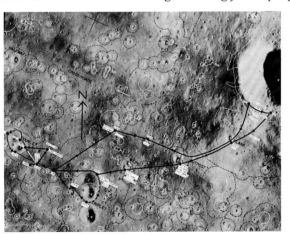

that he'd figure it out when he got there and disregarding their warnings about how difficult it was to find your way around on the Moon. After all, his objective was only a mile away. Shepard had looked at the photos showing the obvious Cone Crater and, as a pilot, figured there'd be no problem. As a lunar traveler on foot, he was finding the situation to be nothing like a pilot's aerial view. Mission Control struggled to orient the astronauts while the scientists in the backroom winced at how little data Shepard was bothering to collect about his lunar rock samples.

The frustrated pilot, swearing at times, dragged the recalcitrant M.E.T. up the slope of Cone Ridge, never seeming to reach the summit even though it appeared to be very close. Judging distances on the Moon was proving to be very difficult. The terrain all looked the same, near and far, grays everywhere, and there was nothing to show whether a crater was small and close or distant and large. Every detail was crystal clear, with no softening of any feature in the distance. It was surreal and disorienting, like losing your depth perception.

The boys in the backroom figured out why Cone Crater summit was overdue: The astronauts must be in the wrong location. They needed to change direction, but they were running out of time. Shepard and his crewmate Mitchell were now carrying the aggravating M.E.T. most of the time rather than fight with dragging it through the dust.

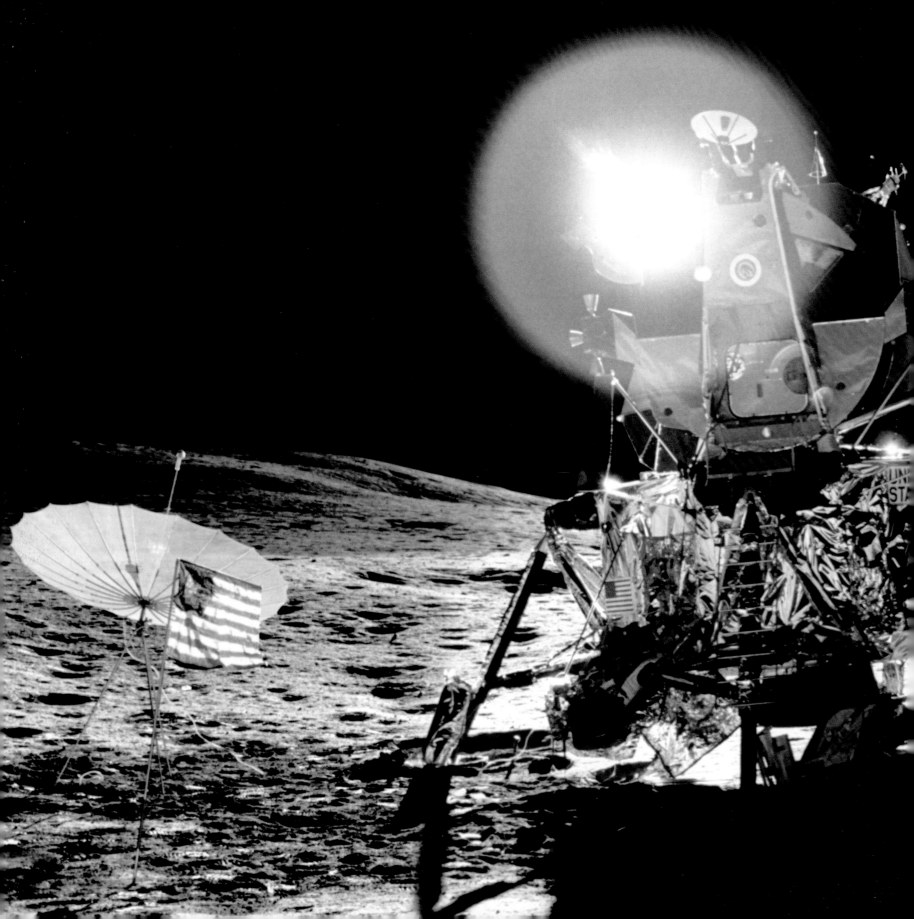

**"LUNAR RICKSHAW"**

*Alan Shepard with the Modular Equipment Transporter, or M.E.T., used only on Apollo 14. The M.E.T. helped Shepard and Mitchell carry more equipment than they could have by hand, but it wasn't easy to drag up the hills or over craters.*

It was like being lost in the desert with all your luggage. Finally, time ran out. The astronauts were ordered back to their LM. "The word from the backroom is they'd like you to consider where you are, the edge of Cone Crater," Mission Control radioed up bravely.

Analysis of the Apollo 14 photos on their return showed that the astronauts had literally been on the summit's threshold. About 60 feet away was the site that would have given them a view into the crater. But Shepard hadn't been interested enough to study the site charts in advance.

Once they were back at the LM, Shepard deployed something he had brought along for his own amusement. He fitted a golf club head to a geology tool handle and dropped an actual golf ball into the dust of the Moon. Restrained in his cumbersome space suit, he had to swing one-handed, but on the third try he sent the ball sailing into the

distance. "Miles and miles and miles!" he said, since those on Earth would never see it land not far away.

Back inside the LM, Ed Mitchell looked back over their struggle. "There were so many things we'd like to have done," he said to Houston. "So many things to do, so many interesting things to look at here—and we didn't even have a chance to scratch the surface. We hope we've brought back something that you can sort out as time goes on." Mission Control assured them that they had done "a great job," but as for the scientific data, the scientists regarded Apollo 14 as the low point of the entire program. Even Apollo 11's brief walk on the Moon had produced better geological observations from the highly focused Armstrong and Aldrin. It was an expensive way to prove a point, but Apollo 14 had accomplished its principal mission and renewed confidence after the harrowing crisis of Apollo 13.

Science was a stowaway to the Moon on Alan Shepard's Apollo 14. But that would change. The H missions were complete, and NASA was ready for an advanced phase of lunar exploration.

## THE SECRET SOVIET MOON

Meanwhile, behind the Iron Curtain, the superpower rivals who had goaded NASA and its Moon program into existence, the Soviet space pioneers who had taunted and intimidated the Americans into fighting desperately for the celestial high ground, were silent and mysterious. What was going on over there?

CIA information had led NASA planners to believe that the Russians were planning to send cosmonauts around the Moon by late 1968. Yet by the time of Apollo 14 in 1970, no Russians had gone to the Moon. Having lost the great race, they now appeared to be acting as if there had never been a race. Had they been in it at all, in the first place? Apollo detractors over the years claimed that the Moon Race was a trumped-up fiction supported by contractors and their congressional representatives to get the $24 billion Apollo price tag funneled into home-state aerospace businesses. For a long time, no one knew what the Russians had really been up to, if anything. With the collapse of the Soviet Union in 1991, all manner of interesting information would come to light.

The Moon Race had been very real, and the Russians were in it until the last minute. It is still not widely known that the Russians had not only designed but tested some of their lunar spacecraft. While we were landing Apollo missions on the Moon, the Russians were secretly testing their LK-1 lander in orbit in 1970 and 1971. We never knew anything about it. It was a one-man ship, built to absolute minimum dimensions to reduce the payload capacity of the giant

rocket that would have to deliver it to the Moon. The LK-1 gave its lone cosmonaut hardly more room than a good coffin, but the Russians built it and flew it unmanned in space, testing it just as we had tested our LM on Apollo 5. The Soviet lander was a no-frills bucket of bolts, but it was real and it would work. Getting it to the Moon, however, was another story.

When Wernher von Braun had designed his mainstay American space exploration rocket for *Collier's* back in the early 1950s, the rocket had a distinctive "bell-bottom" shape to it. The only way von Braun could imagine massing enough power to lift the ship into orbit was by clustering dozens of engines, since it was virtually unimaginable that just a few engines could be powerful enough to lift an orbital rocket, far less a Moon ship. The Rocketdyne F-1 engines changed everything, offering titanic amounts of thrust so that only five were needed in the Saturn V first stage. Thus the Saturn could be cylindrical, the more efficient shape. The bell-bottom shape expressed lower-power engines, and more of them, and while we never built it, the Russians did.

Their N-1 Moon rocket had nothing like the awesome F-1s to power it, nor had the Russians anything like Rocketdyne to design a power plant, so they had to make do with many smaller engines, just like von Braun had once sketched. And while the von Braun team had successfully clustered eight engines in the Saturn I and IB rockets, clustering 32 of them was a vastly more difficult matter. The Russians couldn't get it to work. They rushed the N-1 development in the late 1960s, hoping to beat the

**ALIEN LANDER**

*The Soviet Moon lander was a one-stage, one-man dwarf cousin to the American lunar module. Three secret Earth-orbital tests with unmanned landers in 1970 and 1971 proved that the craft could maneuver as planned. Without a Moon rocket, however, the landers would never reach the Moon. The first of the test landers remained in space until 1983.*

United States to the Moon, but the first flight test of the N-1 was the opposite of von Braun's astonishing, flawless first Saturn V flight. The N-1 malfunctioned one minute into the air and angled over to auger into the ground, exploding into a great deal of wreckage. A second desperate attempt to get the N-1 to work took place only three weeks before Apollo 11. In July 1969, the second, flight-ready N-1 stood on its launch pad in Baikonur, a mighty Iron Curtain Saturn V that the world knew absolutely nothing about. The unmanned Soviet space needle was fueled and readied, hissing and fuming like its American counterpart. It stood some 35 stories high, at 347 feet slightly smaller than the Saturn V because it was carrying smaller spacecraft. The first stage engines were fired, and the giant rocket rose off its pad in a blaze of glory. The Moon was very close, for a moment. Twelve seconds after liftoff, one of the 32 engines ingested a small metal fragment into its fuel injector and exploded. A chain reaction ripped the entire engine assembly apart and ignited the fuel and oxidizer tank system.

The Saturn V launch control complex in Florida was sited three miles away from the launch pad in recognition of the Moon rocket's explosive power. The N-1 stacked up not far short of its cousin in TNT equivalent, and this one detonated with an expanding sphere of annihilation reminiscent of the atomic bomb tests at Bikini Atoll. Launch personnel fled for their lives, running in every direction away from the catastrophe, but the colossal fireball was like a new sun born at Baikonur, and it grew and engulfed them before anyone could get very far. They were like ants before this apocalypse. Over 100 people were killed.

The destruction was visible from space. CIA surveillance photos showed that there had been a launch complex at Baikonur one day, and there wasn't one the next. The N-1 explosion had destroyed everything. It would be years before anyone outside knew what had really happened.

**LOST MOON ROCKET**

*The top-secret Soviet N-1 super-rocket, a model of which appears here, would have carried a cosmonaut to the Moon. Open girderwork connecting the stages allowed ignition before the previous stage had disengaged.*

The Space Race had been engaged as a contest to prove the superior abilities of the superior political system. Curiously, the very instruments of this contest reflected the different systems that brought them into being. American spacecraft demanded a high degree of individual expertise and decision making, requiring the astronauts to be very active participants in each mission, an echo of the expectations inherent in a free and democratic system. Russian spacecraft, on the other hand, reflected the Soviet structure of communism: The cosmonauts were largely passengers, riding in ships controlled by higher authority.

The United States had forged a government-industry partnership that had succeeded in overcoming every technical and managerial obstacle posed by the formidable challenge of the Moon, where the Soviet system was finally incapable of surmounting the same obstacles even with the benefit of their early lead. Time revealed that Nikita Khrushchev had pushed his space program for intimidating stunts, taxing his engineers beyond their limits. They had fostered the impression that the Soviets had developed a three-man spacecraft in 1964, for example, by cramming three cosmonauts into a Vostok capsule meant for one, requiring them to travel without the safety of space suits but calling it "a shirtsleeve environment." Cosmonaut Vladimir Komarov was sent up on a doomed mission in 1967 in a malfunctioning Soyuz spacecraft that had never been successfully tested. Soyuz I resulted in Komarov's death.

Throughout the space race, the U.S.S.R. had concealed its actions in shadows and misrepresentation, revealing only what the government approved, while the United States had shared its adventure with the world, openly broadcasting its successes and failures alike. Soviet superiority had degenerated into smoke and mirrors, which could not be sustained indefinitely. In the end, the contest had proven exactly what it was engaged to prove. Only the American flag could make it to the Moon.

**OVERWHELMING**

*NASA got 7.5 million pounds of thrust out of just five F-1 engines on the Saturn V. The Soviets had nothing even remotely comparable to such a massive engine and had to cluster dozens of smaller engines for their N-1 Moon rocket, which was still less powerful than the Saturn V. Synchronizing the N-1's 32 first-stage engines proved daunting, and all four test N-1s exploded.*

PRESIDENT John F. Kennedy had not launched Apollo in a spirit of exploration. The race to the Moon was for superpower prestige in the arena of geopolitics. As disgruntled scientists came to learn, science was secondary at best in the early Apollo missions. Yet a spirit of exploration had grown within the program. Apollo 11 had commanded a unique kind of awe: No matter what its origins, the mission itself was exploration of the most extraordinary kind and a compelling beacon for the human spirit. When the race was won, and Kennedy's goal had been accomplished, Apollo's overall purpose became much less clear, and it was in the context of this uncertainty that scientific exploration came to fill the void. A unique opportunity in history presented itself: A great power was at hand to be harnessed, and for a brief and wondrous interval, the spirit of exploration took up the reins of this power and drove Apollo to its greatest and most spectacular heights.

# Moon Explorers

## THE J MISSIONS

The first three lunar surface missions had been cautious landings that set us on the ground of this new world but gave us a limited look around. After journeying from another planet on board a titanic rocket-ship with tremendous power and capabilities, man on the Moon could move around no more effectively than his ancestors millions of years ago on the African savannas. Standing on the face of the Moon was a miracle, but now we had the chance to reach farther and empower our celestial travelers with new instruments, new abilities, and new missions into wild and fantastic territories beyond reach on the early Apollo expeditions. The initial landings had given us mastery of extraordinary capabilities. The next three lunar missions would capitalize on those capabilities and embark upon unparalleled journeys of exploration.

**PACKING THE ROVER**

*Technicians ready a J-mission lunar module for Moon service. The folded lunar rover would be stowed in the port side of the foil-wrapped landing stage.*

Landing site parameters were expanded, opening up vast new regions of the Moon away from the narrow strip along the equator. Mission planners who had been restricted to flat, safe territory for the early missions began to target ambitious landings in rugged, wild, mountainous terrain. And once the astronauts arrived, they would stay awhile. Moonwalk time would be extended from Apollo 11's brief two and a half hours to three seven-hour expeditions, allowing the astronauts, in new and improved gear, to range miles from their landing site and explore locations in depth, bringing back hundreds of pounds of Moon rocks and photographs of spectacular landscapes like no one had ever seen before. Above the cratered world, the orbiting command module would carry a whole new bank of instruments, turning it into a scientific observation platform that the crew would fly for up to two days around the Moon even after their return from the surface. Improved video and communications technology would link Mission Control—and world television—directly to the astronauts with sharper, color images, live from the edge of the space frontier. These would be the J-class missions, a thrilling new phase of Apollo.

The two returns to the Moon, Apollos 12 and 14, had been H-class missions, with a maximum of two moonwalks, constrained by the astronauts' ability to walk from the LM and back with a limited supply of air. 'I' missions had been envisioned as orbital exploration, sending a command module without a lander to orbit the Moon for extensive observation. In practice, pressed by time and budget, NASA skipped the 'I' series and went straight to the J missions. The J missions were advanced lunar surface exploration, and they would require a whole new set of gear.

The J missions had been in hopes and plans since before Apollo 11. With the great success of the lunar hardware on the early missions, safety margins had proven generous, and redundant systems were stripped out of the Saturn V to free up lifting power for the lunar module. The Grumman engineers who had worked so hard to trim the LM down to bantam weight for the G and H missions were now allowed to beef up their ship for heavier duty.

The J-mission LM looked almost identical to its predecessors, but inside, the new ships held a lot more equipment, bigger tanks, and an improved landing engine. More fuel would allow more complex landing trajectories, taking the explorers into more challenging terrain. A bigger engine bell would allow for greater thrust to keep the heavier ship in the sky as it approached its landing site. Also hidden within the upgraded LM were greater oxygen and water supplies, which would nearly double lunar surface stay time from 38 to 68 hours.

With the longer stay time, comfort in the LM would be more important than ever to maintain the astronauts' peak capabilities for the moonwalks. Armstrong and Aldrin had endured pretty miserable sleep periods in their cockpit, which was, for sleeping purposes, approximately as comfortable as a stall in a public rest room. Armstrong had sat on the bumpy descent engine cover while Aldrin lay cramped on the floor, both of them in their bulky space suits, which was something like trying to sleep while wearing a suit of armor. This unpleasant experience had led to the adoption on Apollo 12 of a lightweight, collapsible, practical innovation borrowed from ancient sailing ships: the hammock. The J-mission astronauts would enjoy the added comfort of being able to take off their new, more flexible space suits to sleep.

With their stronger engine and bigger fuel tanks, the advanced LMs could carry more gear. The J missions would be equipped with a surprising range of instruments and experimental tools, including core drills and explosive mortar launchers for seismic readings. What the astronauts really needed to extend their explorations, however, was mobility. But how could you pack a vehicle of any kind into the stripped-down, ultra-minimalist statement of pure function that was the LM? Where exactly would you hide, say, a car?

**W**heels on the Moon—a Lunar Roving Vehicle, or L.R.V. That would give the astronauts the mobility they needed. But the lunar module was so carefully packed already that you could hardly hide a box of Kleenex in the thing.

Fitting a Moon rover in there somewhere was a laughable prospect, but Boeing engineers would have to figure it out. The Boeing lunar rover team faced design challenges similar to those that had shaped the LM: pack it with an amazing range of capability, but do it with minimal weight and size. The rover had to operate in the 500° temperature variations between lunar sun and lunar shadow, a range that would render any normal wheeled vehicle inoperative right from the start. It had to work in vacuum, have redundant systems to prevent mission-stopping malfunctions, serve as a cargo transporter, carry a remote-controlled television camera, and also serve as the vital communications uplink directly to Earth. This Moon car had to carry a communications station that could transmit to another planet—and receive. Further, getting lost on the Moon had been possible for Alan Shepard just on foot. Getting really lost miles away from the lander could be deadly. The rover therefore needed to carry its own internal navigation system so the astronauts could locate their targets and then find their way home. Now, NASA said, put all that in a side compartment on the LM no larger than the "trunk" that carried Apollo 11's few science experiments. The space was about the size of a packing crate. Boeing engineers had their work cut out for them.

The completed design that emerged in just 17 months miraculously met all of its design specifications. It was not so much a car as a two-seater roving instrument. The lunar rover was engineered incredibly well, with remarkable capabilities packed into what looked like little more than a metal plate with four wheels made of wire mesh. It steered with a T-bar joystick mounted between the two lightweight, fold-up seats.

## WHEELS FOR THE MOON

*Orange-flavored Tang drink mix carried on Apollo missions was promoted as the "breakfast of the astronauts." To celebrate the J missions, Best Foods gave away a free rubber-band-powered, lunar-rover toy with each jar of Tang.*

*White and black stripes on the rover wheels allowed engineers to measure wheel movement seen in astronauts' 16mm films.*

# The Lunar Rover

Under the direction of Wernher von Braun's team at Marshall Spaceflight Center, Boeing engineers created the lunar rover to extend the reach of the astronauts on the Moon. The well-designed rover was so successful that on Apollo 15 the astronauts traveled 15.7 miles, over three times farther than the traverses covered by all previous landings combined.

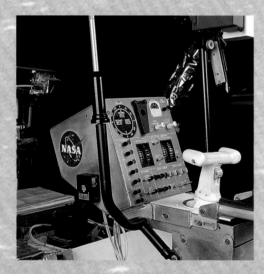

*The rover's T-handle was redesigned from a joystick at the request of astronauts, who found a pistol-grip joystick tiring to hold in pressurized lunar gloves.*

The rover's wheels were made of see-through piano-wire mesh, woven around a core of resilient titanium bands. Puncture-proof and extremely lightweight, the wheels sported titanium "Vs" as tread for traction. Steering worked on both front and back wheels, providing a backup in case of equipment failure.

Like the lunar module, the rover was the commander's to control, but in case of an emergency, the crewman needed to be able to take over. The LM had duplicate controls, but the lunar rover maximized efficiency by placing a single control console between the two astronauts, where either one could reach it.

The control console featured a sophisticated navigation system that kept track of the rover's wheel revolutions and steering commands so that it could always indicate the heading back to the LM, even when the lander was out of sight behind the hummocky terrain of the Moon. Among the high-tech instruments was a sundial-like Sun compass for use in navigation, in case all the technology somehow failed.

Thanks to its 32-inch wheels and 14-inch ground clearance, the rover could cross crevasses 27 inches wide and drive over obstacles almost a foot high. Its low center of gravity and four independent motors gave it the ability to climb hillsides as steep as 25 degrees. Its parking brake, engaged by pulling the T-handle joystick all the way back, would hold the rover on slopes as steep as 30 degrees.

The rover's batteries held enough power to carry the astronauts a total distance of 57 miles, though the astronauts would not have the time nor the safety margin to use this capacity to the fullest. Keeping to a walk-back limit of no more than a six-mile range from the LM would nonetheless open an area of 113 square miles for potential exploration.

The little rover could carry an amazing 1,064 pounds, allowing 400 pounds for each astronaut, including his heavy space suit and gear, plus 264 pounds for a whole arsenal of tools and experiments as well as the precious Moon rock samples. Gear and samples were stored in a rack on the back of the rover as well as in Beta cloth

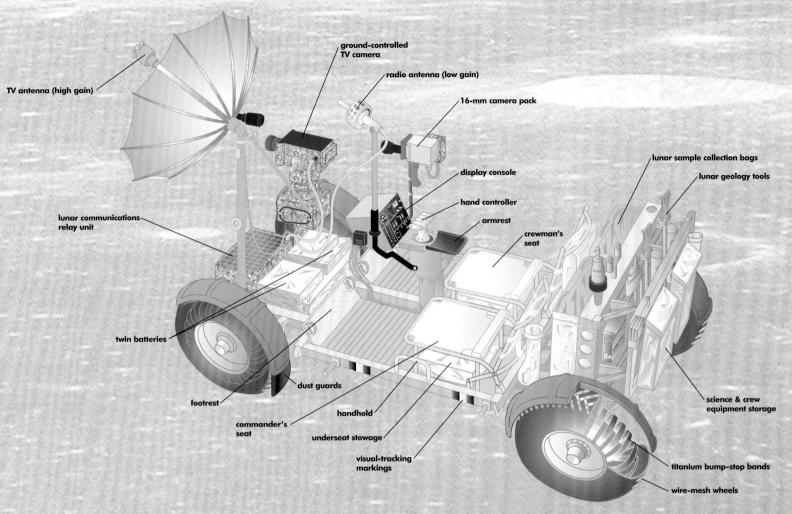

TV antenna (high gain)

ground-controlled
TV camera

radio antenna (low gain)

16-mm camera pack

lunar sample collection bags

lunar geology tools

display console

hand controller

armrest

crewman's
seat

lunar communications
relay unit

twin batteries

dust guards

footrest

commander's
seat

handhold

underseat stowage

visual-tracking
markings

science & crew
equipment storage

titanium bump-stop bands

wire-mesh wheels

*Boeing and its major subcontractor Delco Electronics built three Moon-rated lunar rovers and seven test and training units. Ten feet, two inches long, the rover needed to have a very low center of gravity to maintain stability over uneven terrain in the light lunar gravity. With a full load the rover would not tip over even at pitch and roll angles of up to 45 degrees.*

pouches underneath each of the aluminum-lawn-chair–like seats.

The rover's umbrella-like high-gain television uplink antenna could work only when pointed straight at the Earth, so the television link would be broken whenever the astronauts were driving. At each stop, when time allowed, one of the astronauts would use an optical sight to hand-aim the antenna at the Earth. With the link established, Mission Control could see through the rover's television eye via remote control as the astronauts explored. The rover's stubby white low-gain antenna, mounted on the left side of the center console, carried voice signals only and needed to be pointed only roughly at the Earth, so the astronauts could maintain radio contact while driving. A 16-mm movie camera mounted on the right side of the console captured the passenger's view while the rover was in motion, pitching and bucking over the cratered surface.

Apollo 15's David Scott happily radioed to Houston that the rover was easy to drive, with responsive steering and good traction. The rover opened the vast expanses of the Hadley-Appenine valley to the lunar explorers and on future missions would carry astronauts even farther. Scott liked the rover as much as any American enjoys a good car. This one made the exhausting, long lunar hikes in heavy space suits a thing of the past. Scott concluded, as he drove back to the LM for the first time, "This is a super way to travel. This is great!"

**INSTANT ROVER**

*The remarkable lunar rover folded in on itself twice to make a compact package that could fit into the side of the lunar module. Lanyards would lower the rover on the Moon, where it would unfold by the time it hit the ground.*

Sophisticated instruments, navigation, a communications antenna that could send live TV all the way to Mission Control, and tool and storage racks—the rover had it all. The whole exploration vehicle weighed only 471 pounds, but it could carry over a thousand pounds of load. The little cart could hit a top speed of about 10 mph, which would be plenty, given that mission planners were still nervous about the walk-back limit: In case the rover completely failed, they didn't want the astronauts so far away from the LM that they would roast alive in the broiling lunar sun as their coolant water ran out on the walk back.

The marvel folded up into far less space than seemed possible, journeying to the Moon wedged into one side of the lunar module's landing stage. At the tug of lanyards, the rover lowered like a drawbridge from the side of the LM and unfolded itself completely as it reached the ground. All the astronauts had to do was pull up its seats

and add the attachments to make a complete American exploration car on the Moon. When the Boeing group first demonstrated the deployment operation to the lunar-module builders, the Grumman engineers spontaneously applauded in congratulation at the rover's amazing transformation and remarkable economy of design.

The J-mission astronaut explorers would wear an improved version of the Apollo space suit. Designers had made the advanced suit more flexible, especially in the waist, so the astronauts could sit down in their lunar rovers. The new flexibility would also make moving and working on the Moon easier. On a long moonwalk, an explorer could drink orange-flavored Tang from a tube inside the helmet, an innovation tested on Apollo 14, or enjoy a fruit-flavored food stick mounted near the mouth to help increase his endurance. By the final mission, the designers would even add a Velcro patch that would allow the astronaut to scratch his nose. The explorers would appreciate all these improvements on the long journeys through the moondust ahead.

## APOLLO 15: EXPLORATION AT ITS GREATEST

**A** strange and enigmatic series of channels weave their way across the Moon, airless canyons called rilles. They look like deep riverbeds, but no waters ever flowed on the dead Moon. Rilles begin in curious depressions and flow into the lava plains, some curving like terrestrial streams, others running in essentially straight lines. The Lunar Orbiters had revealed sharper views of more than 400 of these weird features on the near side of the Moon, and puzzled astrogeologists had muttered speculation about some kind of collapsed lava tunnels, but no one really knows how they were formed. What were the rilles of the Moon?

The early Apollo landings had revealed the nature of the *maria*, the lunar "seas." Apollo 14 had ventured into slightly more hilly terrain, but the real secrets of the Moon lay hidden in difficult locales with mountains. We could learn a great deal from the "shores" of a lunar sea, a place where one of the dusty *maria* lapped against a mountainous basin rim. Such a place would be impossible to visit with flight guidelines that restricted the lunar module's approach to a safe, gentle 15-degree slope.

Mission commander David Scott would pilot Apollo 15, and he had carefully studied the data from his predecessors' missions. He was confident that the LM could handle much more difficult terrain and he wanted the challenge, but Scott was something more than a hotshot pilot. Scott had the spirit of a true explorer. For this commander, the new horizons of the Apollo J-mission capabilities beckoned powerfully, and he was determined to press them to the limits.

The site selection team had finally narrowed the choices down to just two for Apollo 15, and Scott sat at the table during the final meeting. One site had emerged as the favorite of the scientists, but then they were not the ones who would have to drop a spaceship into it. The place was called Hadley, where a bay of the great Mare Imbrium washed against the mighty lunar Appenines. The mountains at Hadley-Appenine towered 14,000 feet over the lunar plains of the bay. No one had ever seen anything like them at close range. And at the edge of this small bay was one of those enigmatic canyons, a ribbon of mystery tracing a curving path on the Lunar Orbiter survey photos: Hadley Rille. To complete the treasure of Hadley-Appenine, the geologists had spotted a small complex of what looked like recent volcanic craters, which might prove that the Moon was not geologically dead. The alternate landing site had scientific merit, but not like Hadley. Still, it was the commander whose approval would decide whether to risk the lives and the mission of Apollo 15 in a fragile LM over rugged mountains to reach what appeared to be one of the most remarkable sites on the Moon.

Dave Scott had examined all the engineering data, and he knew the capabilities of his spacecraft. He knew that he had the skill to pilot it to either of the locations on the table. But he had also looked at the fuzzy images of the "treasure site" and imagined the grandeur of the great mountains over the lunar plains.

*Improved J-mission pressure suit, worn underneath the white space-suit cover layer*

# Apollo 15 Explorations

Mission commander Dave Scott piloted the lunar module *Falcon* into the spectacular valley of Hadley-Appenine, landing near his target close to Hadley Rille and within lunar-rover range of the mission's several objectives. Three E.V.A.s from the *Falcon* home base took Scott and Jim Irwin on scientific explorations of Apollo's grandest site.

**S**cott and Irwin had two missions on the surface: geological survey and the setup of their Apollo scientific experiments. The survey traverses would occupy the bulk of the astronauts' schedule. Working with mission planners and astrogeologists such as Lee Silver, the Apollo 15 crew carefully mapped out their intended E.V.A. traverse routes. Dozens of small craters got unofficial names, such as "Elbow," named for its position at a bend in the rille; "Index," which helped David Scott get his bearings among the crater field as he came in for his landing; and "Arrowhead," for its unusual shape. As the astronauts navigated among these landmarks, three objectives directed most of the survey work at Hadley-Appenine.

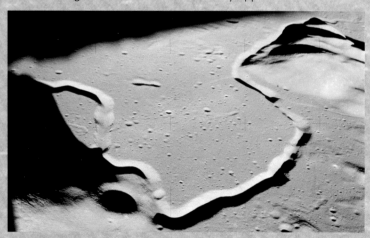

The valley of Hadley-Appenine as seen from the Apollo 15 command module, 69 miles up.

## HADLEY RILLE

**A** primary objective was to investigate Hadley Rille and to study its structure. Hadley Rille begins in a depression, like many rilles, in an area of domes that are probably volcanic—supporting the supposition that lava rivers may have created the lunar rilles. Where it cuts off the bay at Hadley from the open Mare Imbrium, the rille is a mile wide and 1,300 feet deep. Layering in the walls of the rille fascinated Apollo geologists, who desperately wanted to get samples from the rille's floor. Such deep samples might reveal secrets of the rille's origin or details of the Moon's past. Many schemes were concocted to get the astronauts down into the rille or to give them retrieval equipment. A lunar harpoon crossbow was discussed at one point, but none of the schemes were practical, and in the end the scientists had to be content with telephoto images and samples from the rille's edge. E.V.A.s 1 and 3 took David Scott and Jim Irwin to stand at the rim of Hadley Rille themselves, seeing with their eyes fine detail that even their Hasselblad cameras could not record.

## CRATERS

**A** second objective at Hadley was to sample rocks from in and near craters. Impacts gouge out rocks from subsurface layers, making craters windows to older time periods—the deeper, the older. E.V.A. 1 accordingly included the prominent crater

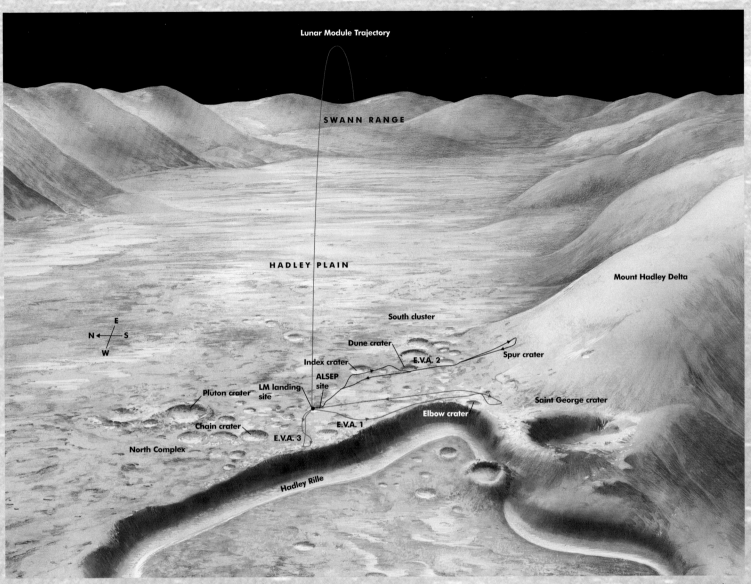

Lunar Module Trajectory

SWANN RANGE

HADLEY PLAIN

Mount Hadley Delta

E
N ← → S
W

South cluster

Dune crater

Index crater

E.V.A. 2

Spur crater

ALSEP site

LM landing site

Pluton crater

Saint George crater

Elbow crater

E.V.A. 1

Chain crater

E.V.A. 3

North Complex

Hadley Rille

*Hadley Rille begins 34 miles northwest of the Apollo 15 landing site (to the left in this view). The channel meanders for about 80 miles along the base of the lunar Appenine mountain range, past the plain of the landing site seen here, which is about 13 miles across. To the southwest, Hadley Rille merges with another, larger channel.*

Elbow, which gouged into the base of Mount Hadley Delta. Many of the Moon's craters are secondary impacts, created by debris blasted out of the ground elsewhere by a primary impact from space. Debris lying within the crater may therefore include

"exotics," or rocks from distant locations, extending the reach of sampling efforts. The South Cluster of craters at Hadley was believed to be a group of just such secondary craters, and E.V.A. 2 navigated the lunar rover through them for investigation.

## MOUNTAIN FLANK

**A** third objective of Apollo 15 was to sample the mountains in search of ancient crust or rocks that would date the massive impact that created the Imbrium Basin. Mount Hadley Delta was part of the Imbrium Basin rim

thrown up during the impact, and on E.V.A.s 1 and 2, Scott and Irwin used the lunar rover to travel up the mountain's flanks for first-hand examination.

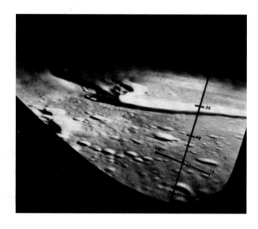

**SURPRISE VIEW**

*Apollo 15 commander*
*Dave Scott trained for*
*his Moon landing using*
*a model with*
*exaggerated surface*
*features. This view out*
*the LM window during*
*the real landing shows a*
*landscape with smooth,*
*subtle features. Scott*
*nonetheless identified key*
*features and landed close*
*to his target point.*

Navigation expert Floyd Bennett had worked out a flight approach plan into Hadley that required a drop almost twice as steep as the old 15-degree glide, so it was possible—on paper. To Dave Scott there was no question. Grandeur mattered in exploration. Apollo 15 would aim for Hadley-Appenine.

**O**n July 30, 1971, Scott stood beside his copilot Jim Irwin at the controls of the lunar module *Falcon* as they hurtled over the dangerous peaks of the lunar Appenines. The computer-controlled braking phase of the powered descent flew them blind, feet forward and eyes up, slowing the spacecraft but maintaining altitude to clear the towering summits of the rugged terrain below. The seconds to the final landing phase counted down, Scott's gloved hands ready at his control stick for manual override. Straining in his harness, he tried to get a glimpse of the terrain through the lower edge of his window. They were coming through the pass, and to his astonishment he saw the peak of Mount Hadley Delta—above him. Jim Irwin saw the even more imposing peak of Mount Hadley rising above the starboard side of the ship. They were at the bay, at the edge of the Mare Imbrium. And then the computer pitched them forward. They were cruising in at 150 mph between the mountains, and David Scott saw a landscape alarmingly unlike the one he had practiced for. The landmarks he knew from the simulators seemed to have disappeared.

The Lunar Orbiter photos of Hadley had not been maximum resolution, since the site was far too rugged to consider for the early Apollo missions. Flight planners had strained to see detail hidden in the film grain, and had exaggerated every feature to build a model of the

terrain through which Scott and Irwin "flew" in the trainer, a camera matching Scott's commands as it traveled over a sculpted moonscape. Hadley Plain was filled with craters, and mission planners had wondered whether the place might be so badly littered with boulders that the lunar rover would never make it through. There was literally no way to know in advance, and Apollo 15 was a calculated gamble.

As Scott flew the *Falcon* into the bay at Hadley-Appenine, he found that the terrain was significantly more subtle than he had expected. Most of the craters were rimless shallow dishes in the regolith. The Bay looked as if it were covered by smooth, luminous gray snow. Irwin called out Scott's critical data while the commander took the flight controller and switched over to manual. Scott could see the rille, and that would be enough to orient him. He cruised in, cutting forward velocity, and began to hunt for a good landing site. He tried to spot the crater patterns he had memorized, as the landing fuel tanks were emptying.

"Six percent fuel," Jim Irwin said coolly.

At 150 feet they started kicking up dust. By 60 feet it was a storm, a gray fog that obscured everything. Scott was bringing the *Falcon* down into nothingness, but it was time to bring them down. He gave up looking out the window and concentrated on his instruments, slowing, slowing, since he was flying blind. The shadow of the spidery lander appeared outside on the fog, dropping in close. "Eight feet," called Irwin, and then the critical pale blue light on the dash illuminated. "Contact light!" At least one of the probes had touched the surface. Loaded with thousands of pounds of extra gear and supplies, the J-mission LM ran an enhanced risk with its larger and more powerful landing engine with its bigger bell under the ship. The flat lunar surface could reflect the LM's thrust right back into the engine, and the J-mission LM was far more likely than the H-mission landers to suffer "blowback" if the big engine bell got too close to the ground.

**FAR-SIDE MEMORIAL**

*Apollo 15 took this*
*photograph of the lunar*
*far side, showing half of*
*the 90-mile-wide crater*
*Hilbert (far left) and*
*the 23-mile-wide*
*Kondratyuk (upper right),*
*named for the Russian*
*mechanic who first*
*conceived the concept of*
*lunar orbit rendezvous.*

Mission planner Fred Haise had stressed the importance of not giving it the chance to explode. Scott instantly cut the engine on contact light, and the heavy *Falcon* dropped the last four feet to the surface with a bone-jarring jolt that jerked the astronauts forward. The ship had tilted back, its rear leg in a crater. But it was settled and stable. "Houston," Dave Scott radioed to Earth, "the *Falcon* is on the plain at Hadley." Apollo 15 was ready to begin a spectacular mission on the surface.

The location surrounded the LM like a great arena. Scott had flown the LM in from the east, over the Swann range of the lunar Appenines, cresting them to reach the plain, which was really a small inlet of the vast Mare Imbrium, the Sea of Rains. Imposing Mount Hadley stood like a sentinel wall at the north end of the plain, while a smaller mountain called Mount Hadley Delta faced it across the plain, demarcating the southern border. Scott had landed, as planned, closer to Mount Hadley Delta. Between the LM and Mount Hadley Delta to the south lay a cluster of larger craters on the flat plain, and to the north was a low hill with its own set of larger craters: the North Complex, which the geologists suspected of volcanism. Defining its western limit, the sinuous canyon of Hadley Rille cut the plain off from the Palus Putredinis, the larger "marsh" opening onto the Mare Imbrium. A flat horizon lay in that direction, broken only by the low silhouette of Bennett Hill in the distance, like an island several miles away. To the north, connected to Mount Hadley by foothills, was Hill 305, the limit of the northern

mountain range. A large crater called Saint George sank into the shoulder of Mount Hadley Delta where the canyon ran to its base and turned to weave out to sea. This was not the anonymous patch of ground that the earlier landers had touched down in; Hadley was a setting of monumental caliber.

No one had ever opened the top hatch of a lunar module on the surface before. It was thought of as the docking hatch, used only in space. But the mission plan included an innovative use of the alternate LM entrance this time. Scott and Irwin, protected in their space suits, bled the air out of the *Falcon*, and Scott opened up the top hatch and stepped up to stand on the descent engine cover. Like a submarine commander's in a conning tower, Scott's head and shoulders emerged from the top of the LM, and before him was a landscape such as no man had ever before seen: great mountains around a lunar plain. He had a 360-degree view of Hadley-Appenine, and he used his unique vantage point to perform a site survey, expertly describing what he could see to the science backroom in Houston, where the eager geology team waited with bated breath. Having excelled at field training, Scott had become a master of field geology, and his perceptive examination brought Hadley richly to life for his colleagues on Earth.

"How's the trafficability?" asked Capcom Joe Allen. Would the team be able to use the rover, or would they be daunted by boulders? Scott assured them that the terrain looked absolutely ideal for the rover. They had a grand program of exploration ahead of them. With the "stand-up E.V.A." complete, Scott and Irwin bedded down in hammocks for the night, sleeping well and comfortably.

**UNPACKING**

*The first order of business after landing was to deploy the lunar rover and load it with instruments, antennas, and gear. The rover would greatly extend the reach of the astronauts on the advanced Apollo missions.*

## DAY 1

**R**esuited in full lunar gear, Scott and Irwin stepped out onto the surface after their first night on the Moon and began their work, unpacking their equipment. The *Falcon*'s tilt made deploying the rover a little tricky since the design relied on gravity to drop it out of the LM and unfold it. But in only a few minutes Scott and Irwin had their wheels, the key to ranging far and wide on the lunar surface. Irwin mounted the television camera and dish antenna on the front and filled the back with their geology tools. The first day's "traverse," as the exploration routes were called, would head straight to Hadley's most intriguing feature: the rille.

The rover surged forward at Scott's push of the T-handle, carrying the two astronauts toward the canyon to the west. Both of the men marveled at the environment of Hadley. The mountains were smooth and rounded, shaped like low sandhills, yet they towered like the Rocky Mountains. And the detail, everywhere, was incredibly sharp, with no air to blur or haze. They could see the "island" of Bennett Hill on the western horizon with startling clarity and the textures on the face of Mount Hadley as if they were looking through binoculars.

Closer at hand, the rover was providing an interesting ride. The light gravity and undulating terrain with its myriad subtle craters bounced and rolled the rover like a dinghy amid the waves. With its low center of gravity and seatbelts the rover was a safe transport, but the two explorers found it quite a rollicking ride as they cruised across the lunar *mare* toward the first rille man had ever examined.

*David Scott's Moon gloves used for training. The fingertips were soft rubber to give a better grip.*

# Apollo 15 Landscape

With towering mountains on either side, a broad valley floor, and a rille canyon, the landscape at Hadley-Appenine surrounded Apollo 15 with the most varied terrain that Apollo astronauts would ever explore. This panorama section was photographed by mission commander Dave Scott at Station 6 on the flanks of Mount Hadley Delta.

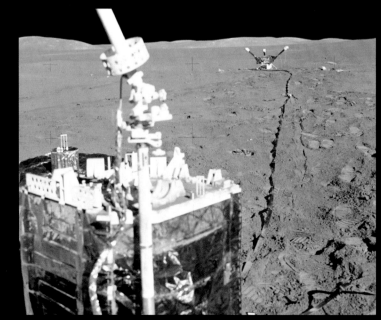

The second E.V.A. of Apollo 15 took Dave Scott and Jim Irwin up the lower slope of Mount Hadley Delta in search of rocks from the Moon's primordial crust. It took a 42-minute drive in the lunar rover for Scott and Irwin to make it from the lunar module to their first sampling station on the lower slope of Mount Hadley Delta. From here they drove diagonally upward, the rover slipping in the moondust but pulling them through. Parking again, they found that the slope was steeper than it looked. Irwin had to stand downhill from the rover and hold it to keep the vehicle from sliding while his commander worked.

Dave Scott, struggling to keep his footing, took this panorama of the valley below them between sampling efforts at the boulder. Mount Hadley lay to the north, in the center of this view, the great mountain marking the northern gatepost of the valley. To the west, at left in the image, the flat terrain of the lunar sea almost conceals the canyon of Hadley Rille. To the east, at right in the image, the Swann mountains form the battlements over which Scott had flown the LM on their landing. The lower slope of Mount Hadley Delta appears in the foreground. From this commanding position almost 500 feet above the valley floor, the Apollo 15 astronauts had an excellent view of the landscape that they would spend a total of three days exploring.

The smooth contours of the Moon make for deceptive landscapes. Mount Hadley looks like a minor foothill might on Earth, but it stands higher than the Rocky mountains in North America, roughly matching the height of Mount Whitney, the tallest peak in the contiguous United States. If Mount Hadley were on Earth, its upper 3,000 feet would be covered in snow, and the treeline would run about two-thirds of the way up its slope. Imagining such familiar cues can help bring scale to the lunar landscape.

**a** Hadley Rille is almost hidden in the flat landscape to the west.

**b** Apollo 15's set of 11 lunar-science experiments, set up here the previous day, measured everything from the lunar magnetic field to heat flow from the core. Built for super-efficiency, the entire set ran on less electricity than one 75-watt lightbulb, the energy supplied by a portable radioactive decay power unit.

**c** In the crystal clarity of the lunar landscape, the astronauts could see their lunar module *Falcon* sitting on the valley floor almost exactly three miles away (see pp. 186–87 for a close-up). Scott had brought the LM in steep from the right of this image, landing to face toward the left.

**d** The Moon has about the same reflecting power as an asphalt parking lot, but the Sun shines so brightly on the moondust that the Moon appears as a bright orb from Earth and a blinding desert on its surface. The glare makes it impossible to see stars in the black lunar sky.

**e** The South Crater Complex formed an obstacle course for Dave Scott on his way to Mount Hadley Delta. Jim Irwin observed that these craters all had rocks piled to their southern sides, supporting the hypothesis that they were made by debris spattered out of a large crater far to the north.

**f** Mt. Hadley rises some 14,800 feet above the plain, its peak about 16 miles away. The diagonal banding pattern appeared to be geological layering, and with a telephoto lens, Scott documented

the phenomenon. Curiously, post mission analysis would conclude that the bands were just a trick of the light.

**g** While the lunar maria look relatively flat from orbit, the astronauts found the terrain hummocky and rolling at the surface. The undulations and slight hills made for pitching, bucking off-road driving, with crater potholes constantly appearing from out of nowhere. Shallow craters were hard to see until you could look down into them.

**h** The Sun blazed down on the landscape from this direction, creating the glare obscuring the nearby mountains. Dave Scott had approached Hadley-Appenine from this angle to have the Sun at his back during landing. While out in open terrain, the astronauts usually kept their mirrored visors down against the Sun's glare.

**i** The Swann Range, mountains of the lunar Appenines, honored the name of Gordon Swann, the Apollo field geology principal investigator: chief scientist in the Mission Control backroom. Following the astronauts via television and radio link, Swann's geology team relayed instructions in real-time to the Capcom, who helped direct the work on the lunar surface.

**J** The flank of 11,000-foot Mount Hadley Delta stretched down to the plain below. It was on this up-thrust mass that Scott and Irwin hoped to find a piece of the most ancient lunar crust. Just a few hundred feet along the slope to the right in this image, they would discover the Genesis Rock (see p. 184 for a close-up).

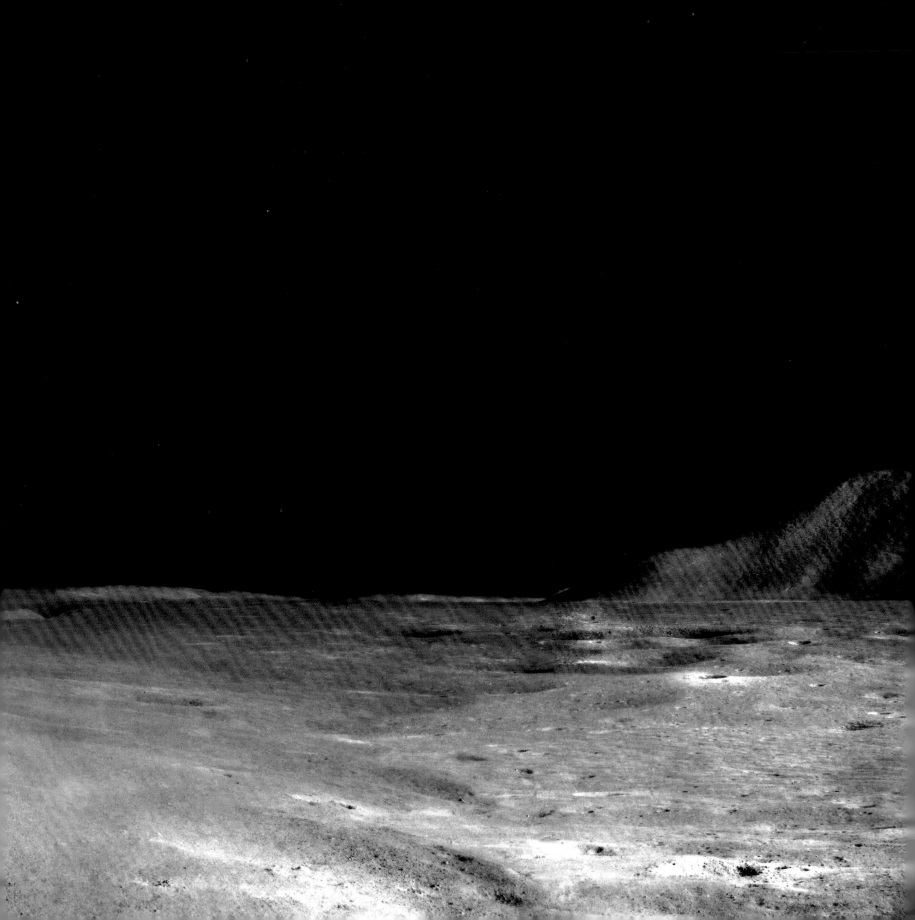

They stopped the rover at the edge of the canyon. It was remarkably even in width and cross section. The channel floor lay over a thousand feet below them. If they were to fall in, they would be hard pressed to struggle out alive in their cumbersome space suits. But the rim of the canyon was soft and curved, with blocks of stone crumbling out, a geological treasure trove for sampling. Scott aimed the dish antenna at the Earth, and Houston got both a picture and active control of the rover's movable camera, their own eye on the Moon. Through this extraordinary conduit, the teams on Earth were there on the Moon with their field scouts. Mission Control and the scientists in the backroom watched in wonder as the astronauts moved among the boulders of this strange land, at the edge of a dropoff that looked sheer and deadly to those who saw it foreshortened on the screen.

In person, Scott and Irwin were able to descend slightly below the rim without danger, turning back before the slope got too steep. The canyon sides were faintly layered, and the boulders lying on the dusty gray regolith of the valley floor were as big as houses. There was no obvious evidence as to how the weird canyon had formed. A silent mystery, the rille ran off to the north toward Hill 305, offering the astronauts a breathtaking view of its snakelike curves.

## MOON CAR

*The battery-powered lunar rover proved to be a dependable vehicle, carrying the astronauts safely through miles of traverses and frequently out of sight of their lunar module. Through the abrasive grit of moondust and the harsh temperature extremes, the rover delivered solid performance, and even in their bulky suits, the astronauts found it easy to drive.*

Pressing on, David Scott and Jim Irwin drove the rover along the canyon rim to reach their next objective, a crater named Elbow. Elbow lay at the edge of the canyon just below the base of Mount Hadley Delta's big slope crater, Saint George, and in this area the astronauts could sample rocks from several different geological environments. The two operated as rigorous scientific field-workers, diligently documenting the source and context of each find, quickly and methodically assessing the locations and moving on, always conscious of the precious limited time they had to gather clues to unlocking the Moon's secrets.

All the way through the traverse, Houston was there with them, participating at the stops via color television more closely than had ever been possible before. Witnessing it all from Mission Control, Joe Allen could even point out to the commander that Irwin's sample bag was coming loose from his backpack and needed cinching up. Houston was an invisible but real presence with them on the Moon.

Scott took a direct route back to the LM instead of hugging the edge of the canyon rille. The two astronauts riding in their electric vehicle crested the low rise that had hidden the LM and crossed the plain, surrounded by the black sky and the gray lunar landscape. They began setting up experiments to complete their day. Parking the rover and climbing the ladder into their little cockpit sanctuary, they were finally back inside after almost seven hours of fieldwork on Day 1.

## DAY 2

After a breakfast from the LM's small but adequate food store, the two explorers put their E.V.A. suits back on, locked their helmets and gloves, and once more emptied the cockpit of its precious air. Out into the vacuum they returned, and the world of Hadley surrounded them again. Outwardly they conducted their work in close touch with Houston, but inwardly each man found the locale inspiring and awesome. As much as they had been trained to function as efficient instruments, they were still men, and the experience was filling them with impressions and a sense of wonder that no machine could share.

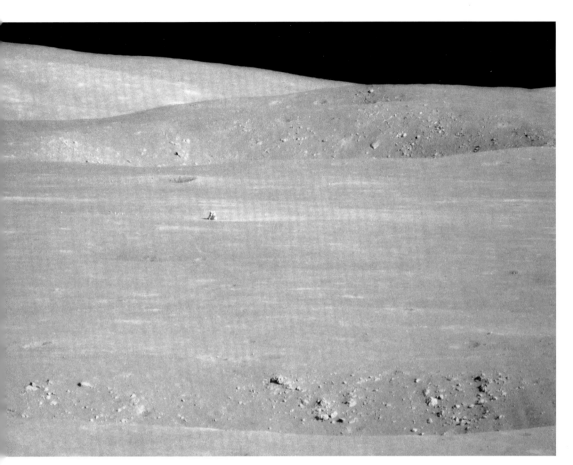

along the left side of this remarkable vista, and their lander sat in the distance. It was *three miles* away. No crew had ever ventured so far before. The mote of gold foil off near the horizon was their spaceship. Only human explorers could have felt such wonder at the sight, and both astronauts marveled at the experience of working in this great frontier. "There's a fundamental truth to our nature," Scott had reflected, upon first stepping onto the lunar surface. "Man must explore. And this is exploration at its greatest."

The astronauts systematically worked the terrain on the slope, putting into practice the many days of field and lab training they had received from their geologist mentors. Scott noticed something, a small white rock. White, here on the gray Moon. He moved

**DISTANT LM**

*Apollo 15 took the astronaut explorers over twice as far from their lander as any previous crew had traveled. This telephoto image shows the* Falcon *on the plain at Hadley, in front of the crater Pluton.*

Heaving and pitching across the soft gray snowfall of Hadley in their rover, the explorers headed straight south, their objective rising before them. Today they would further examine the flank of Mount Hadley Delta and sample a crater on its flank called Spur. Here, their samples would reveal the composition of the Appenine front, which might contain much older components than the *mare* plains. On the flank of Mount Hadley, their goal was a piece of the Moon's origins.

A third of a mile up the slope of Hadley Delta, they found that the training had not completely prepared them for what they would find. It caught them both as they turned around for the first time during their rock-collecting activities. It was the view. The plain of Hadley-Appenine lay beneath them, ringed by the features the astronauts had studied so well that they were familiar on first sight. The canyon ran

to photograph it, describing it. Irwin came to look. It was crystalline, with "twinned," aligned crystal forms that looked virtually pure. It was anorthosite, a rock type that the scientists had been dearly hoping to find. "I think we just found what we came for," Scott said. It was a piece of creation.

Sample 15415 was declared the "Genesis Rock" by the press, and the nickname was not far off. Laboratory analysis would show that this stone had not changed in the past 4.5 billion years, that it was a fragment of earliest lunar crust. It might as well bear the handprint of God. Scott and Irwin were awestruck. Irwin felt an undeniable presence in this fantastic remote place; he felt that they were not alone and that wherever traveled the souls of men, there too would they find their creator. The magnitude of their undertaking was not lost on the men, who felt

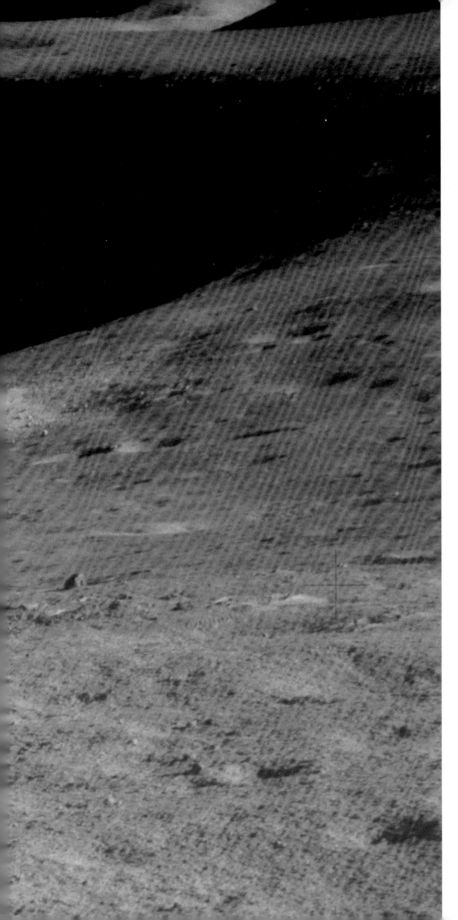

tremendously privileged to represent the hundreds of thousands back on Earth who had worked to put them on the Moon. But there was little time for marveling or reflection; there was always work to do.

Back down on the plain, Irwin finished setting up the experiment packages at a site some distance from the LM to protect them from its liftoff blast. Meanwhile, Scott faced the task of drilling a deep hole for a heat probe. Drilling into the lunar regolith proved to be nearly impossible. The upper few inches of moondust were soft and easily imprinted or shuffled through. But below this loose layer rested a firm and compacted layer that was like what you get if you leave concrete mix in a damp shed. The moondust was made up of pulverized rock particles, which all had sharp, jagged edges, never having been softened by wind or water. When compacted, as they were under the surface, they resisted the core drill like nothing Scott had ever tackled in the field on Earth. It was brutal work to get the core tubes down, and they completely refused to come up again. The tubes were locked into the tightly compacted gray regolith underlayer. Scott exerted himself to the fullest, but it was no use. They would have to leave the core recovery until the next day.

**EDGE OF MYSTERY**

*Jim Irwin works near the rim of mile-wide Hadley Rille. Apollo 15 was the only mission that allowed astronauts to visit a rille.*

## DAY 3

**T**he morning saw Scott fighting to pull the core out again. Even with Irwin's help, he could barely budge it. But Houston insisted that they keep at it, even as precious minutes drained away. Eventually they got it: a ten foot core that ran half a billion years into the antiquity of the *mare*. But it was painfully expensive: It had cost them the time it

*The "Genesis Rock" discovered by David Scott*

would take to reach the North Complex. Were those craters volcanic? Now they would never know. The destination was dropped from the mission plan; the time was gone. The astronauts drove once more to the rille for a final analysis there.

UNITED STATES

Moon. The crag at the left is Silver Spur, named for Apollo geologist Lee Silver. Saint George crater dents the slope of the mountain at the right.

## ORBITING LAB

While his colleagues worked on the surface below, Al Worden carried out extensive photography and scientific observations from the command module. Apollo 15 was the first mission equipped with the Scientific Instrument Module, which faced the Moon and is hidden in this view.

## LUNAR SURVEY

*Jim Irwin works at sample collection using tongs, bending over as far as he is able in the stiff Apollo space suit, which the astronauts often called "hard suits." Mount Hadley towers behind him. Nearby sits the Apollo gnomon, built to appear in Moon photographs so that scientists could observe true vertical and calibrate the colors in the photos to the color scale on the instrument.*

At the very edge of one of the Moon's great mysteries, the two astronauts pondered the enigma of the rille, taking photographs and examining the rille's edge. They hoped that there would be enough data to reveal to the geologists the mysterious force that had shaped this channel. For now, the time was up, and it was time to get back to the LM.

Orbiting above, Al Worden had been operating the brand-new J-mission C.S.M. *Endeavour*, a manned scientific survey spacecraft the like of which had never been launched before. The Apollo

*Aluminum Moon rock box held precious lunar samples for return to Earth.*

spaceships had been designed for expandability from the beginning, and with the greater payload allowances on the J missions, the C.S.M. could carry new equipment just like the lander was doing. When early missions had proven that the fuel safety margins were generous and the Saturn V had been stripped of redundant systems, more gear could be loaded into the available spaces in the spaceships. The LM got the rover; the advanced C.S.M. got the Scientific Instrument Module, or SIM bay, consisting of almost a dozen instruments to measure, sense, and probe the Moon. Al Worden kept busy running these instruments as his comrades traversed the surface. Covering thousands of miles of territory during his revolutions, he operated a laser altimeter, two mapping cameras, sensitive radiation and gas-sensing instruments, and a star camera that provided precise data on exactly where the ship was when it made each measurement. Where its predecessors had been utility transportation, *Endeavour* journeyed into space with the tools of science and would return with a rich harvest of images and data. The SIM bay even included a hangar for a probe called the subsatellite, which Worden would launch into lunar orbit. Far away from the effects of the metal spacecraft, the spinning subsatellite would search for faint traces of the Moon's missing magnetic field, orbiting the Moon for a whole year. The

SIM bay filled what had been an empty space on the earlier ships. It was hard to believe how much it was accomplishing now.

From the examination of the rille, to the Genesis Rock, to the reams of information recorded from the SIM bay, Apollo 15 attained a whole new level of achievement. The advanced lunar missions were probing the Moon and broadening our horizons.

## APOLLO 16: MISSING VOLCANOES

**A**pollo landings had revealed the origins of the lunar *maria*, showing them to be remnants of an age long past. And it had become clear that nearly all the Moon's craters were formed by impacts, not volcanic eruptions. So was the Moon now geologically dead? Or had lunar volcanoes spouted lava and ash in comparatively recent eras? Apollo geologists were determined to find proof of lunar volcanism, proof that the Moon's inner "heat engine" was still active, pulsing with molten blood *somewhere*. Apollo 15 had not been able to examine the possible small volcanoes of the North Complex, and so volcano hunting was high on the list for the mission of Apollo 16.

Only one thing beckoned scientists more powerfully than lunar volcanoes, a target so prominent that a sharp eye can see it from Earth: the crater Tycho. The meteorite impact that created this 51-

mile-wide crater had blasted out bright rays of debris radiating across half the Moon. Comparatively young, Tycho's gouge into the highland crust was not covered by *maria* or by debris rained down from other impacts, and it would offer a look deep into the ancient crust of the

**LUNAR GRAND PRIX**

*John Young test-drives the Apollo 16 lunar rover in this film still. Markings on the chassis and wheels would allow engineers to measure the rover's traction in moondust at various speeds and while turning—information useful for the design of future lunar vehicles.*

Moon. The robotic Surveyor 7 had landed near Tycho's rim in 1968, and the scientists now fervently wanted to send human explorers to this spectacular crater to probe its mysteries.

"You will go to Tycho over my dead body," declared Jim McDivitt in response. McDivitt, commander of Apollo 9, was now the head of the Apollo Spacecraft Program Office and had veto power over proposed landing sites. The scientists pointed out that a blind robot had landed successfully, but McDivitt thought Tycho looked too rugged and dangerous for a manned landing, and that was the end of Tycho.

Apollo 16 was targeted to an alternate, much safer site in some hills near the crater Descartes. The geology team had studied photographs of the area, mapping numerous supposed lava flows and possible ashfalls. From this landscape of forgotten violence, Apollo 16 would bring back proof of the Moon's recent volcanism.

After the loss of Tycho as its target, Apollo 16 suffered a number of other minor disappointments. A vibrating engine caused concern while the crew was orbiting the Moon and interrupted the landing attempt. The command module and LM orbited the Moon in formation for a dozen extra holding rounds before Mission Control decided to send them in anyway. The delay would cut short the moonwalks and trim an entire day off the post-landing orbital science.

Upon landing at Descartes, mission commander John Young and his crewmate Charlie Duke were openly enthusiastic, with Duke capturing a

## DESCARTES HIGHLANDS

*Wearing a collection bag strapped to his life-support backpack, Apollo 16 astronaut Charlie Duke stands on a rise overlooking a lunar vista to the north. Duke can be identified by the lack of red commander stripes on his space suit.*

*Main hatch of Apollo 16 command module. This style of hatch was simpler to open than the original Block I Apollo hatch.*

photo of Young saluting the American flag while jumping three feet off the ground. But spirits fell later when Young accidentally caught his boot on a tangled cable and ripped the cable out of its scientific experiment. The space suits were so bulky that Young couldn't feel the light cable, and with his chest-mounted control pack and camera, he couldn't see his boots as he walked. The damage was irreparable, and the experiment, designed to measure the heat flowing from the interior of the Moon, was ruined.

The Descartes site offered a kind of anonymous rolling terrain, without landmarks like the towering mountains of Hadley or the canyon of the rille. As the Apollo 16 astronauts explored the hills during their three days on the Moon, they discovered that the volcanic rocks they had come to find were nowhere in sight. Every rock the two men picked up seemed to be a breccia, a conglomerated mass created from the violence of impacts. Descartes was uncooperative in other ways as well. Taking their rover 500 feet up the slope of a flat, rounded hill called Stone Mountain, the astronauts hunted in vain for a set of five craters called the Cincos, unable to see over the hillocks that they were only 40 yards away at one point.

On the third and final moonwalk, a crater called North Ray seemed to be the team's last best hope for finding volcanic rocks blasted out of the Moon's bedrock. Upon reaching it, however, the astronauts were uncomfortable going too close to the crater's steep rim and had to make do with samples from around it. A 1,500-foot-wide crater called South Ray offered a beautiful, clean impact with a white halo of interior debris for sampling, but during mission planning, South Ray had been ruled out due to radar soundings that made it look too rugged for the rover to explore. Now that the astronauts were on the scene, they could see that the real crater would have been accessible to them, but it was too late to change the mission plan.

Near the end of the last moonwalk, Houston sent them running toward a large boulder on North Ray's rim which, like many lunar features, turned out to be much farther away than anyone expected. The boulder towered four stories tall, making the astronauts look like toys beside it in the rover's televised image. They called it House Rock. Here was a blasted-out chunk of the Moon that would settle the question of what had formed these highlands. Young and Duke chipped away: It was all breccia.

The conclusion was entirely clear. Apollo 16 did not find a single volcanic rock in the Descartes highlands. The lunar geologists, poring over the photos before the mission, had been so determined to find volcanism that they imagined traces of it where none existed. Apollo 16 ended up finding evidence that the early Moon had been shaped not by volcanoes but long eras of brutal bombardment. We still had much to learn—but so little time left in which to learn it.

## APOLLO 17: THE ULTIMATE TRIP

**A**pollo accomplished its political goal in July 1969 and beat the Russians to the Moon, making the ultimate statement of superior American capability. But the victory had cost the program its prime sustaining force. By late 1972, without the space battle for supremacy against a rival superpower, NASA garnered dramatically less of America's public interest than it had in the heady days of Mercury or at the time of Apollo 11's pioneer landing. The space agency that accomplished so much in creating the incredible instruments and abilities of Apollo failed badly at telling its ongoing stories and sharing the wonder of its adventures with the citizens who paid for it all. NASA never really considered inspiring the public as part of its mission. So the nation had hardly noticed when they again accomplished the impossible and put Apollo 16 on the Moon. But as Apollo 17 stood bathed in the glow of 74 searchlights at Cape Canaveral, people remembered and took notice. For this would be the last time.

The crowds filled the Cape as they had for the first landing mission. Half a million Americans were on hand to watch the miracle that they had somehow brought to pass and almost forgotten. On December 2, 1972, the giant Saturn V stood surrounded by light in the Florida night. The rocket seemed luminous. The spectators could feel its energy from miles away. And for this grand finale, Apollo 17 would mark another first: a night launch. Orbital mechanics had dictated the timing, and the time of day made no difference to the colossal Saturn V.

The blast could be heard 50 miles away. People saw the glow up and down the coast, as far away as South Carolina. Apollo 17 cleared the tower standing on an incandescent column of searing light and rose into the sky, its own sun changing dark into day. The light was like an arc-welder's torch, liquid fire brilliant, and the crackling Saturn thunder rippled through the crowds. Onlookers shielded their eyes from the glare and held their children as they felt the Saturn's staccato thundering blast work its way into the sky with gathering speed. Apollo 17 was on its way to the Moon.

# Apollo 17 Explorations

On the eastern shore of the Sea of Serenity, the valley of Taurus-Littrow lies surrounded by lunar mountain blocks. Gene Cernan landed the Lunar Module *Challenger* in this impressive setting, where the traverse routes would take Cernan and geologist Jack Schmitt ranging across the entire width of the valley.

**O**f the three E.V.A. traverses, the second day's was by far the most ambitious, taking the rover on a run across the valley to the debris slope at the foot of the towering South Massif mountain. Getting to the South Massif site would tax the astronauts and their lunar gear to their limits. Every minute the explorers stayed outside ticked time off their walk-back constraint, the safety limit that would allow them to survive a return to the LM on foot if the rover failed or became disabled. To beat this time limit and still reach the distant South Massif all the way at the far side of Taurus-Littrow valley, Gene Cernan had to drive as fast as he could, avoiding boulders and undulations in the terrain to get to their destination 4.8 miles from the

lunar module. The rover strained to climb a foothill rise called Lee scarp on the way, and the pock-marks of craters within it forced Cernan to zigzag back and forth to crest the low ridge. But the rover made its makers proud and climbed like the ultimate off-road vehicle it was. At the top of the ridge, Cernan and Schmitt drew to a halt at the very foot of the South Massif debris slope and disembarked to begin sampling the area they would call Station 2.

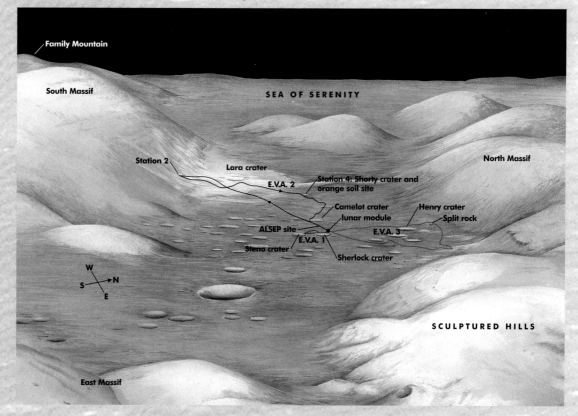

*The tallest mountain at Taurus-Littrow stands about half the height of the peaks at Apollo 15's landing site at Hadley Appenine, and the valley floor here is only about six miles wide. This made for a smaller-scale setting that Gene Cernan and Jack Schmitt could more fully explore, ranging from one side of the valley all the way to the other.*

# Apollo 17 Panorama

Throughout their traverses, the Apollo astronauts stopped to take complete sequences of horizon photographs to document the landscapes they explored. Assembled from photographs taken by Gene Cernan at Taurus-Littrow, this gatefold offers a glimpse of what it was like to be surrounded by the otherworldly vistas of the Moon.

**a** *The astronauts named this section of the valley Tortilla Flats for its pebbled appearance in the orbital photographs. Such names were not "official," but they greatly assisted in mission planning and navigation. The valley floor at Taurus-Littrow was formed from dark basaltic lava flows like other lunar maria.*

**b** *The mountain South Massif, a 7,500-foot-tall block of lunar crust thrust up by the impact that created the Serenitatis Basin eons ago. Its peak is rounded like all the lunar mountain peaks. E.V.A. 2 took Cernan and Schmitt to the base of this mountain, which is 2.8 miles away in this photograph.*

**c** *An avalanche of highland debris from the South Massif mountain slid into the valley floor and rolled across it in a cloud, settling to create an over-layer of light-colored rays stretching out over the dark lava plain. Shorty crater lay within a streak of this light material.*

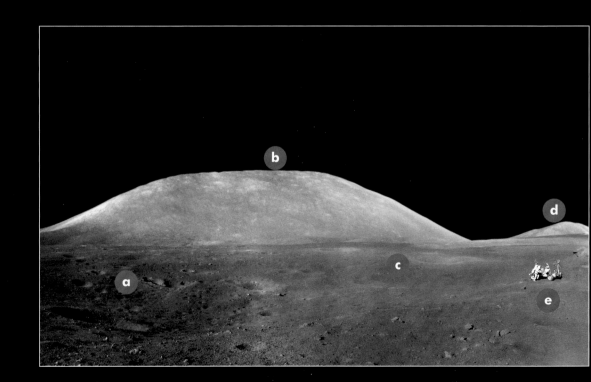

Mission commander Gene Cernan was an astronaut's astronaut. He had barnstormed the Moon with Tom Stafford in Apollo 10, flying in the LM down to just nine miles above the route that Neil Armstrong would follow. He was a solid professional, a commander who seemed born to the post, and like Scott, he had also a sense of wonder. Cernan was one of those who stood out even in a remarkable group of men like the astronauts. He was one of those who seemed chosen by history. When someday starships ply the interstellar void, men like Cernan will command them.

His partner on the surface would be a newcomer to space and the experience of enduring a rocket launch, Dr. Harrison "Jack" Schmitt—the first scientist to head for the Moon. A geologist by training, Schmitt had had to become a pilot and an astronaut second. He had held his own and won a slot for the Moon. Intellectual, deadpan, thoroughly dedicated to his field, Schmitt would be the first geologist to practice his profession on another world.

While Cernan and Schmitt walked on the surface, their cheerful shipmate Ron Evans would pilot the command module and operate the SIM bay full of a new set of instruments for lunar study. Proud of what his country had achieved and full of enthusiasm for the mission, Evans counted himself exceptionally lucky to have made it into the ranks of the astronauts and onto the roster for Apollo 17.

Apollo 17's mission planners were drawn to a landing site called Taurus-Littrow by volcanoes—or, rather, by the hope of finding them. Were volcanoes the mirages of the Moon? Hazy, beckoning

oases that would vanish after a long and desperate journey toward them? Apollo 16 had found only impact breccias in the Descartes highlands rather than the expected volcanic rock. Now the final Apollo mission was targeted in Taurus-Littrow because Al Worden, command module pilot on Apollo 15, had observed what looked very much like dark volcanic cinder cones at that location while he was orbiting the Moon on Apollo 15. The question of the Moon's volcanism still vexed the geologists, and many were still sure that some of the Moon's craters must have been formed by volcanoes. Taurus-Littrow was their last chance to find evidence that the Moon was not a completely dead world.

The site recalled the magnificent Hadley-Appenine valley from Apollo 15. Also at the edge of a lunar sea, the valley of Taurus-Littrow borders the Mare Serenitatis. A dark floor forms a plain between a ring of high, smooth-profiled mountains, bright light gray in contrast to the basalt of the lava-flow valley.

On the "dress rehearsal" mission of Apollo 10 in early 1969, Gene Cernan had cruised over the Moon so close to a landing he could almost feel it. After a span of three years, Cernan had returned into the heavens, again crossing the translunar gulf and again circling the haunting, alien world he had once scouted. This time the ship was his and he was taking it down. That realm of craters and black shadows was going to become his landscape. With complete confidence and not a hint of difficulty, Apollo 17's commander set the *Challenger* down at Taurus-Littrow, and the dust settled around the last and finest LM to make the journey.

Their first E.V.A. took the two moonwalkers only a short distance from the LM, where they set up the scientific instrument station. Several new

On their return from the base of the South Massif during the second E.V.A. traverse of Apollo 17, Cernan and Jack Schmitt drove back across Taurus-Littrow valley, tracing a curving return path to the lunar module. Near their halfway point, the astronauts stopped at a large crater they called "Shorty" and disembarked from the lunar rover for sampling, establishing the site as Station 4. While Jack Schmitt worked near the rover, Cernan walked to the far side of the crater's rim with his Hasselblad camera and took the photographs composing this image.

The panorama presents a roughly 180-degree view of Taurus-Littrow as seen from near the middle of the valley floor. The center of the panorama looks almost due west, the left edge looks south, and the right edge north. Behind the photographer's right shoulder rose the North Massif, and to his back were the Sculptured Hills. The lunar module lay 2.7 miles almost directly behind him.

Shorty crater, which fills the right side of the panorama, was made by an impact big enough to excavate the bedrock underlying the valley's dark *mare* lava-flow surface. The blocks blasted to the crater's rim were pieces of the valley subfloor, allowing lunar geologist Jack Schmitt to work out an improved understanding of the site while on the scene. In such ways, craters provided Apollo astronauts with ready-made excavations, windows into the Moon's structure.

**d** *The Apollo 17 team named this peak Family Mountain. Its crest lies about 14 miles away in this photograph. By contrast, the rise appearing to the right of Family Mountain is only about five and a half miles away. The lack of atmospheric haze on the Moon makes distances difficult to judge.*

**e** *At the edge of Shorty crater, Jack Schmitt works on sampling a patch of orange moondust that he discovered near the boulder where they parked the rover. This orange powder was thought to be Apollo 17's "holy grail"— evidence of recent volcanism and therefore proof that the Moon is not volcanically dead.*

**f** *From across the crater, Gene Cernan could see streaks of the orange moondust. Back in the labs on Earth, the orange soil would test to be volcanic all right, but some 3.7 billion years old, merely churned to the surface by the impact that made Shorty crater. In all six landing missions, Apollo never found evidence of recent volcanic activity on the Moon.*

**g** *Shorty crater is about 360 feet in diameter. Gene Cernan stood on the southeastern edge of the crater to take the photographs of this panorama. The walls of the crater have collapsed over time, slumping into mounds of regolith on the crater floor.*

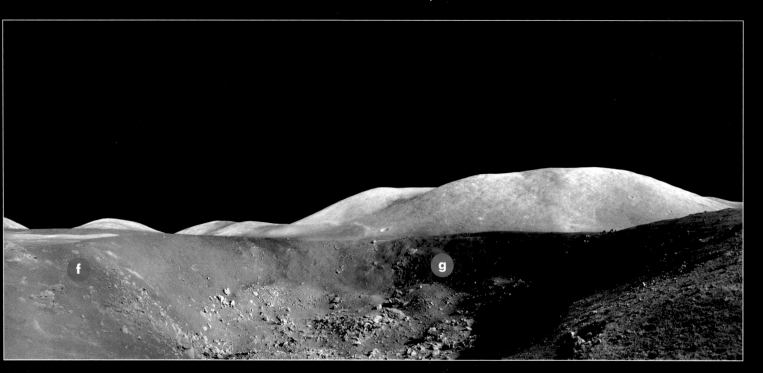

**OFF ROAD**

*The lunar rover handled steep inclines, crater potholes, and loose rocks like a champ, its design proving very effective even in the one-sixth lunar gravity, which would have allowed a taller vehicle to roll over easily. Driving on the Moon was the ultimate off-road experience, and minor damage wasn't about to interrupt it. Below, the replacement fender made of a folded map kept the dust down after a fender extension was torn off.*

experiments made their debut on Apollo 17, including a device to precisely measure the Moon's gravity, an instrument to measure the composition of the tenuous lunar atmosphere, and another that studied micrometeorite impacts, and the material they scattered, by detecting the faint traces of electricity the impacts generated. Schmitt also prepared eight grenades. Apollos 14 and 16 had used scientific grenade launchers, mortars that fired explosive bombs into smooth arcs up to 3,000 feet through the lunar vacuum to detonate on impact with the surface. The shockwaves were then read by sensitive moonquake detectors set up at Apollo landing sites across hundreds of miles. These incredibly sensitive devices triangulated on the shockwaves to read the nature of the Moon's interior since shockwaves travel differently through different kinds of material. On Apollo 17, a local geophone array would serve a similar sensing purpose, and the eight mission

explosives would be placed by hand along the traverse routes, to be detonated by ground control after the astronauts had left the Moon. Jack Schmitt carefully handled the seismic bombs, the largest of which weighed six pounds.

Gene Cernan had meanwhile assembled the lunar rover and taken it for a test drive, finding it in perfect working order. However, in the course of helping Schmitt finish the science station setup, Cernan's rock hammer caught the paper-thin extensible rear fender section and tore it right off. In the bulky Moon suits, one could easily cause all manner of destruction without realizing it.

The fender was hopelessly broken and couldn't be put back on. Without it, driving the rover produced a fountain of moondust that shot up and rained down on the two explorers and all their gear. It was like running a vacuum cleaner backwards.

The moondust threatened to clog moving gear elements and suit seals, but more critically, it dirtied the space suits and darkened them. The dust looked battleship gray on the ground, but when smeared on a suit or inside a plastic sample bag it turned black like coal dust or powdered charcoal. The fine, sharp-edged, abrasive particles worked their way into the gleaming white Beta cloth outermost layer of the suits with the lightest smudge, and while the suits would never be snowy white again, it was imperative that they not stay dark. This was not a matter of fastidiousness; it was a matter of not roasting alive. The lunar day sun blasted with a force unknown on Earth, where the miles-thick blanket of protective atmosphere softens the sun's warm rays greatly, even at the equator. Nowhere on Earth does one face raw, undiminished solar power, but on the Moon there is nowhere to hide except in a space suit. An astronaut's backpack cooled him and his suit by circulating water through the tubes in his longjohns; this water was cooled by allowing minute amounts of it to boil off through a radiator in the backpack. An astronaut could stay cool only as long as his water lasted, and in a dark space suit he would bake like an outdoor grill briquette, burning up his water. Cernan and Schmitt had to spend time brushing each other off so as not to end up roasting. They could feel the Sun's heat even through the 21 layers of their suits. Even low in the sky, the Sun was a force to be reckoned with, producing a surface temperature of 150°F during this 3-day "morning" of the 14-day lunar day.

The dust-showered rover would have to be repaired before Cernan and Schmitt could travel out on their long-range traverses. But with what? Astronaut John Young would figure it out. On Apollo 16 he had encountered exactly the same problem. While the two on the Moon slept, Young in Houston worked through the night on a solution,

*Spring-loaded aluminum Apollo tongs*

wearing a pressure suit to make sure that his fix would be practicable for his colleagues upstairs. In the morning, the Moon men were advised to use a folded, laminated map, duct-taped to form a fender shape (duct tape truly is universally useful), affixed to the rover with clamps they could take off of the LM telescope while they were on the ground. They followed the instructions, being careful not to trap any oxygen underneath the tape, which would cause the tape to burst once they took it outside. The clamps fit, the map stayed in place, and the rover was good as new for the rest of the mission.

Day 2's traverse took the team south across Taurus-Littrow valley, stopping at craters to carry out sampling, and ending at the bright foot of the South Massif, as the mountains around the site were called. The day's big discovery occurred on the way back at a crater they had called "Shorty." Jack Schmitt found orange lunar soil. Not gray, light gray, dark gray, or even the light tan appearance that lunar soil took on from a distance, this was *orange,* and it was no trick of the light. His commander confirmed the find. The geologists were ecstatic. If it was what they thought it was, the orange soil was evidence of volcanic activity. The patch of soil, which looked like someone had spilled powdered orange chalk on the ground, was carefully sampled, bagged, and labeled. And then, exciting as it was, the explorers moved on, racing against time to cover the full range of their ambitious objectives.

On their third day, Cernan and Schmitt drove north, to the other side of Taurus-Littrow valley. They reached the foot of the great North Massif and kept driving, climbing its slope for a ways. They could see their objective from quite a distance: a huge boulder that had rolled down the mountainside to nearly its base and had cracked into five huge pieces. They called it Split Rock, and you could just about see it

*The painstaking geological survey work of the later Apollo missions required improved tools. Jack Schmitt, opposite, uses a lunar "rake" to collect gravel-sized samples, large enough to contain useful data but small enough to be packed in quantity. Tongs, left, helped the astronauts pick up rocks since bending over in their pressure suits was difficult.*

**FIELD DAY**

*Jack Schmitt revels in the successful conclusion of his first day of geological fieldwork on the Moon. Schmitt proved that a sufficiently dedicated scientist could become a well-qualified astronaut.*

from 70 miles up in orbit. Cernan brought the rover in, and the two busily worked it, hammering off pieces, sampling soil around it, and trying to determine its nature. There was so little time. At one point, however, Cernan paused and looked across the valley. They were a couple of hundred feet above its floor. And there, about two miles away, was their lander, the *Challenger*. He took a telephoto image of it, then a panoramic sequence with the regular lens as his colleague worked on the boulder. It was an extraordinary place they were in, and Cernan was determined to take back more than rocks—he wanted to take back what it felt like to be here.

Schmitt was all business; he was a professional geologist, and he was in his element, whether or not there was air around him. When Cernan urged him to look up at the miracle in the sky at one point, Schmitt demurred, saying "When you've seen one Earth, you've seen them all," as he kept at his tasks. Cernan knew he would be the last man on the Moon for an unknown length of time, and when others asked him what it was like to be there, he wanted to be able to tell them. For years afterword, Cernan's few moments spent just looking and soaking it all in would prove to be priceless human experience because he was able to powerfully convey it all to audiences around the world through his extraordinary lectures. The mission would be accomplished, and fully, but Cernan would definitely come back with more than rocks.

All too soon, their time on the Moon at Taurus-Littrow came to an end. For half a week there had been people sleeping on the Moon, closing up their tiny cockpit to make miniature night, shuttering the windows, and turning in as people prepared for sleep in Houston, where the clocks gave the same time as those on the Moon. This tiny outpost maintained its human rhythms even in this ancient and other-worldly place.

As they drove back to *Challenger* for the last time, Cernan's mind was full of impressions: the incredible detail visible everywhere from the fine texture of a rock on the ground to the heights of the mountains high above them; the dark floor of the valley, as dark as anything known on the Moon; the bright, almost glowing hillsides; and the weirdly smooth contours of everything, even the huge mountains that formed the horizon underneath the inky blackness of the sky with its single blue-white ornament. There was grandeur here, around the two men approaching their golden chariot. Schmitt compared Taurus-Littrow to the Grand Canyon in sheer spectacle. If only their countrymen could share this extraordinary experience. The television broadcasts from Apollo 17 were the best and clearest yet, but the nation had other things on its mind, and NASA had never been particularly good at communicating the thrill of its endeavors to the public. Either the newsmen got excited and found their own stories to tell, or they didn't and the public got bored. Only Apollo 8's Christmas flight, Apollo 11's first landing, and Apollo 13's near disaster had broken through as such powerful stories that they made themselves. Here the J-missions were accomplishing fantastic adventure, and the public hardly knew, partly because there was no one to bring it alive for them, no NASA spokesperson who conveyed the adventure of what was really happening now to the people who had grown tired of paying for it. It would be up to men like Gene Cernan to carry the spellbinding magnificence of it all to others, through personal contact, one by one, over the years to come.

## DISTANT HOME

*Apollo 17 landed farther away from the visible Moon's center than any previous mission, making the Earth appear lower in the sky at Taurus-Littrow than it had at other landing sites. On Apollo 11, the Earth had appeared almost directly overhead. Since the Moon always keeps the same face to the Earth, the blue planet always hangs in one place in the lunar sky at any given location on the Moon. Some astronauts reported that they could see the planet's rotation over time.*

EXPLORERS

207

## SPLIT ROCK

*This boulder was so big that the astronauts could see it from lunar orbit. Here astronaut Jack Schmitt carries the gnomon after sampling and collecting fragments of "Split Rock," which had rolled down the slope of the South Massif before breaking into pieces. At far right of the photograph, just above the rock, the astronauts' lunar module Challenger can be seen as a distant speck sitting at the right edge of a lighter area.*

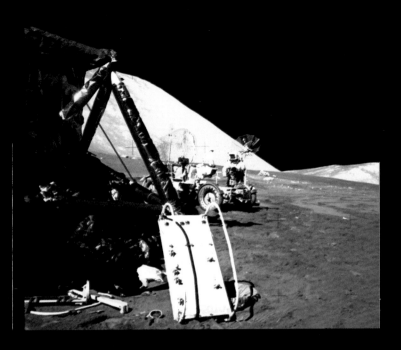

## BASE OF OPERATIONS

*The* Challenger *carried a set of scientific instruments in addition to the lunar rover. The landing site soon became littered with the detritus of human activity.*

## MISSION ACCOMPLISHED

*Exploring the Moon was dirty, grueling work. After three days of operations on the surface, the astronauts were coated in moondust grime and exhausted. Jack Schmitt took this photograph of Gene Cernan back inside the LM cabin after their third and final excursion on the lunar surface.*

## DEPARTURE

**C**ernan stood at the ladder of the *Challenger*. Schmitt was already inside. Cernan was breathing heavily from the work of passing rock boxes up to Schmitt for stowage inside their spaceship. But there were words that needed to be said. "As I take man's last steps," he almost gasped, "from the surface, back home for some time to come—but we believe not too long into the future . . ." He fought to get his breath. "I believe history will record that America's challenge of today has forged man's destiny of tomorrow. And as we leave the Moon at Taurus-Littrow, we leave as we came, and, God willing, as we shall return, with peace and hope for all mankind."

The rover had been parked 500 feet east of the LM, at a place they called the VIP spot. From here, Houston's television eye would have a good view of the blastoff of the cockpit stage. The countdown reached zero, and in a silent explosion, the gold foil burst away from the landing stage in a shower of particles. The cockpit rose smoothly and quickly into the black sky.

Inside the LM, Cernan and Schmitt felt as if they were in a high-speed elevator. There was no loud rocket sound, no hard buffeting, just the feeling of rising. After a few hundred feet they were pitching over,

gradually angling so that they would curve into orbit, where they would catch up with Ron Evans in the command module *America*.

The lunar rover's twin batteries were still working. The Boeing engineers had given the rover double the power they thought it would need, just to be safe. The little car's remarkably powerful television antenna remained pointed at the Earth. And the camera eye of Houston could still move. The camera operator had followed the LM into the sky until he couldn't see it

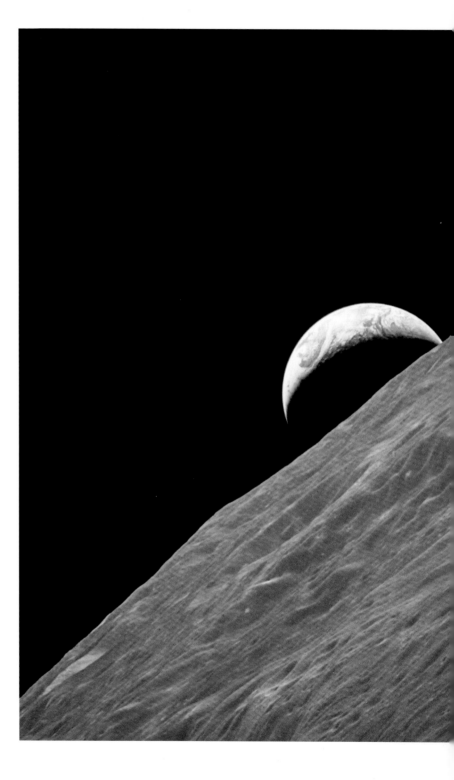

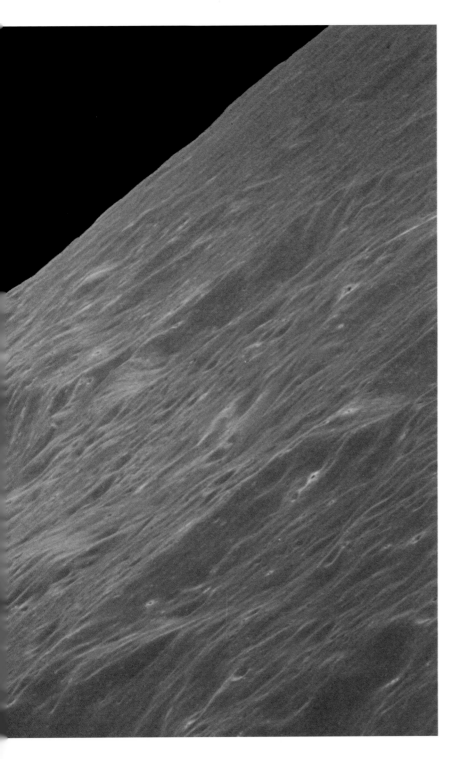

anymore. Now the camera on the dutiful rover panned back down to the empty landing stage. The rocket-blasted foil had all settled to the surface, to uncanny perfect stillness, never to be disturbed by the slightest breeze. There was not a single movement of any kind, except of the camera itself. The men were gone. The camera looked back and forth, almost hesitantly. There was no one, nothing. Eventually its batteries would run down. But the Earth would have stopped listening, and the camera link would be turned off, long before they died.

## HOMEWARD BOUND

In orbit above the Moon, Cernan masterfully brought the *Challenger* in to dock with *America*, and they were reunited with Ron Evans. The mission had gone incredibly smoothly. They spent another day in orbit, continuing scientific observations, and then headed home.

Challenger had been returned to Taurus-Littrow. The jettisoned lander's cockpit had crashed into the South Massif just as planned, to give the moonquake detector network something else to listen to. Now the *America* prepared to fire its powerful main engine to break the bonds of lunar gravity.

The main engine of the C.S.M. was the Service Propulsion System, or S.P.S., visible as the huge bell at the base of the spacecraft. This was one of the unavoidable bottlenecks of the Apollo mission design: On this single engine the astronauts' lives depended because if it failed to fire, they were stuck orbiting the Moon. It sat 16 feet below their couches, its guts buried inaccessibly in the heart of the service module, and if it failed, there was nothing they could do to fix it. Their oxygen would last them about five days, and then they would each suffocate. The ship would not, of course. It would keep orbiting, an expensive and elaborate metal coffin that would circle the Moon with its dead. The possibility was gruesome, but it was also real. This was risky technology, at the edge of human capability.

**PERSPECTIVE**

*As Apollo 17 departed the Moon, the Apollo program left behind 6 Apollo landing stages, 3 lunar rovers, and some 60 scientific experiments scattered across the silent landscapes. As Gene Cernan's crew began their voyage home, they saw for the last time the view of the Earth that only Apollo made possible.*

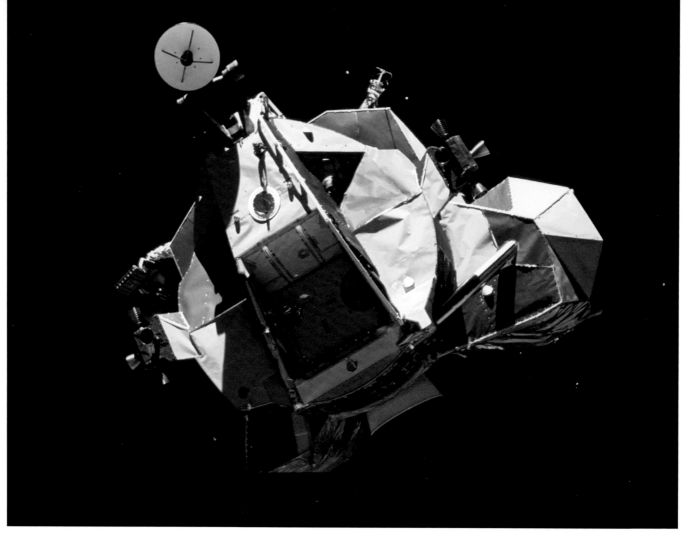

The astronauts had ensured that the engineers were well aware of the importance of the S.P.S. This return engine was therefore made as foolproof as was humanly possible. As well as every part of the Saturn V and its Apollo spacecraft had been thought out and worked through, the S.P.S. had commanded special attention. What if an igniter failed? A small part, a simple failure, could make all of the fuel useless. The S.P.S., accordingly, had no igniters. It had a thrust chamber, and valves with backups. And it had—this was the trick—hypergolic fuels. Hypergolics were extremely difficult to deal with, but they were your friend when you wanted a sure-fire ignition. Hypergolic fuel is so powerfully reactive that each component will instantly explode on contact with its counterpart. Tanks of the hypergolics were connected to the S.P.S. in the simplest possible way, and all that had to happen was that the valves had to open. The hypergolics came out, and *kaboom*. Guaranteed ignition.

The S.P.S. also had the virtue of having been designed back when the engineers were still thinking of the Apollo tailsitter. It was, in fact, designed for a much larger ship, making it the equivalent of a 12-cylinder engine packed into a Volkswagen. There would be power to spare. If the astronauts made it back to their command module, they were going to get home, and that was the engineering bottom line.

Ron Evans hit the switch, and the hypergolics emerged into the thrust chamber. In the pure vacuum there was an instantaneous reaction, and the engine fired with tremendous force. A gray, battered world over two thousand miles wide held them in its gravitational grasp, and it was now a contest of all its planetary might against the power of this one engine and its 20,500 pounds of thrust. The S.P.S. burned and drilled and hammered, and the three astronauts were pressed into their seats. The Moon receded. The astronauts were going home.

## CISLUNAR SPACE WALK

**D**uring the long coasting flight through the Earth-Moon reach called cislunar space, there was one more adventure to be had. Ron Evans may not have gotten to walk on the surface of the Moon, but he would get to walk in the void. His SIM bay had priceless treasures in it now: the film he had shot of the Moon rolling by below him. The instruments could relay their findings through signals, but the film had to be retrieved, and it had to be done before they got back to Earth because the service module wasn't coming with them.

With all three astronauts protected in their space suits, Evans depressurized the *America* and opened the hatch. Connected to the life-support mechanisms inside by a tether, he emerged into the blackness without a backpack to hamper his movements. Hurtling from the Moon to the Earth, they were traveling at thousands of miles per hour. But in open space, there is no sensation of speed while coasting, and the ship seemed completely motionless.

Handholds were built onto the face of the conical command module. They led up to the peak of the cone, where they could have been used to get a crew into or out of the LM in case the docking hatch had failed. They also led down to handrails that were new on the J-mission service modules, handrails that Evans could use to work his way down to the cameras. The sensation of being out in the total void was thrilling to Evans. There was no up or down out here. Was he riding atop his spacecraft with an endless sky above him, or hanging above a bottomless abyss stretching to the end of the universe? "Talk about being a spaceman!" he exulted. "This is it!" Clutching the handrails as tightly as if his life depended on them, he made his way down to the SIM bay. Waiting for him there was a special fitting into which he could slip his space boots, a restraint providing anchorage while he worked at the cameras and opened them up to get the film magazines. Mission commander Cernan watched from the open hatch of the *America*. For the J-mission command module pilot who could not walk on the Moon with his crewmates, this film recovery mission was a welcome bonus, and Evans relished the entire experience, living it to the fullest. This was high adventure. The Earth was over 150,000 miles away.

## REENTRY

**A**n Apollo spacecraft returning from the Moon approaches the blue Earth at almost 25,000 mph, 32 times the speed of sound itself. At such speeds a vessel crosses the gulf between worlds in days. Upon its return home, the craft must then negotiate a transition to the realm of air, wherein space-travel velocities turn the soft, free air of gentle human breath into a raging, screaming force that rips off skin and surface and tears into metal itself, burning the offender white-hot, molten.

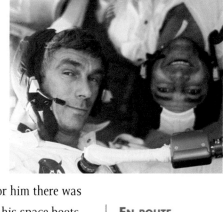

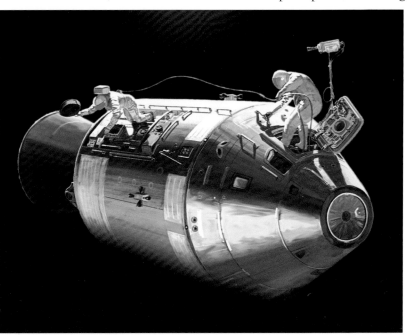

*Retouched NASA art depicts Evans's space walk to retrieve film from the scientific instrument bay. This dramatic adventure was difficult to capture well on film and so never made an impression on the public.*

The *America* transformed itself for the reentry into Earth's atmosphere. The service module that had served so well in space was now jettisoned: It would be fatal deadweight in reentry. The umbilical that had transferred power and air into the capsule disengaged, and the cylindrical service module floated away from the capsule holding the three men. Ron Evans now operated *America* on a small reserve of battery power.

The Earth grew large as the transition to atmosphere loomed. Their trajectory had been very carefully determined in advance. Too steep and they would be incinerated by the friction of reentry. Too shallow and they would shoot through the curve of the atmosphere and back out into space. Without the rocket power of their service module, they would not be able to get back into proper alignment, and they would be lost. The entry corridor had to be accurate to within half a degree of angle at the critical moment.

The air began to grow denser. They could feel it. Reentry had begun. The great space capsule designer Max Faget had wrestled with the problem of bringing an Apollo command module back to Earth. The Mercury and Gemini capsules had endured nothing like the incredibly high-speed reentry of a Moon return. The stakes, and the demands, were much higher in Apollo. There was no way to fight it with rocket power; even the burly S.P.S. could not have begun to slow them sufficiently, and the small capsule itself could hold only tiny thrusters. Instead, Faget would use the strength of his enemy—air friction—to manage the craft's reentry. The squat cone of the Apollo capsule hit the atmosphere blunt-end first, which slowed its speed, but it could

## RETURN TO EARTH

*On their way home in December 1972, the Apollo 17 astronauts photographed the classic image of the full Earth, below, that has since been reprinted countless times. After splashdown in the South Pacific, mission commander Gene Cernan, right, emerges from the command module* America, *the capsule's foil thermal shielding shredded by the ordeal of reentry.*

# Apollo Reentry

High-speed reentry into the Earth's atmosphere required a complex trajectory sequence. Returning from their lunar mission, Apollo astronauts would round the Earth and plunge into reentry at a point directly opposite the Moon. The reentry was timed with the Earth's rotation to bring the crew down to a point in the Pacific Ocean where a U.S. Navy aircraft carrier recovery team awaited.

**A** team of women at North American Aviation hand-built the Apollo command-module heat-shields by injecting phenolic resin into the hexagonal chambers of a honeycomb structure, one by one. Every small chamber had to be completely filled, with no air bubbles or gaps: Three lives would depend on each shield.

An Apollo capsule hit the atmosphere at about 400,000 feet above the Earth, or 76 miles up. From this point the space-craft would travel a "double-skip" roller-coaster trajectory for fifteen hundred miles before it reached the ocean waves. The spacecraft's small rockets produced 94 pounds of thrust, enough to shift the capsule's orientation and steer it through the fiery obstacle course of potential overheating.

For the first 38 miles, the capsule plunged in a nearly straight line. Glowing ionization quickly increased until it blocked radio signals. The g forces grew to a crushing peak of 6.35 g forces. A 180-pound man feels a weight of 1,143 pounds under such intense deceleration. Thrusters tilted the capsule more upright at this point, giving it lift, reducing its speed, and allowing some of the accumulated heat to burn away with the ablating resin in the honeycomb shield. The lift sent the capsule back upward and over a trajectory rise to then tilt backward and plunge a second time. Heat built up again, leading to another rise, another plunge, and a return to 5.99 g forces. After this point, the worst was over, and the capsule began falling rather than shooting across the sky. The command module had covered over 1,450 miles of its reentry course and would soon be in sight of the waiting U.S. Navy recovery forces.

*Three parachutes lower the America to the sea at about 25 miles per hour.*

*Navy frogmen deployed from a Sikorsky Sea King helicopter have fitted the Apollo 17 capsule with a flotation collar to prevent it from tipping over. The astronauts were winched aboard the copter and given a chance to clean up on the flight back to the aircraft carrier.*

*Recovery crane aboard the U.S.S. Ticonderoga pulls the America from the sea.*

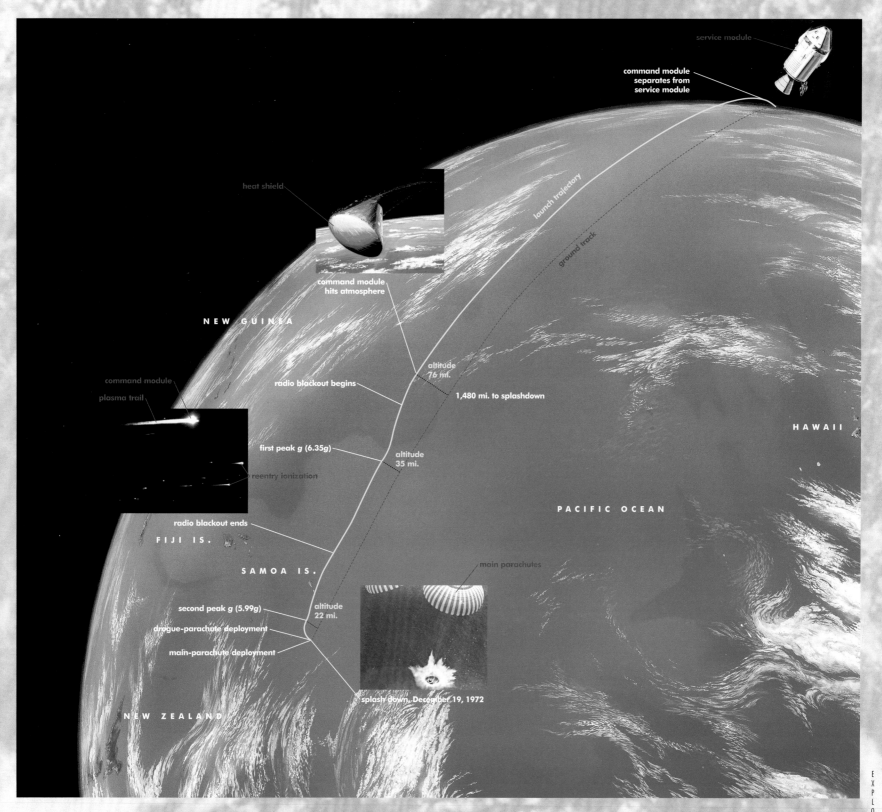

service module

command module
separates from
service module

launch trajectory

ground track

heat shield

command module
hits atmosphere

NEW GUINEA

altitude
76 mi.

radio blackout begins

1,480 mi. to splashdown

command module

plasma trail

first peak g (6.35g)

altitude
35 mi.

HAWAII

reentry ionization

radio blackout ends

PACIFIC OCEAN

FIJI IS.

SAMOA IS.

main parachutes

second peak g (5.99g)

altitude
22 mi.

drogue-parachute deployment

main-parachute deployment

splash down, December 19, 1972

NEW ZEALAND

Reentry brought the Apollo command modules down in the South Pacific, where there was the greatest possible margin for error in the trajectory. The Block II Apollo capsules were designed to withstand a hard ground landing, but such an accident would risk injury to the crew. In practice, splashdowns became so accurate that planners began to worry about hitting the aircraft carrier.

not endure the full brunt of a direct reentry indefinitely. Its thrusters could do nothing against such speeds and forces, but they could change the orientation of the capsule, and therein lay the solution. Blunt end forward, the shape produced drag. Angle it slightly, though, and it produced lift. By tilting the capsule slightly at just the right moment, Ron Evans had the power to make the atmosphere shoot the *America* upwards again, before it got too hot from direct reentry. When it had cooled and slowed, he would angle the craft for drag, and they would begin to drop and endure full reentry force again, until it got too strong, and Evans would take them up for another roller-coaster arc. Two of these maneuvers would balance the *America*'s endurance against the force of the atmosphere and slow them in stages: Such was the plan of Max Faget's design.

In the space of a few minutes, the crew would twice feel deceleration equivalent to six times the force of gravity. As air friction powerfully braked their hurtling speed, the astronauts were pressed into their couches, forced like leaden barbells until their own bodies seemed to weigh half a ton. Then the pressure would ease.

Cernan, Schmitt, and Evans lay strapped into their couches as the atmosphere thickened. An incandescent haze developed outside their windows as the temperature rose and rose. The atmosphere tore at the ship, stripping its outer foil covering into shreds and raging at the heat shield until it was hotter than the F-1 engines had been during the Saturn V launch. The men held fast as *America* was buffeted and the temperature rose to 5,000°F, the temperature of the Sun's corona. They could occasionally see chunks of something shooting past their windows. The heat shield was flaking off.

They could not contact Houston during this time; the furious conditions of reentry surround a ship with ionized plasma and completely block any transmissions in or out of the spacecraft. The final drama of reentry was faced alone, and Houston heard only radio silence, counting the seconds until the hoped-for re-acquisition of signal.

Reentry had already killed three space travelers. Soyuz 11 had come through reentry to a successful landing in the U.S.S.R., but when the recovery crew opened the hatch, they found three corpses, the cosmonauts killed by decompression from a leak in the capsule sustained just before reentry. Unlike Cernan and his crew, they were not wearing space suits—the Russian capsule was too small to permit three of them.

Below the Apollo 17 astronauts, the heat shield was turning white-hot, melting and slipping away, exactly as it was supposed to do. A honeycomb structure in the shield was filled with a dense resin that would absorb the intolerable heat and then flake and burn off, taking the heat with it—*ablating,* as the designers called it. The ablative heat shield was another way of sidestepping the overwhelming strength of the air-friction enemy. The Apollo engineers had faced such opponents on paper, and in their slide rules, and like martial artists, they had overcome greater power through skill and strategy.

## JOURNEY'S END

The capsule was now plunging freely through the air with its human cargo like a truck dropped from an airplane. At an altitude of 23,000 feet, the top ring of the command module blew off with explosive bolts, exposing the recovery apparatus. Mortars fired small drogue parachutes, then at 10,000 feet fired the mains. Three great round red-and-white-striped chutes, 60 feet across, blossomed and lowered *America* to the Pacific for splashdown, within sight of the waiting U.S. Navy aircraft carrier U.S.S. *Ticonderoga.*

A powerful Sikorsky Sea King helicopter, already hovering nearby as they hit the water, retrieved the astronauts and brought them to the

carrier, where their spacecraft was recovered shortly later. The recovery crew saw not a gleaming instrument of exotic perfection, but a blasted, torn, and ragged survivor, its titanic strength utterly exhausted, a husk now, a shell. The capsule they hauled out of the ocean was all that remained of the Apollo 17 Saturn V. The journey had spent, incinerated, smashed, or blistered into atoms every other part of the colossal, 363-foot white rocket, leaving only this burnt and brutalized 9-foot capsule. A great shining army had set out over the horizon, and a lone squadron had returned, savaged beyond recognition, collapsing into the arms of its rescuers, dead. Such was the price of reaching for another world.

Three men, however, stood unharmed by the tremendous forces through which they had journeyed for the past 10 days. And their capsule had perfectly protected and preserved the treasure trove from their destination in the sky: Over 200 pounds of the Moon itself had made the journey with them, along with Ron Evans's SIM bay film and the Moon explorers' own record in still and motion pictures.

The space travelers had set a spate of records in their adventure. They had walked on the Moon for 22 hours. Compared with any previous mission, Apollo 17 had carried out more lunar surface exploration, stayed longer, brought back more Moon rock, shot more film, and collected more data. It had been spectacular. In more ways than one, it was the ultimate trip.

## MISSION ACCOMPLISHED

*Mission commander Gene Cernan pays his respects to the symbol of the nation that put him on the Moon. The flag raised by Apollo 17 was the flag that had been displayed in Mission Control since the beginning of the Apollo program.*

THE Moon carried the American flag, and this wonder seemed only the beginning. A thousand scientists were studying the lunar explorers' treasure, the Moon rocks more precious than diamonds, and the silver orb had begun to reveal its secrets. American industry was prepared for the next stage of exploration, brainstorming exotic new technologies and new capabilities that could carry astronauts longer and farther. Wernher von Braun conceived a new way to use his Saturn V Moon rocket, and his rocketeers in Huntsville were given approval at last to design America's first space station. Our foot was on the threshold of the future . . . but Apollo's time was running out. The magnificent effort had been sustained only by powerful forces of leadership and superpower competition in space. Kennedy's inspiration could not last forever. Beyond the Moon Race and under a new administration, Apollo would reach its international conclusion, and the world would witness the last chapter in an age of wonders.

# Beyond Apollo

**SKYLAB**

*America's first space station orbits the Earth in 1974, as seen by astronauts on the third mission to the station. Spacewalking astronauts successfully rigged the gold sail as a sunshade over a damaged hull section.*

## MYSTERIES OF THE MOON

**W**hile it still hung in the sky, completely out of reach, the Moon was thought to be the Rosetta stone of the solar system. There, on that celestial face, might be written the secret words of the world's creation, unaltered by time and Earth's living processes, unobscured by seas and soil, awaiting the arrival of man. The scars of ancient cataclysms on the Moon might be the traces of the original Age of Formation, the birth of the solar system. Apollo had set out to read those secrets.

Sixty scientific experiments probed the Moon's enigmas in the course of the Apollo landings. Thirty more orbited the pale world in the science bays of the upgraded command modules. And 841 pounds of Apollo lunar rock samples made the journey to Earth to be distributed to more than a thousand scientists around the world for intensive study. While the Moon retains a good measure of mystery, Apollo revealed much about its structure and formation.

Moonquake detectors, beginning with the one that Buzz Aldrin set up during Apollo 11, have measured the travel of shock waves through the Moon's interior, revealing its nature. Explosive charges, like those set up by Jack Schmitt on Apollo 17, gave the seismic instruments more to listen to, with still larger shock waves produced by the deliberate crashing of spent Saturn V third stages and lunar-module cockpits into the Moon. The composite data from Apollo seismic stations show that the Moon has a rigid crust 20 to 40 miles deep, four times thicker than Earth's.

The lunar crust is made up of light-colored, lighter-weight elements that floated to the surface like froth when the Moon was still a molten mass in the volcanic Age of Formation. During this age elements cooled and crystallized to form the Moon's

## These schematic views reveal the geological structure of the Apollo landing sites.

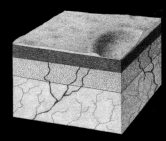

**A11** *Near the crater West, Apollo 11 touched down on a flat mare plain formed during the Age of Lava Seas, when dark lava flowed through mantle cracks to fill giant impact basins. The Age of Moondust pulverized the lava surface into powder.*

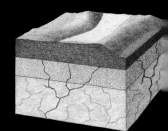

**A12** *Apollo 12 landed in the Ocean of Storms, another lava plain overlain by a thin layer of moondust no more than about 15 feet thick. Below the lava layer are inferred to lie Age-of-Bombardment debris and below that original crust.*

**A14** *Apollo 14 visited a highland site with a lava plain some distance away. The rocks under the thin moondust layer here were not lavas, as found on Apollos 11 and 12, but smashed breccia rubble from the Moon's Age of Bombardment.*

**A15** *A colossal ancient impact shoved primordial crust up to form the mountainous basin rim visited by Apollo 15. While the valley here was filled by a more recent lava flow, the mountains held samples of the Moon's most ancient crust from the Age of Formation.*

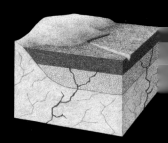

**A16** *Apollo 16's highland hills were expected to show evidence of recent volcanism but turned out to be great lumps of smashed breccia from the Age of Bombardment, pulverized by micrometeorites into a thin surface layer of moondust.*

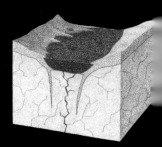

**A17** *Apollo 17 visited a complex site with a valley formed by a block of dropped ancient crust. Impact breccia and basin rim crust form the surrounding mountains, and the valley is filled with lava from the Age of Lava Seas.*

MARE FRIGORIS
(SEA OF COLD)

Plato

MARE IMBRIUM
(SEA OF RAINS)

Archimedes

**15**

MARE SERENITATIS
(SEA OF SERENITY)

**17**

MARE CRISIUM
(SEA OF CRISES)

Aristarchus

APPENINE MTS.

MARE VAPORUM
(SEA OF VAPORS)

MARE TRAQUILLITATIS
(SEA OF TRANQUILLITY)

Copernicus

Kepler

**11**

MARE FECUNDITATIS
(SEA OF FERTILITY)

**12**

**14**

OCEANUS

**16**

PROCELLARUM
(OCEAN OF STORMS)

MARE NECTARIS
(SEA OF NECTAR)

MARE NABIUM
(SEA OF CLOUDS)

Tycho

**Numbers indicate the six Apollo lunar landing sites by mission.**

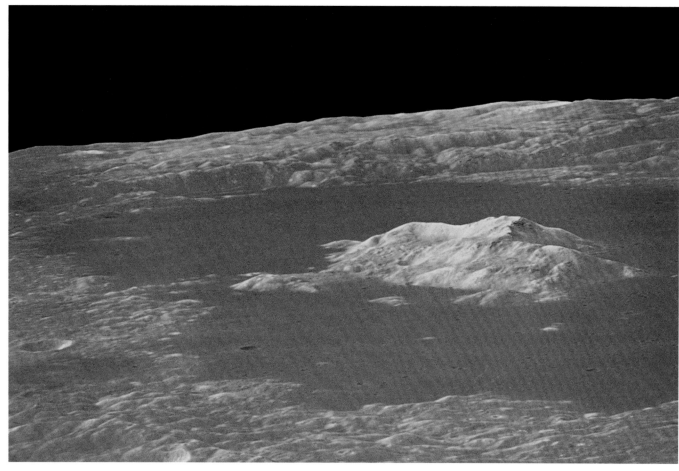

**LIGHT AND DARK**

*Photographed here from the orbiting Apollo 15 command module, the lunar far side crater Tsiolkovsky clearly shows the distinction between bright lunar highlands and lowlands flooded with dark lava from the Moon's interior.*

surface. On the slopes of towering Mount Hadley Delta, Apollo 15 found a piece of this original crystalline crust: the Genesis Rock that dated back a spectacular 4.5 billion years (see p. 185). The Moon itself is believed, like the Earth, to be only 4.6 billion years old, so the Genesis Rock is about as old an artifact as an expedition could possibly find. The ancient stone reveals that the lunar surface in the Age of Formation contained almost pure anorthosite, a light-colored rock crystallized on the primordial magma ocean.

The Moon was originally thought to be a world unchanged since its Age of Formation, but Apollo revealed a more complex story. Apollos 14 and 16 investigated lunar highlands, or *terrae,* expecting to find rocks from the original crust or traces of recent volcanic eruptions. The astronauts instead found the highlands made of smashed

*Anorthosite is almost white, pure crystalline rock cooled on the primordial molten surface, the "floating cream," of the original magma.*

debris, fragments of old anorthosite pulverized and transformed by the heat of impact. Countless meteorites had blasted the original crust into crumbled and conglomerated rock fragments called breccias, and through these samples Apollo discovered the Moon's Age of Bombardment. A heavy "thunderstorm" of flying rock and debris in the early solar system assaulted the Moon's crust from about 4.3 billion to 3.8 billion years ago. The Age of Bombardment left a carpet of breccias so thick that Apollo 16 found nothing else in the Descartes highlands.

The lunar evidence reveals that the Earth must have suffered the very same such brutalizing by meteorites and asteroids during the Age of Bombardment. We do not see its traces here because Earth's surface is rarely more than a mere 500 million years old, constantly recycled in our thin, hot, active crust by continental drift and the forces of wind, water, and life. Our living skin has healed. The Moon, by contrast, presents the bleached bones of a planet's skeleton.

At the foot of the lunar highlands lie the dark, flat plains of the Moon, the *maria,* or seas. Apollos 11 and 12 touched down on smooth *mare* surfaces to discover that the *maria* were made of dark lava from the Moon's interior. After the Moon's primordial surface had cooled, huge asteroid impacts punched into the rigid crust, cracking it deeply enough for lava from the underlying mantle to seep through. This darker, denser mantle rock, called basalt, flowed freely as lava, filling the ancient impact basins in an Age of Lava Seas. From Neil Armstrong's samples from the Mare Tranquilitatis to Apollo 17's samples from the Mare Serenitatis, basalts brought back to Earth revealed the Age of Lava Seas to date between 3.8 billion and 3.2 billion years ago.

By about three billion years ago, the Moon had become mostly quiet. The storm of giant meteorites had abated, and the lunar interior had cooled. Further, smaller impacts merely left craters rather than punched through the crust. Occasional large meteors dug into the bedrock below the shallow *maria* and splashed rays of lighter crust material far across the seas. Apollo 12 landed at a site crossed by rays from the crater Copernicus, and the rays of Tycho stretch across half the Moon. But such great impacts had become rare. Scientists thus expected that the Moon would lie relatively unchanged during this time. But Apollo would discover a final Age in the Moon's history and explain a lunar mystery.

Without wind and rain to soften the edges of fresh rock, lunar highlands were expected to look like young mountains on Earth, jagged and sharp like the Tetons, just as Chesley Bonestell used to paint in his visions of the Moon we would one day visit. It was a surprise to both astronauts and geologists when Apollo showed us that the mountains of the Moon were smooth, more like old, weathered mountains such as the Alleghenies. Even after Frank Borman's crew on Apollo 8 first saw the gentle lunar contours from orbit, Apollo 15's commander

Breccia can contain fragments of anorthosite or other rock types, smashed and recombined by impacts into a conglomerate.

Dave Scott expressed a final note of confirmation that the great mountains at Hadley-Appenine were "very smooth. The tops of the mountains are rounded off. There are no sharp jagged mountain peaks or large boulders apparent anywhere." Apollo 17 found exactly the same kinds of contours in the mountains of Taurus-Littrow. What force had softened these landscapes on the airless, waterless Moon?

Every Apollo mission found the lunar surface covered with pulverized Moon rock called regolith. Neil Armstrong took advantage of space left in his lunar rock collecting box and scooped regolith into it until the box was full. This became NASA's first sample from the Age of Moondust, and it held the answer to the smooth contours of the lunar landscape. In the billions of years since they were molten, the lunar lava seas have been pulverized by an endless hail of fine particles and small meteorites, crumbling the surface into a fine-ground powdery layer of moondust.

The meteoritic forces that had created the moondust had also softened the lunar mountains. The astronauts found that when they picked up a rock, it tended to be smoother on top and more angular below. The rocks' upper surfaces, like the mountains, had been exposed to eons of micrometeorites raining down from space. Meteorites, which would have burned up in an atmosphere like Earth's, have worked like a sandblaster over the last three billion years to smooth the ancient rugged edges, whether of stone or mountain. The Age of Moondust has left a layer of pulverized powder over all the Moon. So it turned out that there *was* an erosive force on the Moon, a kind of unexpected celestial weather from which the blanket of our atmosphere protects us.

Basalt is a fine-grained, dark lava-flow stone. Heavier than anorthosite, the basaltic lava lay underneath the original crust and flooded up later through major crustal cracks.

## MOON ROCKS

*Three of the Moon's four ages are represented by the three most important rock types brought back by the Apollo missions: anorthosite, opposite, from the Age of Formation; breccia, below, from the Age of Bombardment; and basalt, above, from the Age of Lava Seas. From any of these rock types, the Age of Moondust created pulverized regolith on the surface.*

# The Moonscape

The scarred surface of the Moon reveals its history to the trained eye. The lack of familiar features like vegetation and rivers can make the moonscape appear strange and cryptic at first, but the lunar landforms are actually rather easy to learn. Apollo gave us a better understanding of the Moon's characteristic features, many of which can be observed through a good amateur telescope.

The oldest parts of the Moon that we see are the bright *terra* highlands. The Moon's original surface was made of the molten mineral "cream" floating atop the magma oceans during the Age of Formation. This crust cooled to form the "deep bedrock" underlying the moonscape. The Age of Bombardment blasted this surface with rock meteorites, smashing the upper portion into a thick brecciated layer of rubble. Giant impacts that shoved bedrock upward at impact basin rims brought some of this ancient crust to the surface again. These greatest impacts cracked the lunar crust so deeply that dark basaltic lava from within the Moon's mantle welled up to fill the impact basins during the Age of Lava Seas.

As the lava seas cooled, they formed *mare* crusts that sometimes wrinkled, cracking them and allowing upwelling still-hot lava to form wrinkle ridges. Irregular "hot spots" beneath the cooling *mare* crust could create bulges called domes. Hot spots that erupted through the crust flowed new lava to form volcanic domes or fumaroles of the kind familiar on Earth.

Other hot-spot upwellings that pierced the cooling lava crust may have created the rille channels of the Moon. Sinuous rilles may have melted their way through the surface crust like lava rivers, while others running in straight lines may have been formed along fault lines. Still other rille channels may be "graben type," the result of a section of crust dropping between fault lines.

Meteorites have continued to hit the Moon since the Age of Bombardment, though gradually smaller in size and less often. Craters formed while the plains were still cooling could have their floors flooded with lava. Later impacts into "dry" lava seas merely smashed the layers of stone into rubble. Some of these later impacts dug through the shallow lava to splash out rays of lighter-colored crust below. Other impacts sent clusters of debris impacting in crater chains of three or more craters radiating

**terra**
**mare**
**terra**
**mare**

**crust**
**lava flows**
**floor of large impact basin**
**rock debris**
**ancient crust**
**mantle**
**1,080 miles**
**mantle**
**220–280 miles?**
**core**

*A look into the interior of the Moon shows its major components: ancient crust, impact rubble, and lava flows within impact basins. With an equatorial radius of 3,963 miles, the Earth is over three and a half times larger than the Moon.*

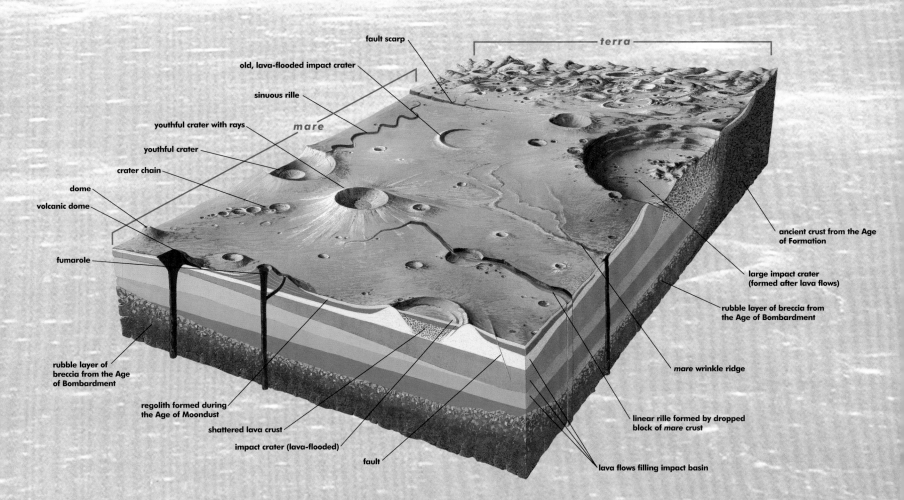

fault scarp

terra

old, lava-flooded impact crater

sinuous rille

mare

youthful crater with rays

youthful crater

crater chain

dome

volcanic dome

fumarole

rubble layer of breccia from the Age of Bombardment

regolith formed during the Age of Moondust

shattered lava crust

impact crater (lava-flooded)

fault

ancient crust from the Age of Formation

large impact crater (formed after lava flows)

rubble layer of breccia from the Age of Bombardment

*mare* wrinkle ridge

linear rille formed by dropped block of *mare* crust

lava flows filling impact basin

outward from their point of origin. Fine meteorites falling in the eons since the lava seas were hot have pulverized the whole lunar surface into the powdery

mix of rock fragments called regolith during the still-ongoing Age of Moondust.

The Moon's core is small and only partly molten. Lumpy

mass concentrations, or mascons, within the mantle make the Moon's gravity field irregular, challenging the stability of spacecraft orbits. The surface crust is

thin and rigid. Some faults and resulting cliff-like scarps can be seen in the *maria,* but these appear to be much rarer on the Moon than on Earth.

*Active plate tectonics produce young, jagged mountain ranges on Earth (Tetons, left), but mountains in the cold, rigid crust of the Moon are all very old and look smooth and weathered like old ranges on Earth (Alleghenies, right).*

## MYSTERY

*The crater Aristarchus, seen prominently here from an Apollo spacecraft, has been the site of a high number of reported glows or mists of light, seen not only by amateur astronomers but occasionally by professional observers and astronauts. Unpredictable and almost impossible to record, the "transient lunar phenomena," or T.L.P., continue to cause doubt and controversy. Dismissed by some astronomers as optical illusions, they may be evidence of as yet unknown lunar geological activity. The fact that T.L.P. seem to be more frequently reported in certain specific areas suggests that they may be real phenomena and not merely telescopic illusions, as were the canals of Mars.*

The Apollo discoveries helped shape an understanding of the Moon's surface structure, but the questions of the Moon's formation remained baffling until scientists had spent years with the Apollo data. It took a decade and a half for a scientific consensus to emerge about the origin of the Moon, and the conclusion was striking and unexpected. It is now believed that a planet the size of Mars collided with the Earth very early in the Age of Formation, smashing off material that eventually formed into the Moon. The portion of early Earth that was blasted into space by the collision consisted of the lighter elements that had floated closer to the surface of the molten Earth, leaving the Moon much less dense than its parent world. The heavy elements of the Earth had sunk to form our white-hot core, where they still remain today, combined with the core of the world that hit us.

The primordial Moon had a core in motion from the raw force of its formation, giving the young planetoid a magnetic field which has long since faded as the world grew cold and still. Moon rocks have traces of magnetism, showing that there was once a magnetic field around this world, but the global field is now so faint that only sensitive instruments like those placed by Apollos 12 and 14 can detect it. Without a magnetic field, a world is unprotected from the abrasive force of the charged particles thrown outward in the Sun's powerful solar wind, and atmosphere is stripped away over the eons, leading to the fate of breathless Mars. The Moon, small and lightweight, had even less gravity than Mars with which to hold onto any gases. The solar wind stripped the rest away, leaving the invisibly tenuous few molecules of atmosphere that the Apollo instruments detected ghosting around the lunar sphere.

"A ruined world, a globe burnt out, a corpse upon the road of night," in the words of explorer Sir Richard Burton. And yet, there are the lights. Since the 1500s, observers have been recording rare flashes and glows visible on the surface of the Moon. Often red in hue, these glows have illuminated or obscured familiar lunar features. The lights were so fleeting and so baffling that many discounted their existence. "Transient lunar phenomena," or T.L.P., they were dubbed, a suitably ambivalent name, but they were finally documented without question in the mid-20th century. The Russian astronomer Nikolai Kozyrev had recorded spectrographic traces of escaping gas in the crater Alphonsus during 1958, and the Lowell Observatory tracked three glows near crater Aristarchus that lasted almost an hour in 1963. Similar glows were occasionally reported by the astronauts from closer range. Neil Armstrong and the Apollo 11 crew observed unidentifiable illumination in Aristarchus using binoculars on July 19, 1969. There remains no accepted explanation for the T.L.P.

The rille canyons have not yet been well explained either, and at a place called Schroeter's Valley the lunar enigmas come together in a kind of Bermuda Triangle of the Moon. Schroeter's Valley is a huge sinuous rille canyon over five miles wide. Uniquely, it holds a smaller rille in its floor. Winding its way near Aristarchus, the Valley has long been known as one of the most frequently reported sites of T.L.P. glows. Scanning the valley from orbit, the instrument-packed service module SIM bays of Apollos 15 through 17 were equipped with ultrasensitive instruments to measure any detectable molecules of lunar atmosphere. Over Schroeter's Valley they detected radon, an element known to be released from the Earth in volcanic events. The Apollo lunar seismometers detected no clear evidence of lunar volcanism, but *something* is going on up there. Subtly, at the edge of perception, the Moon is taunting us with its secrets. As Apollo 17 concluded, the mysteries beckoned our return to the world in the sky.

**WHEN WORLDS COLLIDE**

*During the Age of Formation, a planet the size of Mars struck the Earth, sending out a debris cloud that coalesced into the Moon. The core of this rogue world was imbedded in our planet and sank into the interior where it remains today, helping to give the Earth its powerful, protective magnetic field.*

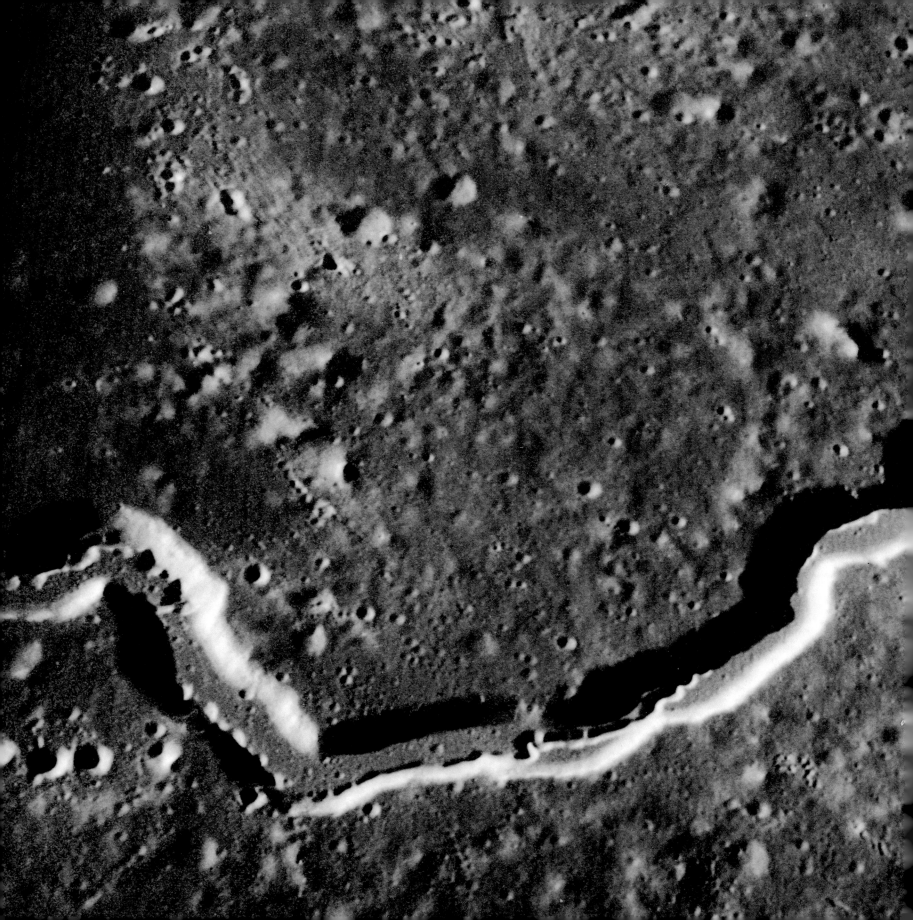

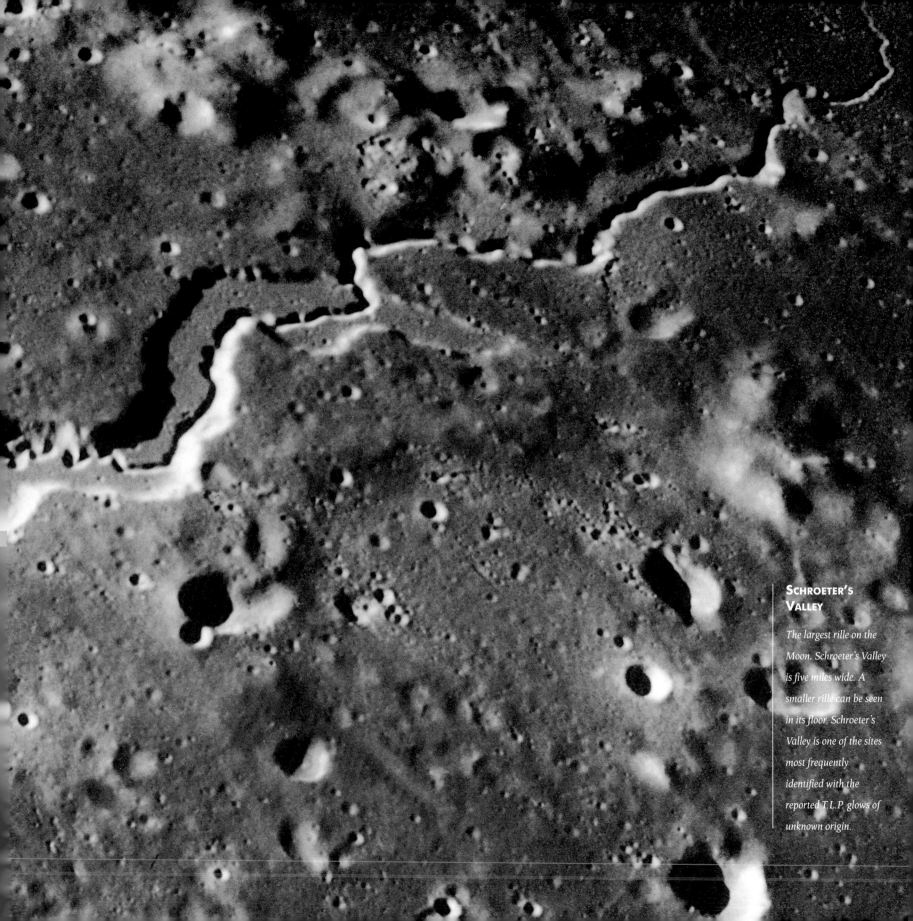

## SCHROETER'S VALLEY

*The largest rille on the Moon. Schroeter's Valley is five miles wide. A smaller rille can be seen in its floor. Schroeter's Valley is one of the sites most frequently identified with the reported T.L.P. glows of unknown origin.*

## LUNAR EXPLORATION DREAMS

**T**he Apollo program planned for 20 missions. Flights 18, 19, and 20 held exotic possibilities because by these later missions the program would be efficient. The final phase of Apollo would capitalize on the huge investment in technology and expertise, and from this foundation it would reach farther, more effectively. By the time of Apollo 17, the next three Saturn V rockets, which were in the budget since the beginning of Apollo, were already built and ready.

Landing site prospects for Apollo 18 through 20 included not only the T.L.P. sites of the crater Alphonsus and the mysterious Schroeter's Valley, but even the extraordinary goal of a landing on the far side of the Moon. The Russian *Luna 3* had discovered the far-side crater Tsiolkovsky. The geologists were eager to get a ground mission to this incredible site, with a dark *mare* floor and bright white mountain peaks in the center. There were major differences between the near and far sides of the Moon: the far side was, inexplicably, almost empty of *maria,* and an Apollo landing would shed light on this enigma. A far-side landing, it could be done. Flight planners had initially recoiled at the proposition because a site on the far-side of the Moon would have no direct communication with the Earth. But a network could be set up. Communication satellites were on hand that could be placed in lunar orbit by a Titan II rocket, the same workhorse that had lofted the Gemini capsules. Astronaut-geologist Jack Schmitt campaigned with determination to see the far-side landing gain approval.

Additional surface transportation options for the astronauts had been explored as well, which could allow them to range even farther from their lunar module than the lunar rover had. If the walkback constraint were eased with increasing confidence in the life-support backpacks over time, then the engineers could have a field day exploiting the weak lunar gravity. TRW and Bellcomm had developed design concepts for a miniature version of the LM landing stage that could pack into the space of the rover. It formed a two-seater lunar flyer, or "Mooncopter." The lunar flyer could carry a crew soaring over the surface for miles and miles, to a wide variety of otherwise inaccessible sampling sites, resulting in the equivalent of many missions at once. The flyer looked much too dangerous to flight planners, but the astronaut pilots couldn't wait. Just when all the high-tech piloting challenges had been mastered, here was an even hotter prospect. There would be no shortage of volunteers.

Grumman had meanwhile devised a whole sheaf of ways to capitalize on the proven technology of its now-beloved lunar module. The reliable lander could now be built upon and its capabilities expanded at a small fraction of the cost of the LM's original development. An unmanned LM could be sent to the Moon in advance of a landing crew, setting down automatically like the robot Surveyor probes had done, carrying no crew cockpit or ascent engine but instead a huge load of supplies. This unmanned supply LM would be a "lunar truck." The astronauts would follow and land close by. The supplies carried by the lunar-truck LM could extend a mission's duration by weeks. Alternatively, a cargo LM sent in advance could carry a larger mobile laboratory vehicle, like a rover but more substantial, even enclosed with a pressurized cockpit. In such an exploratory vehicle the astronauts could travel great distances from their lander, camping in it during extended traverses.

Extended stays on the surface of the Moon not only would allow more of the same kind of exploration but would make possible the penetration of regions too dangerous and rugged for a LM landing. Lunar modules could be landed as close as possible to a particularly fascinating target, and then well-equipped explorers could travel for days if necessary, safely on the ground, to reach canyons or rugged highlands that could be hazardous to a LM. There were extraordinary sights on the Moon, some even visible through Earth telescopes, that would make thrilling exploration prospects. The Straight Wall, for example, on the edge of the Sea of Clouds southeast of Apollo 14's landing site, is some kind of huge scarp, a cliff running in a nearly straight line for dozens of miles. No one knew its nature. An extended mission could visit such a marvel. Other possibilities would include the polar regions of the Moon, which were suspected of many things, even of holding frozen water.

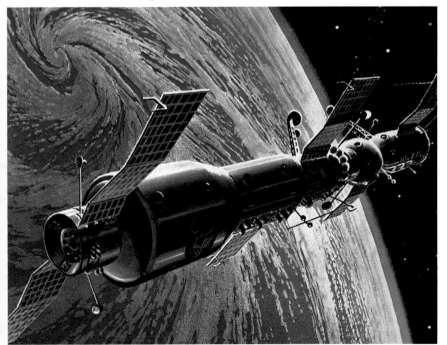

NASA had run the missions of late 1968 and 1969 at a furious pace to meet Kennedy's deadline. The ambitious launch schedule was originally conceived to complete the Apollo program of exploration with Apollo 20 in 1971, the launches occurring every two months. However, after the successful first landing, the schedule was relaxed to three-month and then six-month intervals. The dates for the last three missions were extended beyond the launch of a planned Apollo space station in 1973.

## THE APOLLO SPACE STATION: SKYLAB

Apollo still held surprising possibilities of many kinds. When Apollo 17 splashed down, many in NASA had already been working for some time on a bold space station project. The Soviets, ever our prime movers, had set it in motion. In 1969 the CIA had come to the president with intelligence that the Soviets were planning a space station of some kind for 1971; America would respond to maintain the vital prestige that space exploration was all about. The new Soviet goad was another salutary influence—and a welcome one to planners like von Braun. The space station would be, for a change, an asset we got to keep. The desperate pace of Apollo had used up everything we had sent into space, leaving us without the space infrastructure that von Braun had long envisioned. But we did have the spaceport launch complex in Florida and Mission Control in Houston, and, planners worked out, we already had what it would take to create a space station.

Manned exploration had taught us much about the conditions of space and allowed engineers to rethink the space station concept. Weightlessness did not appear to pose significant dangers to our astronauts, and so the gravity-generating great rotating ring of Noordung's designs and Bonestell's *Collier's* paintings was not required. A nonrotating, zero-g station could be much smaller and easier to build. We could, in fact, build a very good space platform out of something we already had.

**SALYUT**

*A Soviet Soyuz spacecraft (far right) docks with a pioneering Salyut space station in this artist's rendering. Between 1971 and 1982, the Soviets launched seven Salyuts, small stations designed for increasingly long orbital life spans, Salyut 7 lasting four years.*

# Advanced Apollo

From 1966 to 1970, NASA's Apollo Applications Program (sometimes called Apollo X) planned for space missions beyond the initial lunar landings. Efficiently using existing rockets and Apollo spacecraft with minimum modifications, Apollo Applications envisioned further exploration of the Moon, orbiting space stations, and new kinds of missions in space.

**F**our lunar landing missions were slated for post-Apollo exploration in the Apollo Application Program schedule published in 1967. These advanced missions would extend scientific studies across broader reaches of the Moon and support longer stays on the lunar surface. Two-week surface exploration missions would use dual Saturn V launches and specialized lunar modules. A first launch would carry an unmanned "LM truck," designed like a standard LM with a new upper stage. Never intended to leave the Moon, the LM truck's upper stage would need no flight controls or engines and would instead hold expanded living quarters, a lunar exploration vehicle, and supplies for the long expedition. Astronauts on the LM truck delivery mission would orbit the Moon carrying out scientific surveys but not landing, sending down only the truck. The second Saturn V of the dual-launch mission would bring a landing crew in a "LM taxi," specially modified to maintain its liftoff capability after sitting dormant for two weeks. Living in the LM truck shelter with its improved sleeping arrangements, the landing crew would unpack its exploration vehicle and set up scientific stations in locations far and wide. The LM truck could carry advanced lunar surface equipment, including a new 100-foot lunar drill that could

*The "mooncopter" lunar flying vehicle would allow astronauts to set up remote scientific stations far from the landing site.*

penetrate billions of years into the Moon's geological past.

Instead of a lunar rover, a LM truck could also carry the "lunar flying vehicle," which looked something like a Space-Age two-seater lunar motorcycle. Bell Aerosystems had developed this daring concept beginning in 1965 as a way to give astronauts great mobility even during short stays on the Moon. The lightweight mooncopter, as it was sometimes called, could fly 50 miles from the lunar module, opening up vast reaches to exploration and offering a spectacular platform for reconnaissance photos.

A more advanced version of the LM truck would carry a form of lunar rover called the Mobile Lunar Laboratory, or MOLAB. There would be no room on the MOLAB LM truck for living quarters, but the MOLAB itself would become the expedition shelter: It included a pressurized cabin and would allow the astronauts to drive for days into wild and unexplored territory, reaching into challenging terrain too dangerous for a lunar landing.

Still longer stays would be possible with the "lunar-surface station." An unmanned Saturn V could deliver a lunar-surface station to the Moon, equipped with both a lunar rover and a lunar flyer, along with supplies for a 96-day stay. This mission would use an Apollo service module with its powerful main engine to help land the heavy station. A modified command module would carry four astronauts on the second launch of the mission. Two landing crew would descend by LM taxi, and two would live in lunar orbit for three months, their long sojourn supported by a supply module carried on the first launch.

With budget for further spacecraft development could come a heavy-duty landing vehicle that would carry a MOLAB and a substantial lunar-base module.

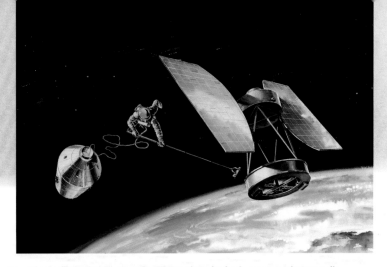

*The Apollo Applications Program envisioned new kinds of missions employing Apollo spacecraft, including satellite grappling for repair and examination. The Space Shuttle would eventually carry out missions like this.*

Depending on the configuration, such a heavy landing base could support up to six astronauts for a year and a half, with crews arriving by LM taxi.

Among its many studies Apollo Applications also researched ground-landing retro-rockets and para-wings as alternatives to ocean splashdown for capsule recovery to eliminate the need for the large and expensive naval-recovery force.

The Apollo Applications Program lunar missions were canceled when NASA's budget declined during the Vietnam War. Only the lunar rover from these starry-eyed plans ever made it to the Moon, but the Apollo Applications space-station concepts would come to grand fruition in a project called Skylab.

*Extended-stay dual-launch lunar missions would first land an unmanned LM truck carrying a shelter module or a mobile laboratory vehicle. Landing crew would then touch down in a LM taxi.*

Always on the lookout for ways to make the most of existing resources, von Braun had come up with the idea of refitting an S-IVB Saturn V third stage *as* a space station. The Saturn V was well able to loft such a load into Earth orbit; it had done the job many times already. This time, there would be no fuel in the third stage; instead it would hold a four-story space station. All the weight of a Moon-bound Apollo spacecraft package could be allocated for equipment for the station. McDonnell Douglas, builders of the Saturn V third stage, won the contract for the orbital "Saturn workshop" and built what came to be called Skylab.

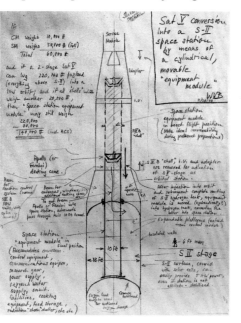

Von Braun envisioned several Skylabs orbiting the Earth, serving as observation and scientific stations, platforms for research on human biology in weightlessness, and bases for further exploration.

The first Skylab was allocated the Saturn V rocket that had been built for Apollo 20; it seemed a reasonable trade-off for launching a space station. A permanent hardware asset! Von Braun loved the idea. The Skylabs would be the beginning of America's enduring future in space.

Douglas built two Skylab stations, plus a third one as a trainer, and the crews trained extensively at Marshall, making much use of the neutral buoyancy pool, where they worked underwater to practice for weightlessness. Veteran Apollo astronauts would lead the first two crews to this outpost in the sky. They could hardly believe the magnitude of the craft they were training for.

Skylab was huge. With 12,711 cubic feet of habitable volume, it formed an absolutely enormous space for astronauts who were used to the cramped confines of the Apollo command module and lunar module.

Two lower decks held sleeping quarters, an actual bathroom (and a shower), a galley, an exercise station with bio-monitoring devices, and a scientific station. Two more decks' worth of space were open, allowing the crew exercise space and providing for the flexibility of other uses as new needs arose. Around the walls of this large atrium were extensive storage lockers for months' worth of supplies.

Adjoining the main body of Skylab was an annex, a hallway-like scientific section including a great deal of Earth observation instrumentation, and the Apollo telescope mount, which would carry a set of five telescopes into space, high above the realm of clouds and atmosphere to observe the Sun in unprecedented detail and clarity.

At the end of this scientific annex and the telescope mount was a multiple docking adapter, so that more than one Apollo command module could dock at a time to exchange crews or carry out multiple missions.

Great solar wings would extend from the main station, and a huge X of panels would radiate from the telescope mount, powering the station with the inexhaustible energy of the Sun. It was an ambitious space station, a magnificently grand design. In one step it would provide the United States with a large facility in space.

Saturn IB rockets would carry the crews up to the station. These Saturn V precursors, like the one flown by Wally Schirra on Apollo 7, had been built back in the mid-1960s and had never been needed since the proving flights had all gone so well. The rockets had been stored carefully and were still in great shape. Refurbished, the nine-year-old Saturn IBs were all that NASA needed to ferry a command module up to the station, so Chrysler's Saturn rocket would see service again.

The crew rockets would launch from the active Apollo pads, not the old Launch Complex 34, where the Apollo 7 Saturn IB had been

sent up. A giant "milkstool" trestle was built as an elevated base to bring the smaller Saturn IB vehicle up to the height where it could conveniently use one of the mobile launch towers that had been built for the giant Saturn Vs.

NASA prepared for the unexpected with Skylab. For the first time we would have orbital rescue capability on standby. North American Aviation created a command module rescue ship modification kit, which could pack in five astronaut acceleration couches instead of the usual three. Two astronauts could go up and rescue a full Skylab crew in case anything went wrong with their return vessel while they were in orbit. The setup was admirably complete.

The Russians sent their first space station up on schedule in 1971. We had started too late to catch them, but then, we were still sending astronauts all the way to the Moon. The Soviet pioneer was called Salyut ("Salute"), and it was a compact module designed to last several months in low Earth orbit. Our station would come a little later, but the NASA engineers reveled in the fact that our station could practically hold the entire Salyut in its main atrium. Skylab was a giant, and it was possible only because we had that incredible ticket to space, the mighty Saturn V, which the Russians could not match.

While the first U.S. Skylab crew rocket waited on pad 39B, the unmanned Skylab station blasted into orbit from pad 39A in 1973. The Saturn V performed magnificently as always, but launching a space station was new for us, and we had a painful lesson coming. The rugged Saturn V could take the buffeting and dynamic air pressures of

*Skylab crew sneakers featured triangular plates built to twist-lock into the flooring plates for secure footing in weightlessness. In practice the twist-locks turned out to be cumbersome and were rarely used.*

launch, but these forces proved too much for the outermost components of Skylab I. As the Saturn drilled through the point of maximum dynamic atmospheric pressure, the 730 mph slipstream battered Skylab's outer hull and ripped away part of the station's outer covering, a thin micrometeoroid shield. Staging retro-rockets then tore the portside solar wing off completely, and owing to the damage, the second wing failed to deploy once the station reached orbit. The station had no wings—far too little solar power—and it was overheating from the force of the Sun without its outer shield.

The first Skylab crew had been ready to launch the day after the station itself. As the grim telemetry told Mission Control that the station had not survived the boost intact, mission plans were immediately suspended. NASA and its contractors worked around the clock to devise a fix that the first crew could carry out in orbit. In just ten days they had worked out the procedures and trained the astronauts, as news media followed the dramatic situation closely.

Pete Conrad, commander of Apollo 12's Moon landing, led this first crew, and when they rocketed into orbit, they were ready for some real work. They arrived to find Skylab filled with breathable air but sweltering at almost 100°. Conrad and his crew first set about shielding their orbital platform from sunburn.

Through a small scientific airlock in Skylab's side, they deployed a huge foil "parasol" that had been cleverly stowed in their command module. With this fix, the temperature in the station dropped,

**DAMAGED**

*Skylab's launch damage is evident in this photograph, below, from the first crew's fly-around inspection. The left solar wing is missing, the right one is jammed, and the station's exposed back is blistering in the Sun.*

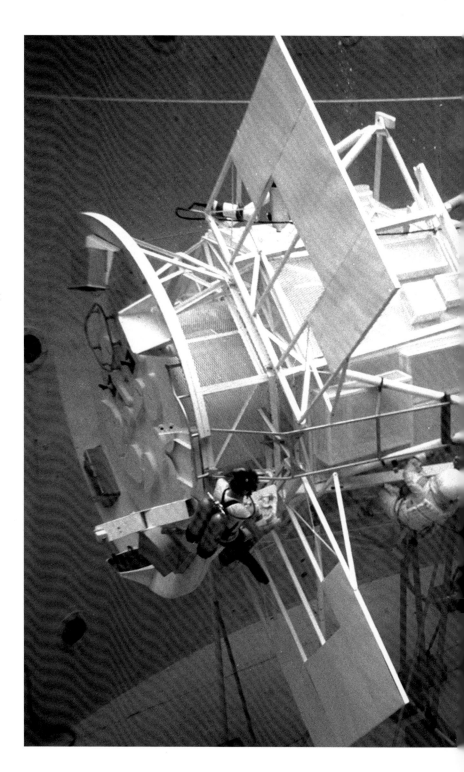

but they were still struggling with too little power. Wearing a bulky Apollo space suit, Conrad ventured outside on a critical space walk, working at the portside solar wing to release it until it deployed as planned. The station now had one functioning wing. With the margin for error NASA built into all their Apollo hardware, one solar wing was enough for full functionality on board the station. Delighted at their repairs, Conrad's crew settled in for their mission, which lasted an entire month in space.

**AQUANAUTS**

*In a 40-foot-deep tank at Marshall Space Flight Center in Huntsville, full-size replicas of Skylab sections (such as the telescope mount seen here) allowed astronauts to train for their spacewalk procedures in an environment that simulated the weightlessness of space.*

After they had returned to Earth, a second crew roared into orbit for a 54-day mission, commanded by Conrad's fellow Apollo 12 moonwalker, Alan Bean. This second mission continued the improvement of the space station's condition, carrying out further spacewalks to cover the parasol with a larger foil sheet anchored with lanyards over the exposed area of the station. Bean's mission was followed by a third crew, which stayed an amazing 84 days. Each crew kept up an intense schedule, running a tremendous variety of experiments and observations, their telescopes trained on the mysteries of the Sun and peering down at the Earth below.

The astronauts did not merely travel in Skylab, they lived on this island in the sky. It was America's first long-term outpost in space. And when the crews came home, we still had the station. Soon we could have more: The second Apollo space station had already been built and awaited launch.

We were learning a great deal about space station design because the crews learned what worked and what didn't work up there in orbit. But there was a specific reason that these endurance flights were proving that crews could deal with the effects of weightlessness: a much longer journey, to the next destination much farther away. Skylab, in addition to carrying out a multitude of scientific experiments, was laying the groundwork for a manned mission to Mars.

# Skylab

The descendant of a clever idea to refit spent rocket stages as space station components, Skylab was capable and complete. A giant orbital workshop, Skylab offered 13,000 cubic feet of habitable space. After the first Skylab crew repaired the damage the station suffered during its launch, Skylab became a great success, accomplishing all its major objectives.

**E**ver conservative and always planning ahead to maximize productivity, Wernher von Braun came up with a number of ideas for repurposing Apollo hardware to build modular space stations. Skylab was the direct descendant of sketches von Braun had toyed with in 1964.

The so-called Saturn orbital workshop was originally envisioned to be made out of a fuel tank in space, launched on an economical Saturn IB rocket. Von Braun envisioned using spent S-IVB third stages, which could be drained of their last propellants, pressurized with air, and then outfitted with interior equipment. This workshop core could be expanded with add-on modules delivered by subsequent launches, such as an airlock, a multiple docking adapter, and "LM labs," lunar-lander spaceframes modified into scientific modules. Two of the composite orbital stations were planned by 1967.

Months after the first Moon landing, von Braun was given approval to redesign the Apollo space station for launch with a full-power Saturn V. The Saturn V could lift a load five times heavier than the spent-stage conversion workshop, so the new workshop core could be completely fitted out before launch. In fact, the workshop could have all its modules assembled together in advance. The LM lab became the Apollo telescope mount, its base still octagonal like a LM landing stage. The tinkertoy-style orbital workshop became a complete "space-station cluster" far more capable than any orbital workshop would have been, and in 1970 this grand new incarnation was renamed Skylab.

Skylab would be fully constructed and pretested on the ground and filled with 20,000 pieces of supplies and equipment. It was the ultimate version of the Saturn orbital workshop concept.

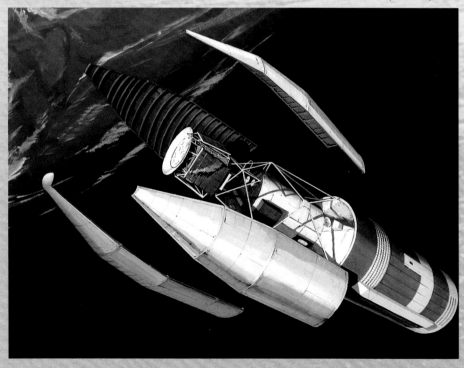

*In orbit, Skylab's nose cone shroud disengaged to reveal the science annex and telescope mount, which then rotated and extended its solar panels.*

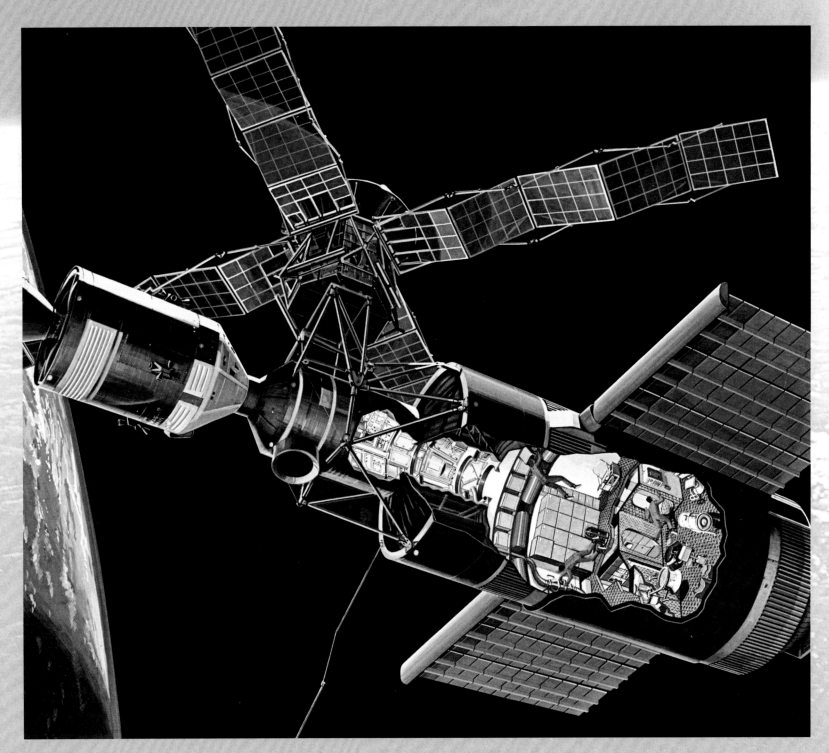

This cutaway view shows the size of the huge Skylab space station and its general interior layout. Sun and Earth observation instruments were manned in the narrow section to the left, the solar telescopes built into the center of the X solar panels. The crew quarters were in the larger section of the station to the right, with storage lockers forming a ring around the main atrium in the middle.

Apollo command modules docked with Skylab to bring the crews aboard.

## SKYLAB SCIENCE

**S**kylab crews carried out several kinds of scientific missions. In the medical bay, astronaut doctors put their crewmates through tests on an exercise bike and other equipment, measuring and doc-umenting the human body's response to life in space. The medical data on long-term expo-sure to weightlessness would assist in determining the feasibil-ity of a manned Mars mission. Meanwhile, the eight solar tele-scopes in the telescope cluster peered at the Sun in multiple wavelengths, revealing sunspots, solar flares, and the Sun's com-plex surface, dramatically advancing scientific knowledge. And while the solar telescopes looked up, Earth resources experiments looked down. Skylab flew over 75 percent of the Earth's surface, recording vis-ible indications of such things as crop health and regional envi-ronmental damage from drought and pollution. Skylab astronauts photographed the Falklands ocean current for the first time, precisely documented poorly mapped areas of South America, and peered inside hurricanes better than any weather satellite had been able to do, revealing new information about internal storm structures. NASA was also interested in developing space as a location for American industry, and so the upper deck of the station core featured a micro-gravity lab where space technology experiments were conducted, including materials-processing experiments such as crystal growth and weightless laser manufacturing. Skylab even tested a prototype astronaut jet-pack—the cavernous main atrium being large enough for tumbling maneuvers.

## ORBITAL LIFE

**L**ife aboard Skylab was in some ways far more comfortable than Apollo astronauts had experi-enced. The bathroom had a toilet and a door that closed, as

Astronauts Gerry Carr and Bill Pogue demonstrate the power of zero g aboard Skylab.

well as an air filter. The galley let astronauts prepare their food to taste and gave them a table to sit around together and a win-dow through which they could see the beauty of the Earth out-side. The crewmen each had private sleeping quarters, small rooms fitted with comfortable vertical sleeping bags.

Skylab living also had its dif-ficulties. The astronauts found it easy to move large equipment in weightlessness, but little items were forever tumbling away from them, spilling out of storage lockers in ten directions at once and vanishing into the myriad nooks and crannies of the huge facility. The crews learned to check the air-circulation intake grating for small lost items swept

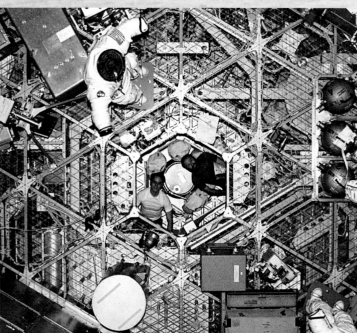

A view down into the crew section of Skylab. Lightweight latticework formed flooring and walls. The Apollo space station offered impressive work and living space, but its utilitarian structure was visually "noisy" and could be disorienting for crews who wanted more of a sense of up and down.

there over time by fan-driven air currents. The zero-g toilet was not the easiest thing in the world to use, and the weekly showers in a collapsible plastic tube required tedious effort to vacuum up stray floating water droplets. No one liked the uncomfortable fireproofed uniforms or the drab interior colors of the station, and Skylab's hodgepodge of spaces mixed "up" and "down" confusingly or had no orientation at all. But overall, the station performed superbly, and the crews were happy with it.

All the Skylab crews kept up a demanding schedule of work, constantly carrying out experiments throughout the station, making photographs, participating in medical tests, and spacewalking to retrieve film canisters and reload the camera magazines. The three missions together conducted 2,400 experiments.

*Skylab seen from below. The main docking port is at the front, with the auxiliary port on the underside of the white section. The telescope mount above the docking adapter shows the octagonal shape originally conceived using a LM landing stage.*

## SISTER STATION

**S**kylab I was a tremendous success, and Skylab II was planned for launch sometime in 1975 or early 1976. This second station would be an advanced international model, serving as a rendezvous point for American and Soviet spacecraft in the joint Apollo-Soyuz test project and receiving payloads from future space shuttle missions. The rockets, spacecraft, and space station were already built, and Skylab II operations were budgeted to cost just $220 million to $650 million. In the turmoil of the early 1970s, however, the program was canceled and the fleet of Apollo space vehicles deactivated. The "lost" space station Skylab II can be visited today on display in the Smithsonian National Air and Space Museum in Washington, D.C.

## LEGACIES

**T**he lessons learned from Skylab have shaped the new International Space Station in important ways. Gone are the cluttered, disorganized spaces of Skylab in NASA's new space station modules. Dark floors and light ceilings maintain a helpful (if arbitrary) sense of up and down. Skylab's utilitarian "exposed equipment aesthetic" has been replaced by a clean, well-organized environment, and the old world of browns by a new realm of brushed aluminum and white. Fitted panels aboard the new space station prevent small items from floating into inaccessible spaces or getting lost, making for a setting that in some modules looks very much like the attractive futurist spacecraft designs seen in the film *2001: A Space Odyssey*. Skylab helped us appreciate the important functional benefits of such designs. Our first space station is still making contributions today.

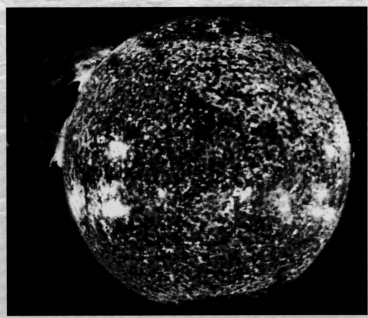

*Skylab photograph of a solar flare bursting hundreds of thousands of miles into space. Skylab's solar telescopes dramatically advanced scientific knowledge of the Sun.*

## VON BRAUN'S VISION: THE INTEGRATED SPACE PROGRAM

**W**ernher von Braun had seen his 1950s comprehensive plan for space exploration get sidestepped by Kennedy's political deadline for the Moon landing. The crash program of Apollo got us to the Moon and won the Space Race, but von Braun's dream had always been one of exploration, and the race had left us with little hardware to show for all our effort. Our Saturn Vs kept coming back as burnt-up little capsules. Von Braun reenvisioned his comprehensive recommendation, taking into account the realities that had come to pass, and also taking into consideration the assets that we had built and retained, both in hardware and in technology and expertise.

On August 6, 1969, only two weeks after the first Moon landing, von Braun, already looking far ahead, presented to the presidential Space Task Group his vision for a new Integrated Space Program, developed with his Marshall and industry colleagues, especially a keen planner named Georg von Theisenhasen. This new space program was to begin with Skylab I, followed by a second Skylab, using them very deliberately as stepping stones to future goals: a permanent base on the Moon and a manned mission to Mars. The entire program was planned using multipurpose modules to maximize efficiency. With as much proven Apollo hardware as possible, the Integrated Space Program projects would build on the resources already invested and continue to challenge American industry with ever greater technological needs.

NASA had already been developing the next generation of rocket engines for just such grand ambitions. They were nuclear. Nuclear Engines for Rocket Vehicle Applications, or NERVA, were the focus of a development program proceeding well at a test site in Nevada. The interplanetary nuclear engines would be used only in space, and their strength was that they would use only half as much fuel as standard engines. Von Braun could confidently predict a successful flight-ready model by the 1980s, and it was this superefficient engine that could hurl spacecraft all the way to Mars.

Several NERVA stages would have to be assembled in orbit to build the Mars exploration spacecraft, and it would take serious muscle to get them upstairs. But we would have it. Von Braun's Marshall engineers had already designed a Saturn V super-heavy-lift rocket, with stretched stages to hold more fuel and with strap-on solid rockets to vastly increase the already-gargantuan power of the Saturn, reaching the power levels once envisioned for the mighty Nova. These "Saturn Plus" rockets would thunder skyward from a new heavy-duty pad, 39C, to be built on land already set aside for it, just north of 39B. Five Saturn Plus heavy-lift rockets would boost NERVA stages into orbit, where they would be assembled into an interplanetary space vehicle aimed at Mars. Another Saturn would loft the Mars spacecraft to be placed at the nose of the five NERVA stages.

The Mars spacecraft was essentially a version of the Skylab module, a habitat for the astronauts during their 221-day journey. Adjoining it was a 29-foot-tall lander shaped just like an Apollo command module because Max Faget's favored shape was well understood in reentry conditions. The lander would use a combination of heatshield reentry and retro-rocket in Mars's thin atmosphere, combining characteristics of both the Apollo command module and the lunar module. After supporting a four-man crew on the surface for several weeks, the upper part of the lander would return to the habitat stage in Mars orbit, just as the cockpit stage of a LM rejoined its C.S.M. The entire mission would take a year and a half. And it was all possible. The greatest technological problems had been, for the most part, already solved. It all awaited us.

### NERVA

*Nuclear rocket engines superheated their propellants to create thrust, a less powerful but more efficient design than traditional chemical rockets. Prototype NERVA engines were developed and successfully tested in Nevada.*

### MARS RETURN

*In this concept painting from von Braun's proposal to Vice President Spiro Agnew's Space Task Group in 1969, a manned Mars spacecraft reignites its nuclear engine to head home. The forward stage is a crew-quarters module similar to the main section of Skylab.*

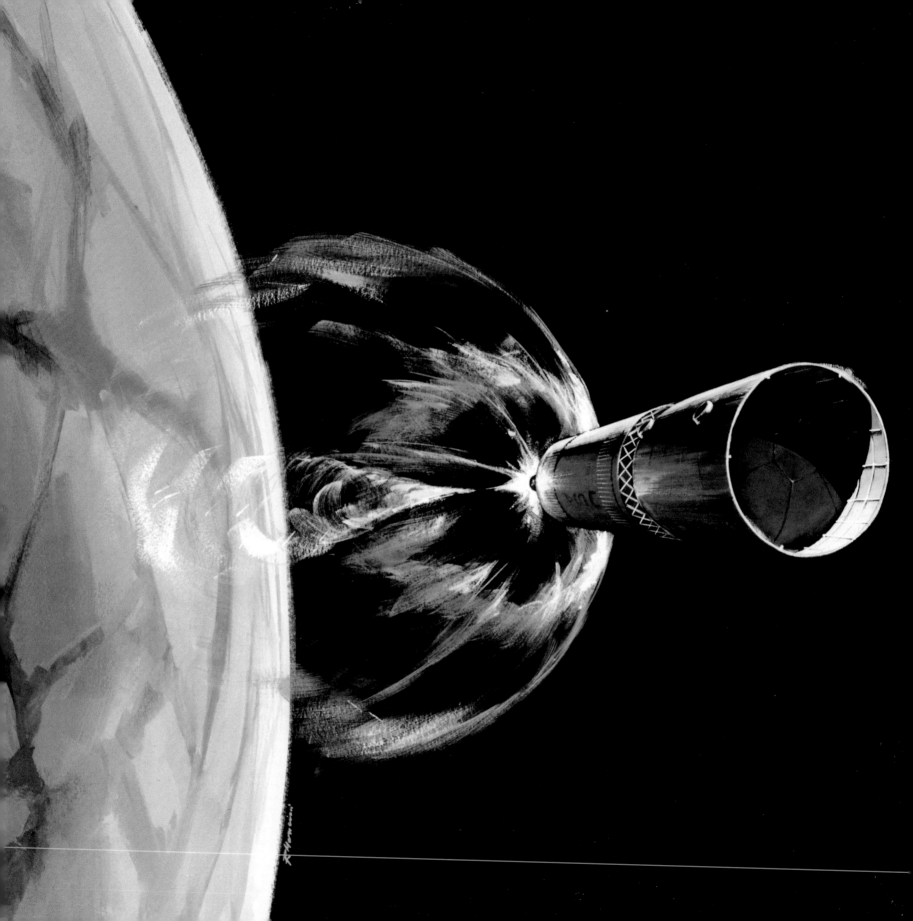

# A New Plan

Without a clear goal beyond winning the Moon Race, NASA was in danger of drifting. Wernher von Braun proposed an Integrated Space Program for 1970–1990. Reusable common components and maximal use of Apollo systems already developed made the plan logical and cost-effective, supporting a lasting infrastructure in space as our reach extended to the planets.

Under von Braun's Integrated Space Program, the main workshop module of Skylab would be developed as a standardized mission module in the early 1970s and adapted for a wide range of uses. One would be orbited around the Moon in 1975 to establish a six-man lunar-orbit space station. Two mission modules could be linked to form a second-generation Earth-orbit space station in the same year. Over the years, six more mission modules would be added to the Earth space station core to build a massive permanent space base capable of housing an international crew of 100 by 1986. Space base would serve as a lunar and planetary mission staging post and offer a comfortable environment in which nonastronaut scientists and industrial workers could easily operate. Still another mission module would be boosted into geosynchronous orbit 23,000 miles up, where the high-orbit station would hang stationary over Earth like a communications satellite.

A heavy-duty lunar module–type lander called the space tug would be developed by 1975, allowing the landing of heavy payloads on the Moon. By 1979, we could land a mission module as a lunar-surface base for six men. With expansion by 1981, there would be 24 astronauts stationed in lunar orbit; seven more mission modules landed on the Moon would establish a lunar colony of 48 astronauts by 1984. The lunar colony would go beyond science and also begin industrial work, mining resources for power and manufacturing.

Key to supporting the expanded lunar operations, as well as planetary exploration, would be the NERVA nuclear shuttle, whose engine was already in development at NASA when von Braun made his proposal in 1969. The nuclear shuttle would be an unmanned rocket stage sent into orbit by an

*While one mission module orbits the Moon as a lunar space station, another module has just been landed by the space tug as a six-man lunar-surface base in this scenario for 1979.*

*The Mars mission module, powered by a nuclear-shuttle stage, orbits above after a 280-day journey from Earth. On the surface, the three-man landing party makes mankind's first explorations of another planet.*

upgraded Saturn V and available as a reusable booster to send large payloads into geosynchronous orbit, to the Moon, or beyond. Launched half-full of propellant to save weight, the nuclear shuttle would be topped up and periodically refueled by a visiting space shuttle, which was supposed to be providing low-cost orbital delivery of small payloads by 1975. Von Braun could have a nuclear shuttle ready by 1978 to support the placement of the geosynchronous Earth-orbit station in 1980.

In 1981, three nuclear shuttles would be bound side by side in orbit to create the power plant of America's first manned interplanetary spacecraft, destined for Mars. The two outermost stages would thrust the spacecraft into trans-Mars injection, breaking the pull of Earth's gravity. After this burst of power, the outrigger nuclear-shuttle stages would separate and return to Earth orbit for reuse in hauling payloads to the Moon. After a 280-day interplanetary voyage filled with pioneering stellar and solar

observations and experiments, the remaining nuclear-shuttle stage would slow the vessel into orbit around Mars, and the mission would stay for 80 days. For the 290-day return trip to Earth, the nuclear shuttle would come to life again, sending the mission around the Sun. To cut the vessel's speed, the ship would swing close to Venus on the way back, carrying out

radar mapping and sending down probes. After a heroic two-year mission, the crew would be received on space base before returning to Earth on a space shuttle. "If early explorations prove interesting," von Braun wrote, the same hardware could be used to establish a 12-man Mars ground base by 1986 and a 48-man colony by 1989.

In the end, restricted by budget concerns and pressured by President Nixon, NASA had to choose between the Integrated Space Program and the costly space shuttle. But the program mission module saw successful space service as the core of Skylab, and the long-range plan still serves as a logical and exciting blueprint for future exploration.

*The Mars landing crew blasts off LM-style after concluding a historic exploration in this scenario for 1982.*

## THE CURTAIN

**A**t least it did in von Braun's imagination. But Apollo would never even launch its planned final three missions. The year 1967 had been the peak year of funding. As soon as we were on the homestretch to achieving the single goal that had driven NASA since Kennedy's pledge, the space budget began gradually to wind down, oblivious to the enthusiasm of the people involved who mistakenly believed Apollo was about exploration or space science. A new president with new priorities and policy goals had taken office in 1969, and a different torch had been passed. Richard Nixon would oversee an early end to Apollo.

Nixon was not alone in his lack of enthusiasm for space. The public had largely lost interest. The Apollo J-missions were spectacular projects, and the color television beamed back from the galloping lunar rover did spark a brief resurgence of interest in the program. But by Apollo 17, America was no longer paying attention. Vietnam, social unrest, urban riots, and ecological decay seemed too pressing and too alarming for the nation to be looking to the stars. The Moon and our dreams of the new ocean would be abandoned.

NASA Director Tom Paine canceled Apollo 20 in 1969 and Apollo 18 and 19 in 1971 to please the Nixon White House, which wanted an end to the program identified with the Democrat Kennedy. If Nixon was going to support anything in space exploration, he wanted something distinctive that could be his own mark on history: His legacy would be the space shuttle. Apollo Applications, including the further use of Skylab or the launch of the already-built second Skylab or the two remaining Saturn V

super-rockets, were all canceled. Most of Apollo's German rocket scientists were pushed into retirement, von Braun was "promoted" to a powerless position behind a desk in Washington, and the millions of dollars' worth of space-ready Apollo hardware was scrapped and turned over to museums.

## APOLLO-SOYUZ: CLOSURE

**A**pollo would make one more journey into space before its curtain fell. In its last gesture, it would close the loop that had set it in motion. Apollo's final hour took place in 1975, during the last approved project of the Apollo Applications Program. A final Saturn IB crew rocket would be fired on a mission called the Apollo-Soyuz Test Project, an orbital docking with a Russian spacecraft. After all the years of competition with the Soviets in space, Apollo's last mission would be one of union.

To one man, Apollo-Soyuz meant more than he could easily express. Deke Slayton had been the only one of the original Mercury Seven astronauts who never made it into space. Grounded early by a minor heart irregularity, this superb test pilot, groomed for single combat on behalf of his nation, had had to stand by on the ground and watch his comrades fly up into metaphorical battle. Slayton had taken the consolation post of chief of the Astronaut Office and had done his job well, but he never got over the bitter feeling of having been cut out of a role he was born to play. By 1975, Slayton was 51 years old. But space medicine had come a long way since he had been grounded in 1962, and as a result of his determination and a thorough new heart examination, Slayton had finally been cleared for flight. Apollo-Soyuz, the last Apollo mission, would put one of our first astronauts into space for the first time. It would make a fitting closure in more ways than one.

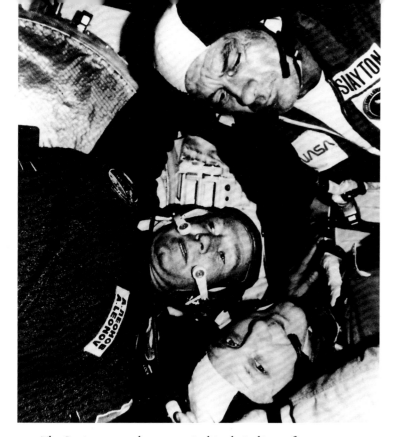

The Soviets were almost comical in their discomfort at interacting with Western journalists on the project. Openness was simply not a familiar procedure behind the Iron Curtain, and reporters were flown into the Soviet launch facility at Baikonur only under cover of night. The U.S.S.R. consistently provided inaccurate information regarding its location and even its correct name, to the chagrin of the reporters who pointed out that the U.S. Strategic Air Command knew its location with military precision. The Soviet cloak-and-dagger way was simply too ingrained to be abandoned, no matter what logic suggested.

The last Apollo command module soared up to rendezvous with its Soviet counterpart, the American ship carrying on its nose not a LM but a docking adapter that would allow the two foreign craft to join. Through the small passage within the adapter, the two crews greeted each other. Amid this historic exchange, Mercury astronaut Deke Slayton reached out and grasped the hand of Soviet commander Alexei Leonov, the first spacewalker, and a new era in space began as an old one died. This international cooperation between the old enemies would take a long time to bear fruit, but by the end of the century Russian

and American astronauts would be serving together on space stations built by both countries. Apollo-Soyuz was the beginning of this destiny. Born of a political contest and forged to accomplish a political goal, Apollo in its last bow was perhaps the most honest it had ever been, making a purely symbolic political gesture and uniting hands that had shaken as fists in an earlier time.

## AFTER APOLLO: SPACE SHUTTLE AND A REPLACEMENT SPACE STATION

**A**fter the end of Apollo, Skylab still circled the Earth, awaiting the return of astronauts to our orbiting outpost. The tremendous power of an Apollo Saturn V had placed this heavy laboratory in orbit, and it would not be easy to repeat this feat. Skylab was a hard-won asset in space, and it would need tending in order to survive.

From above, the Sun beat on Skylab with a hail of charged particles—the solar wind from which our atmosphere protects us. From below, the tenuous wisps of the uppermost atmosphere gradually slowed the station in its orbiting path. From the drag of these effects, the Apollo space station would lose altitude over time. Skylab had no orbital maneuvering thrusters of its own, but NASA planned a dramatic rescue mission for the space station at the beginning of the next era in space. The Space Shuttle would be sent up to rescue Skylab and boost it back into a higher orbit. The station would then become the Shuttle's destination in the sky as it ferried astronauts and experiments to and from the huge laboratory.

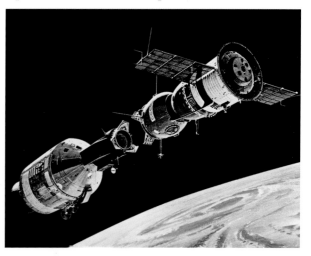

*NASA artwork of the U.S. and Soviet spaceships docking in Earth orbit. The Apollo command module carried the docking adapter.*  **251**

# U.S. Rocket Power

NASA's space vehicles grew rapidly during the 1960s, from the little Mercury Redstone missile to the majestic Apollo Saturn V. Towering twice as high as today's space shuttle, the Saturn V could lift four times as much tonnage, and its main engines remain by far the most powerful ever designed. One can appreciate the Moon rocket better in context and comparison.

Five ten-ton engines boost the Apollo 11 Saturn V at liftoff.

Any rocket that can carry an astronaut is a substantial piece of engineering, but NASA's Saturn rockets stand out as gigantic and powerful even among their peers. Consider as a baseline the Gemini, launched on the air force Titan missile: This was a two-man spacecraft that could stay aloft for two weeks and, with orbital refueling, reach heights of 850 miles. The Gemini capsule could even have been sent around the Moon, and such a possibility was actually considered when it looked like the Apollo ship might be delayed in development. The Gemini Titan was a very capable space vehicle, and yet the Saturn IB rocket dwarfs it in size and ability, just as the Saturn IB is dwarfed in turn by the colossal Saturn V. Apollo and Saturn were truly works of monumental stature.

The sizes and cargo-to-Earth-orbit ratings of the rockets shown on the opposite page give a good impression of their relative capabilities, but you can also think of it this way: The suborbital Mercury Redstone was the bicycle of the space program. It allowed for short hops, but it couldn't take you very far. The orbital Mercury Atlas was then the motorcycle, with the power to take one man much farther. The Gemini Titan II rocket was a Volkswagen Beetle with some gear in the back seat. It could carry two men and was of such a basically sound design that in an updated form it is still in production today. (The air force uses Titan IV rockets for satellite launches.) The Apollo Saturn IB was a small pickup truck. It could hold three men and sported a cargo area behind them. The Saturn V was NASA's Ford F-350 heavy-duty truck: It could carry three men and a full load of equipment anywhere they needed to go, including the Moon. For a short-range trip such as to Earth orbit, the Saturn V could haul an entire prefabricated mobile home to its destination, as it did with the Skylab space station.

In this light, the space shuttle might be considered the 1981 Lamborghini of the space program. Exotic and sophisticated, it is also extremely expensive to operate and maintain, and its limited luggage space is not exactly ideal for construction jobs, requiring the new space station to be built with many launches of small components. On the other hand, the shuttle is a tremendous leap forward in reentry capability—from the tiny Apollo capsule that alone came back from a Saturn V mission, we now see the dramatic return of entire huge shuttle orbiters, carrying crews of up to seven astronauts.

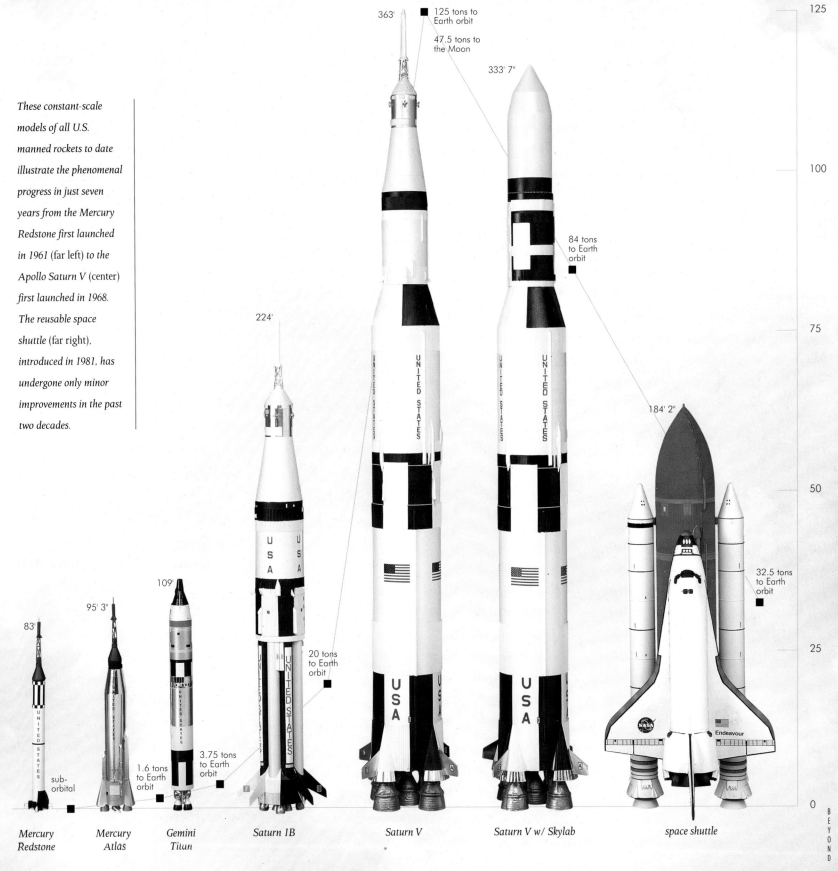

*These constant-scale models of all U.S. manned rockets to date illustrate the phenomenal progress in just seven years from the Mercury Redstone first launched in 1961 (far left) to the Apollo Saturn V (center) first launched in 1968. The reusable space shuttle (far right), introduced in 1981, has undergone only minor improvements in the past two decades.*

363'

■ 125 tons to Earth orbit

47.5 tons to the Moon

333' 7"

84 tons to Earth orbit

224'

184' 2"

32.5 tons to Earth orbit

109'

95' 3"

20 tons to Earth orbit

83'

1.6 tons to Earth orbit

3.75 tons to Earth orbit

sub-orbital

Mercury Redstone

Mercury Atlas

Gemini Titan

Saturn 1B

Saturn V

Saturn V w/ Skylab

space shuttle

125

100

75

50

25

0

Unfortunately, without a clear visionary behind it, without a clear goal, and without the "old heads" in NASA engineering, the shuttle program ran very differently from Apollo, and it would come in grossly over budget and years late. Originally slated for 1978, the shuttle's planned completion slipped by one year and then another. Skylab waited precariously in its decaying orbit.

By 1979, the Apollo space station was marooned in space without hope of rescue. NASA had spent $20 million developing an orbital boost engine for Skylab, but there was no way to deliver it: The shuttle was nowhere near completion, and we had scrapped all our powerful Apollo Saturn rockets. We no longer had the capability to send men into space or to rescue our space station. It was too late. On July 12, 1979, Skylab was finally ensnared irreversibly in the Earth's atmosphere. Caught in the burning friction, the station plunged at last through reentry's furnace, breaking into pieces and tearing itself apart over the Australian Outback. Small parts of the station were found by ranchers and locals over a wide territory and brought back as curiosities. The space shuttle finally blasted off in 1981, but without the 100-ton legacy of the Apollo space station, there was nowhere for it to go.

Apollo astronaut John Young had walked on the Moon during Apollo 16, and he piloted the huge and exotic shuttle into low orbit several times in the early 1980s, as did several Skylab astronauts. They found the shuttle's crew space roomy by Apollo standards, and the craft's reusability was remarkable, but on

## TOO LATE

*The Space Shuttle was to fly up and rescue Skylab on its third mission, but during Skylab's deorbit in 1979, the first operational orbiter Columbia was still undergoing testing. The shuttle is shown in March 1979, mounted atop a Boeing 747 carrier aircraft.*

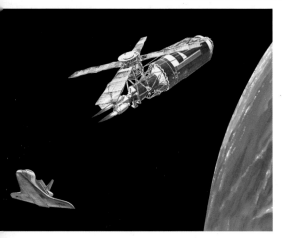

*The Skylab rescue mission would have docked a booster rocket pack into Skylab's main docking port.*

the other hand the shuttle had limited capabilities. Standing half the height of a Saturn V, it was far less powerful than a Moon rocket, and the shuttle could make it only into low Earth orbit, with an absolute maximum altitude of 400 miles. Even the Gemini capsules of 1963 had gone higher, reaching altitudes up to 853 miles. While the Saturn V could boost a 125-ton payload into Earth orbit, the shuttle could carry less than one third of that weight.

Most problematic was the shuttle's lack of purpose, which made it a completely different exercise from the tightly directed Apollo effort. The shuttle program's purpose seemed to be tautological: to build a space shuttle. Post-Apollo NASA had talked about the shuttle making access to space cheap and easy, but the shut-

tle turned out to be tremendously expensive to fly and complex to operate, and it cost more to put satellite payloads into orbit with the shuttle than it did with off-the-shelf unmanned rockets. Nonetheless, NASA used the shuttle for such purposes in order to give it something to do.

Two decades after Skylab was allowed to plunge to its destruction, NASA is engaged in the building of a replacement space station whose construction will require over 30 shuttle launches carrying small loads and cost over 10 times what was already spent on Skylab. The purpose of this new station is not clear, it has no specific objectives, and in spite of the colossal new investment, America does not even control access due to the involvement of international partners.

Beyond the shuttle? Beyond the space station? No one knows. Without the clear vision and leadership of men like Wernher von Braun

*This "Shuttle-C" would have more than tripled the shuttle's lift ability, allowing us to build a space station more efficiently with larger, pre-assembled components.*

and NASA's early chief James Webb, NASA has drifted without long-term goals. Afraid to champion a lunar base or a manned Mars mission that would stretch and challenge aerospace companies like Apollo once did, NASA has shrunk from a Congress considered unsympathetic to grandiose space exploration plans. Apollo had strong leadership, vision, and clear goals with hard milestones and a deadline. Today no organizing goal or purpose motivates NASA or the shuttle fleet, and there is no presidential leadership in space policy. Our vision is short-term at best and pork-barrel politics for aerospace contractors at worst. From the perspective of today, it seems incredible that we were ever able to reach the Moon. But once upon a time, we were.

## APOLLO'S LEGACY

**A**t the dawn of the twenty-first century, what does Apollo mean? A generation has grown up to whom the Moon landings are ancient history. But the race to the Moon was a touchstone moment of great significance. Exploration, and still less science, form only a portion of Apollo's importance. The ideological, national, social, and psychological implications of Apollo loom larger.

To frame the Moon Race in the spirit in which it was conceived, it was a Cold War battle to demonstrate the superior ability of the superior system, capitalism versus communism. Beating the Soviets was the primary driving energy behind Apollo. And the battle did prove out the more capable system. America made it to the Moon in full strength, while the Soviet Union could not even succeed with its more modest Moon landing plans. The reasons are many, but among them the power of free enterprise ranks high. There was no Boeing, no Rocketdyne, no Grumman in the Soviet Union working feverishly to outrank their rivals in the open market and surpass their competition for Apollo contracts. Free competition motivated American workers whose livelihoods were related to the quality and brilliance of their work, and we saw extraordinary, impossible things accomplished by ordinary Americans. The American flag on the Moon is such a powerful symbol because it is not a vain one. America, like no other nation, *was* capable of the Moon.

It is also interesting to observe the character that the Moon Race brought out in each of the two competing systems. The Soviet Union's rhetoric was filled with combative boasting in the name of communism. When America reached the Moon, however, we did so not amid bombastic fanfare but with surprising humility. On Apollo 8, Frank Borman's crew read not state-approved propaganda but Genesis. The plaque on Apollo 11's *Eagle* read, "We came in peace for all mankind," and pictured all the lands of the world, with the United States not even marked separately. And when Gene Cernan took the last step off the Moon during Apollo 17, speaking from his heart and not from any script, he said, "We leave as we came . . . with peace and hope for all mankind." Who were these people who both personally and nationally could experience awe at what was humanly possible, and express it not in hubristic pride but in a sense of humanity's essential oneness? Who were these people who could be sobered by the magnitude of what they were granted to accomplish and who could share this bitterly hard-won victory with every nation on Earth? How extraordinary this was. This generosity of spirit, no less than the achievement itself, was a statement of the potential in the American identity. We were capable of both great and terrible things; Apollo brought out the very best in us.

Somehow along the way, Apollo transcended its origins. We did beat the Soviets, but across the petty superpower finish line we found a legacy so overwhelming that it remains incompletely assimilated today. Apollo revealed the magnitude of what was really possible, in America and for the human spirit. It revealed that "impossible" is only, as von Braun observed, a lack of "the will to do it."

**EAGLE'S PLAQUE**

*Neil Armstrong uncovered this plaque mounted on the LM's leg during his walk on the Moon. Rather than asserting national pride, the plaque calls the astronauts simply "men from the planet Earth," making a profound and moving statement of humanity in an era of international strife and pain. The plaque remains at Tranquility Base today.*

### MAN AND SUPERMAN

*Apollo demonstrated mankind's power to reach beyond earthly boundaries, as shown to advantage in this photograph taken by Gene Cernan during Apollo 17. Jack Schmitt and his home planet appear beside the flag.*

### PERSISTENCE

*Loved by his team and by the astronauts, Wernher von Braun (far right), on an engineering inspection, worked toward his dream of space flight through years of frustration and disappointment. His optimism, industry, and determination reflected what came to be the spirit of Apollo.*

### AMERICAN MOON

*The achievement of the Moon landing was a benchmark for all humanity, but it was also an American statement. No less than the glowing white architecture in Washington, D.C., the Moon reminds us of the heights we have reached and the potential within us.*

It seems that, in America at least, we really can do anything. The implications are sobering when one considers all the other goals to which we might turn our human powers. Ever since July 20, 1969, we have used this observation casually in the common phrase, "If we can put a man on the Moon, why can't we . . . ." The realization is there, but it still seems unreal, theoretical. Our greatest problems still beset us, racial harmony and social justice still out of reach, our environment's purity incompatible with prosperity: problems seemingly too large for us to solve. Apollo proved otherwise, but perhaps that extraordinary dash to the Moon happened so fast, and disappeared so quickly, that we could not take it all in at the time. It is surprising, and a little sad, that there exists no Apollo Monument in Washington, D.C., shining in the day and gleaming in the night to remind us of what is possible when we rise to our best.

Apollo mobilized the resources of America and inspired hundreds of thousands of people who outdid themselves in creating the technology and the ability to achieve the goal. Yet Apollo killed no enemies.

It was an unprecedented new kind of project for our culture. We must look to the pyramids of Egypt or the cathedrals of Europe to find parallels that partake of this special kind of major national goal apart from war.

Such monumental works arise because they express shared beliefs that unite a people, just as the quest for the Moon expressed America's shared beliefs in capitalism, technology, and American capability. Apollo was a great pyramid, a national cathedral of 20th-century America. The nation that raised the Empire State Building and wrested the power of the universe from the center of the atom combined sky-scraping technological daring with unimaginable explosive fury and brought to pass the Saturn V, against which all our other instruments and structures pale. Its rivals are the pyramids and cathedrals, and few others, precisely because the Saturn V is impossible without the massive, focused resources and the vision and drive it took to organize 400,000 builders.

The Moon remains our trophy. And one day, the achievements of Apollo will inspire us to find our astonishing strengths again. One day we will look up at the Moon, knowing that Apollo was a glorious prelude and not, as it seems now, a peak we look back on wonderingly, amazed that we ever climbed so high.

We will surpass Apollo. Whether that means further space exploration that requires the focus and strength of our abilities in technology and organization, or whether that means some new kind of endeavor that cannot be guessed today, that once again requires a massive union of our very best and more, a synergy beyond the sum of our parts—whatever that new objective may be, we will one day surpass the achievement of Apollo. In reaching beyond it, we will at last fulfill its promise, a promise that lies waiting today, waiting for anyone to look up at in the glow of the night sky, a promise recorded in the footprints on the Moon.

## IMPRINT

*Like the haunting footprints left in caves during the Ice Age, this footprint on the Moon will endure thousands of years into the future, carrying the same message: We were here.*

*The final lunar-mission
patch frames a
retrospective golden
Apollo with a futuristic
American eagle, its wings
again touching the Moon
and its head stretching
out toward the planets
and into deep space,
symbolizing the paths of
tomorrow. High above
the Earth in an Apollo
spacecraft, one felt the
limitless possibilities of
the future.*

I am a marked man. One cannot behold all the lands and seas of the Earth in a single glance and remain unchanged by the experience. Returning to Earth from the Moon poses the challenge of finding a perspective within yourself that can encompass what has happened to you, that can accommodate the matters of ordinary life as well as the memory of having looked into the endlessness of space and time from another world. I once stood upon the dust of the Moon and looked up, struggling to comprehend the enormity of the message that we found in Apollo. All that is here. In this book, you have stood by my side, and you have felt what I felt within the midst of those extraordinary adventures. This book *is* the story of Apollo. As I close these pages, the wonder and the glory surround me, and I remember: I have been there; I have lived in Camelot. The destiny Apollo forged remains for the future. It lives in a tomorrow that will one day dawn just as did the days of our landings on the Moon.

# Landfall

## BY GENE CERNAN
### Mission Commander of Apollo 17

# Apollo Mission Summary

**APOLLO 1**
*January 27, 1967*
A fire in the command module during a preflight test of Apollo 204 kills astronauts Roger Chaffee, Guss Grissom, and Ed White. The operation is renamed Apollo 1 in Spring 1967.

*[There were no Apollos 2 and 3. The command modules destined for these missions were disassembled in parallel to determine the cause of the Apollo 1 fire.]*

**APOLLO 4**
*November 9, 1967*
The first flight test of the Saturn V Moon rocket sends an unmanned rocket into Earth orbit with all stages live on its first launch.

**APOLLO 5**
*January 22, 1968*
The first space test of the lunar module puts an unmanned prototype lunar lander in Earth orbit using a Saturn IB rocket.

**APOLLO 6**
*April 4, 1968*
A second and final Saturn V unmanned test flight (into Earth orbit) reveals engine system vibration problems called "pogo," which lead to early engine shutdown. Pogo is analyzed and solved for future flights.

**APOLLO 7**
*October 11–22, 1968*
Astronauts Wally Schirra, Donn Eisele, and Walt Cunningham prove out the redesigned Apollo command and service module in Earth orbit on the first manned Apollo flight.

**APOLLO 8**
*December 21–27, 1968*
Launched on the first manned Saturn V, Frank Borman, Jim Lovell, and Bill Anders become the first men to orbit the Moon and behold the phenomenon of "earthrise" for the first time.

**APOLLO 9**
*March 3–13, 1969*
On the first manned test of the lunar module, Jim McDivitt and Rusty Schweickart test-fly the lander in Earth orbit and practice rendezvous techniques with Dave Scott in the command module.

**APOLLO 10**
*May 18–26, 1969*
On a full dress rehearsal of the lunar landing, Tom Stafford and Gene Cernan pilot the lunar module to within 50,000 feet of the Moon, while John Young mans the command module "mothership."

**APOLLO 11**
*July 16–24, 1969*
*Sea of Tranquility*
Neil Armstrong and Buzz Aldrin accomplish the first manned landing on the Moon, while Michael Collins orbits above in the command module.

**APOLLO 12**
*November 14–24, 1969*
*Ocean of Storms*
Alan Bean and Pete Conrad demonstrate precision landing techniques, touching down 600 feet from the Surveyor 3 probe that landed on the Moon two and a half years earlier. Richard Gordon conducts observations in lunar orbit.

**APOLLO 13**
*April 11–17, 1970*
An explosion of an oxygen tank 55 hours into the mission forces astronauts Fred Haise, Jim Lovell, and John Swigert to circle the Moon without landing, using their lunar module as a lifeboat.

**APOLLO 14**
*January 31–February 9, 1971*
*Fra Mauro Highlands*
Astronauts Alan Shepard and Ed Mitchell make the first landing on lunar highlands. Stuart Roosa mans the command module in lunar orbit.

**APOLLO 15**
*July 26–August 7, 1971*
*Hadley-Appenine*
Dave Scott and Jim Irwin explore for three days on the Moon, traveling miles away from the landing site in the first lunar rover. Al Worden circles the Moon, making observations with a large instrument module.

**APOLLO 16**
*April 16–27, 1972*
*Descartes Highlands*
Equipped with the second lunar rover, Charlie Duke and John Young explore the Moon's central highlands for three days in search of lunar volcanoes. Ken Mattingly makes observations from lunar orbit.

**APOLLO 17**
*December 7–19, 1972*
*Taurus-Littrow*
Gene Cernan and Harrison Schmitt use the last lunar rover to carry out the most extensive explorations men ever accomplish on the Moon, concluding the Apollo landings. Ron Evans mans the instrument bay in orbit above.

# Select Bibliography

Some of the best works written about Apollo appeared in the heady days shortly after Apollo 11. These could not cover the entire history of the program, which had yet to run its course, but they have provided some of the best combinations of narrative overview and research to date. Since then, solid writing on Apollo has been largely for the aficionado, whether it is behind-the-scenes political history or technical or personal memoirs, though in very recent years we are starting to see a broader range of good Apollo titles. My hope is that the present volume will provide an encouraging gateway into the existing body of Apollo literature. Once Apollo's traditional jargon and basics are familiar, the eyewitness accounts and even straight mission transcripts become riveting documents of highest adventure. Following is a very selective account of some of the material out there.

## I. PRIMARY SOURCES

Godwin, Robert, ed. *The NASA Mission Reports.* Ontario: Apogee Books, 2000–2001. In one or two volumes per mission, Godwin presents the Apollo mission press kits and also includes post-flight debriefing transcripts, primary documents of great interest that were originally classified and never before published. These volumes include a wealth of NASA diagrams and photographs, and exhaustive CD-ROMS of images and motion pictures.

Bonestell, Chesley, and Willy Ley. *The Conquest of Space.* New York: Viking Press, 1949.

Ley, Willy, and Wernher von Braun. *The Exploration of Mars.* New York: Viking Press, 1956.

Ryan, Cornelius, ed. *Across the Space Frontier.* New York: Viking Press, 1952.

Von Braun, Werhner, Fred L. Whipple, and Willy Ley. *Conquest of the Moon.* New York: Viking Press, 1954.

These four books vividly record the brink of the Space Age, when it was all dreams and plans, before any man-made satellites ever existed. In addition to the beautiful paintings and diagrams, they include a great deal of engineering and technical detail. For those jaded by the politics and bureaucracy that has beset space exploration in the modern era, a look at these books can burnish the dream anew.

Von Braun, Wernher. *The Mars Project.* Urbana, Ill.: University of Illinois Press, 1953. This was von Braun's early, technical work on the subject, omitting the story he wrote to dramatize the concept.

Verne, Jules. *From the Earth to the Moon.* Translated by Lowell Blair. New York: Bantam Classics, 1993. Originally written in 1868, Verne's account is still entertaining for its satiric view of America and remains impressive for its sheer audacity in confronting the magnitude of engineering a Moon shot. It is no wonder that this book inspired the rocket builders.

## II. SECONDARY WORKS

Barbour, John. *Footprints on the Moon.* New York: The Associated Press, 1969. Barbour provides an inspiring and exciting account of the missions leading up to and including Apollo 11. His story captures the wonder of the time and includes many details that have since dropped out of the standard histories. Particularly strong for pre-Mercury and Gemini, which get less coverage elsewhere.

Benson, Charles D., and William B. Faherty. *Gateway to the Moon* and *Moon Launch!* Gainesville: University Press of Florida, 2001. Fine paperback republication in two volumes of *Moonport* (1978), the excellent official account of the creation of the Apollo Saturn launch facilities at Cape Canaveral.

Bilstein, Roger E. *Stages to Saturn: A Technological History of the Apollo Saturn Launch Vehicles.* Washington, D.C.: NASA, 1980. The outstanding, technical, but highly readable official account of the development and construction of the Moon rocket stages and engines.

Bizony, Piers. *Island in the Sky: Building the International Space Station.* London: Aurum Press, 1996. Bizony provides an excellent outside perspective on the tortured politics of the International Space Station and places it in context with early space station concepts, particularly Skylab.

Brooks, Courtney G., James M. Grimwood, and Loyd S. Swenson Jr. *Chariots for Apollo: A History of Manned Lunar Spacecraft.* Washington, D.C.: NASA, 1979. Exhaustive official history of command and lunar module development and use through Apollo 11.

Cernan, Gene, and Don Davis. *The Last Man on the Moon: Astronaut Eugene Cernan and America's Race in Space.* New York: St. Martin's Press, 1999. Cernan's memoir, which is stronger on his career and earlier flights than on Apollo 17's expedition to the lunar surface.

Chaikin, Andrew L. *A Man on the Moon: The Voyages of the Apollo Astronauts.* New York: Penguin, 1998. Chaikin's engaging book presents in effect a composite memoir of the Apollo astronauts, focusing on their experiences rather than technical explanation or political background. For the astronaut's point of view, this is the best single volume on the entire Apollo program.

Collins, Michael. *Carrying the Fire: An Astronaut's Journeys.* New York: Farrar, Straus, and Giroux, 1974. Candid memoir of the Apollo adventure by Apollo 11's command module pilot; a good personal account filled with poetic and vivid descriptions and Collins's wry, self-effacing humor.

Compton, W. David. *Where No Man Has Gone Before: A History of Apollo Lunar Exploration.* Washington, D.C.: NASA, 1989. Official history of figuring out how to get to the Moon, then exploring it.

Harford, James. *Korolev: How One Man Masterminded the Soviet Drive to Beat America to the Moon.* New York: Wiley, 1997. The first English account of the life and personality of von Braun's opposite number in Russia.

Harland, David. *Exploring the Moon: The Apollo Expeditions.* Chichester, U.K.: Praxis Publishing, 1999. Takes you step-by-step with the astronauts through every part of the lunar explorations to every crater and every rock. Also includes dozens of panoramas assembled for the first time by the author into seamless images of the Apollo moonscapes. There is no other book like this for taking you to the surface of the Moon.

Hechler, Ken. *Toward the Endless Frontier: History of the Committee on Science and Technology, 1959–1979.* Washington, D.C.: Government Printing Office, 1980. Congressional debates and decisions regarding Project Apollo.

Heiken, Grant H., David T. Vaniman, and Bevan M. French, eds. *The Lunar Sourcebook.* New York: Cambridge University Press, 1991. Collects world research on lunar geology and science into a modern technical reference volume.

Kelley, Thomas J. *Moon Lander: How We Developed the Apollo Lunar Module.* Washington, D.C.: Smithsonian, 2001. Memoir of the Grumman engineer who led the LM design and construction team. Dense, dry, and technical, this account provides a frank and honest look at how the company worked in creating the LM.

Kraft, Christopher C., and James L. Schefter. *Flight: My Life in Mission Control.* New York: Dutton, 2001. Engaging inside memoir of the man behind the Apollo flight directors at Mission Control, filled with personal stories of this Apollo nerve center.

Kranz, Gene. *Failure Is Not an Option: Mission Control from Mercury to Apollo 13 and Beyond.* New York: Berkeley Publishing Group, 2001. Memoir of the man best known as the lead flight director at Mission Control during Apollo 13. Forthright and engaging, Kranz's account tells the story of how dedication and discipline made Mission Control an effective team at the cutting edge of exploration and technology.

Launius, Roger D. *NASA: A History of the U.S. Civil Space Program.* Melbourne, Fla.: Krieger, 1994. A concise history of American space exploration including three chapters on Apollo. Features both narrative and historical documents.

Light, Michael. *Full Moon.* New York: Knopf, 1999. Deliberately disorienting, this art book offers large prints of Apollo images painstakingly scanned from NASA master negatives. A 2001-style narrative-free experience.

Logsdon, John M., ed. *Exploring the Unknown: Selected Documents in the History of the U.S. Civil Space Program.* 5 vols. Washington, D.C.: NASA, 1995–2001. These volumes reprint 500 key documents from 20th-century space history.

Lovell, Jim, and Jeffrey Kluger. *Apollo 13.* New York: Houghton Mifflin, 2000. Originally published as *Lost Moon* (1994), this account stands out among the Apollo memoirs as a strong narrative and not just a personal career history with anecdotes.

Mellberg, William F. *Moon Missions: Mankind's First Voyages to Another World.* New York: Ian Allan, 1997. A good concise summary of Apollo from its earliest beginnings through Apollo 17.

Murray, Charles, and Catherine Cox. *Apollo: The Race to the Moon.* New York: Simon & Schuster, 1989. Basing their work on a large number of interviews, Murray and Cox provide the best account of Apollo from the flight control and engineering points of view, focusing on behind-the-scenes political intrigue and backroom discussions.

Ordway, Frederick I. III, and Mitchell R. Sharpe, with a foreword by Wernher von Braun. *The Rocket Team.* New York: Crowell, 1979. Accessible account of von Braun's rocketeer team, their German war background, their emigration to the United States, and their work at Marshall.

Schirra, Wally, and Richard N. Billings. *Schirra's Space.* Annapolis, Md.: Naval Institute Press, 1995. Schirra's accessible, irreverent, and often jovial memoir of his many adventures at the heart of American space exploration.

Stoff, Joshua, and Charles Pellegrino. *Chariots for Apollo: The Untold Story Behind the Race to the Moon.* New York: Avon Books, 1999. Far less comprehensive than its title would suggest, this loosely written book focuses on Grumman and the lunar module, largely omitting discussion of the Saturn V or the command module.

Wilford, John Noble. *We Reach the Moon.* New York: Bantam, 1969. Wilford's superb paperback is a combination of narrative and explanation, including clear diagrams and illustrations. Wilford skillfully paces his story and treats the important questions associated with Apollo (e.g., "Is this trip really necessary?").

Wolfe, Tom. *The Right Stuff.* New York: Bantam, 1983. Wolfe is the best writer to ever tackle space history, and his coverage of project Mercury is, as ever, crackling with color and humor.

World Spaceflight News Staff. *Apollo and America's Moon Landing Program: Command Module (CSM) Reference.* Mount Laurel, N.J.: World Spaceflight News, 2000.

————. *Apollo and America's Moon Landing Program: Lunar Module Reference.* Mount Laurel, N.J.: World Spaceflight News, 2000.

————. *Saturn V: America's Apollo Moon Rocket.* Mount Laurel, N.J.: World Spaceflight News, 2000.

These three titles offer technical detail and hundreds of diagrams and illustrations of these vehicles and their subsystems unlike anything else in print.

Zimmerman, Robert. *Genesis: The Story of Apollo 8: The First Manned Flight to Another World.* New York: Four Walls Eight Windows, 1998. The story of Apollo 8 as told through the thoughts and experiences of the astronauts and their families. Zimmerman also takes care to frame the mission in the social and historical context of 1968.

### III. Web Sites

http://www.apolloarchive.com/
Kipp Teague's Apollo Archive serves as a comprehensive reference source on the Apollo program, especially strong for its collection of high-resolution images.

http://www.hq.nasa.gov/alsj/frame.html
Dr. Eric Jones has compiled the Internet's heavily researched Apollo Lunar Surface Journal, a fully annotated and illustrated record of the communications during the Moon explorations; an exceptional resource.

http://www.astronautix.com
Mark Wade's on-line Encyclopedia Astronautica is an unparalleled resource featuring entries on rockets and space programs, from the earliest to the latest, including performance data, histories, diagrams, and reports on programs that were cancelled as well as those that flew.

http://images.jsc.nasa.gov/iams/html/pao/pao.htm
Johnson Spaceflight Center's on-line digital images collection is an excellent source for images, organized by program and mission.

## Acknowledgments

Many people behind the scenes in "Mission Control" and its vital backrooms helped make this book possible. Among them, I owe special thanks to the following. Trish Graboske, publications officer at the Smithsonian National Air & Space Museum, supported this book from its inception and was instrumental in getting it off the ground, and Linda King at NASM got the ball rolling in the first place. Von Hardesty welcomed me into the world of professional space and aviation history. His enthusiasm and guidance came at a critical juncture. Irene Willhite, archivist at the U.S. Space & Rocket Center, is truly the queen of the von Braun papers and many other treasures in Huntsville. Her consistent support afforded me a vital look into von Braun's personal records and into his character, an experience that shaped this narrative. Young space expert Andrew Chandler helped prepare archival items for photography. Frederick C. Durant III welcomed me into his home to admire Bonestell originals and to hear stories of his friendship with von Braun. Ron Miller first revealed to me the wonder of the Plan for Space. Bob Johnson at Kennedy Space Center arranged for my thrilling visits to the sites of Apollo, and Thurston Vickery took me around, under, and inside the crawler-transporter. Margaret Persinger at KSC kindly loaded the project with gold and diamonds in the form of rare images from the days of Apollo. Bob Jacques and Judy Pettus at Marshall gave me a look into the fascinating image archives there, and John London and Jeff Hamilton arranged a memorable tour of the great test stands. Outstanding space historian Dave Harland provided very helpful eagle-eyed technical review and sharpened my understanding of a great many details, though only I am accountable for errors that remain. Roger Launius, NASA chief historian in Washington, contributed collegial correspondence and much-appreciated support as well. Two of the men who made the Apollo voyages served as test pilots for the book, made sure it "flew true," and offered special contributions: Wally Schirra stepped in with kind enthusiasm and good humor, and Gene Cernan generously offered his support for the project's smooth splashdown. I also thank my illustrators and the Tehabi team: Mark Santos, who pieced together Apollo photographs into our new high-resolution panoramas; Brian Lemke, whose illustrations offer some of the best cutaway views of Apollo spacecraft yet published; Gary Hincks, whose artworks provide new perspectives on key Apollo events; Vicky Vaughn, who worked long hours to create this book's design and to find its extraordinary range of photographs; and "Capcom" Garrett Brown, who championed this book's lofty goals and persevered through a project filled with both discovery and challenge. Finally, ever since the night of July 20, 1969, when we watched Neil's first step together, Mrs. Charles D. Wright has supported my interest in Apollo and shared with me a sense of wonder about space exploration. Thanks, Granma. —DWR, November 15, 2001

# Index

Italicized page number indicate photographs.

# Photography and Illustration Credits

© 2001 David West Reynolds/Phaeton Group: 103c, 103f, 167b, 234a, 256a

AP/Wide World Photos: 137

© Bettmann/CORBIS: 70, 153

Bill Eppridge/TimePix: 134–135

© Bonestell Space Art: 15, 25b, 27b, 28b–d, 29b, 29c

Copyright © 1957 by The New York Times Co. Reprinted by permission: 34a

Courtesy Frederic W. Freeman Trust: 30a

Courtesy of Los Alamos National Laboratory: 246

Courtesy of NASA/JPL/Caltech: 13a, 13b, 58b

Courtesy Ron Miller: 16, 218

David M. Harland: 187a

Deutsches Filmmuseum Frankfurt am Main: 23b

© Disney Enterprises, Inc.: 32b–d

Gary Hincks Illustrations: 103b, 139, 173b, 193b, 217b, 228b, 229b

Genesis Space Photo Library: 115a, 235

Genesis Space Photo Library/NPO Energia: 12, 161, 163

Illustration by Ron Miller: 231

Illustrations by Brian Battles: 85, 93, 95, 224b–g

Illustrations by Brian Lemke: 69b, 87–90, 121b, 169b

Institute & Museum of History of Science: 17a, 17b

Jerry Olingers Movie Material Store, Inc.: 23c

Lockheed Martin Space Systems Company–Michoud Operations: 256b

Lyndon Baines Johnson Library and Museum: 41

Models and Photographs by Glenn Johnson: 55b, 162, 253

NASA: 1 (AS11-40-5880), 2–3 (AS11-40-5875), 4–5 (AS14-66-9277, AS14-66-9278, AS14-66-9279), 7 (AS-11-44-6551), 8a (AS7-7-1877), 8b, 10a (AS7-7-1877), 14a (AS7-7-1877), 18, 23a (AS11-44-6552), 25a, 26–27a (AS11-36-5293), 26b, 28–29a (AS11-36-5293), 32a (AS11-36-5293), 33, 35 (GPN-20001-008), 37a (AS11-44-6552), 37b, 37c, 37d, 38, 38–39 (S62-8774), 42 (GPN-2000-1009), 43, 46 (64-36914), 47 (KSC-63C-1414), 48 (GPN-2000-1180), 49 (S65-30427), 50–51 (GPN-2000-1408), 51a (S66-54455), 51b (GPN-2000-1420), 52 (65-59949), 52–53 (S65-63194), 54 (GPN-2000-125), 55a (AS11-36-5293), 56 (66-59907), 56–57 (NSSDC-66-732-1D), 57, 58–59a (AS11-44-6552), 58c (GPN-2000-1979), 59b, 59c (PIA02976), 60–61 (65-51659), 62 (KSC-66C-4722), 63a (AS7-7-1877), 64 (66-41853), 64–65 (GPN-2000-618), 66 (KSC-67PC-17), 67 (67-HC-21), 68a (GPN-2000-1834), 68b, 69a (AS11-44-6552), 71 (S66-41851), 72 (68-33750), 73 (KSC-68PC-197), 74–75 (AS7-4-1582), 76–77 (AS7-7-1877), 77a (AS7-7-1748), 77b (AS7-4-1584), 78a (S68-50713), 78b (AS7-3-1545), 79 (AS7-8-1933), 80 (72-35188), 81 (GPN-2000-1274), 82 (GPN-2000-048), 82–83 (8007298), 84, 86a (KSC-1PP-825), 86b (GPN-2000-616), 91a (KSC-1PP-825), 91b (MSFC 68 MS-G 1305D), 92 (65-H-206), 94a (AS17-148-22727), 94b (64PC-82), 95 (AS17-148-22727), 96a (KSC-68C-8693), 96b (66PC-76), 96c (72-PC-429), 96e (66C-6962), 97, 98a (KSC-68P-614), 98b (68-51093), 99 (KSC-68PC-338), 100 (KSC-68PC-327), 101 (S68-55742), 102–103a (KSC-1PP-825), 102b (KSC-69PC-416), 103d (S66-10996), 103e (S66-11006), 104 (68-51306), 105 (PIA00224.11077), 106–107 (AS8-16-2588), 107a (AS8-13-2344), 107b (AS8-17-2670), 108a (AS8-12-2209), 108b (AS8-12-2052), 109 (AS8-13-2224), 110 (68-56531), 111 (AS8-14-2383), 112a (AS7-7-1877), 113 (AS11-40-5850), 114 (68-18733), 116 (EL-2000-433), 116–117 (67-50927), 119, 120–121a (AS11-44-6552), 120b (69-25668), 122–123a (AS11-44-6552), 122–123c (S69-39262), 122b (EL-1996-217), 123d (AS9-21-3212), 124–125 (AS9-19-2919), 125 (AS9-20-3064), 126–127 (KSC-69PC-78), 127a (S69-17809), 127b (S69-34333), 128 (AS10-27-3873), 129a (KSC-69PC-295), 129b, 130 (KSC-69PC-338), 131b (KSC-69PC-399), 132–133 (KSC-69PC-413), 132a (KSC-69PC-387), 132b (KSC-69P-631), 136 (AS11-44-6581), 138–139a (AS11-44-6552), 138b (AS11-37-5437), 140 (AS11-37-5454), 144a (AS11-40-5868), 144b (AS11-40-5942), 145 (AS11-40-5903), 146b (AS11-37-5528), 147 (AS11-44-6642), 148a (69-H-1421), 148b (69-60069), 149 (AS12-51-7507), 150–151a (AS11-44-6552), 152 (AS12-48-7133), 154 (AS13-59-8500), 154–155 (AS13-62-9004), 156a (GPN-2000-1313), 156b (70-19764), 157a (S70-50764), 157b (GPN-2000-1146), 158–159 (AS14-66-9305, AS14-66-9306, AS14-66-9307), 160 (AS14-68-9405), 164 (AS17-134-20476), 165a (AS7-7-1877), 166 (71-HC-684), 167a, 168–169a (AS11-44-6552), 170 (71-31409), 171a (S71-22401), 172–173a (AS11-44-6552), 172b (AS15-87-11718), 174 (S71-40390), 175 (AS15-88-11985), 176 (S17-41836), 177a (GPN-2000-1140), 178 (AS15-87-11845), 182 (GPN-2000-1122), 183 (AS15-84-11324), 184–185 (AS15-85-11451), 185 (S71-42951), 186–187 (AS15-88-11866), 187b (AS15-88-11974), 188 (GPN-2000-1129), 189b (72-37002), 190–191 (GPN-2000-1123), 191 (AS16-113-18339), 192 (72-H-864), 193a (AS11-44-6552), 200 (AS17-145-22252), 201a (GPN-200-148), 201b (AS17-137-20979), 202–203 (AS17-134-20435), 204 (AS17-134-20425), 206 (AS17-134-20530), 207 (AS17-137-20960), 208–209 (AS17-140-21496), 209a (AS17-134-20462), 209b (AS17-145-22224), 210–211 (AS17-152-23274), 210a (S72-55421), 210b (S72-55423), 212 (AS17-149-22859), 213a (S71-39614), 213b (AS-17-162-24053), 214 (AS17-148-22727), 214–215, 216–217a (AS17-148-22727), 216b (S72-55834), 216c (S72-56147), 216d (69-21783), 217c (69-15592), 217d (S66-11003), 217e (71-43543), 217f (S66-10991), 219 (S72-55937), 220–221 (AS17-134-20380), 222a (AS17-145-22285), 222b (AS10-34-5026), 223 (SL4-143-4706), 224a (AS11-40-5947), 226a (AS15-91-12383), 226b (69-45025), 227a (75-23543), 227b (S71-45477), 228–229a (AS11-44-6552), 230 (AS15-88-11980), 232–233 (AS15-93-12628), 234b, 236–237a (AS11-36-5293), 236b, 237b, 237c, 238, 239a, 240 (SL2-4-265), 240–241, 242–243a (AS11-36-5293), 242b, 243b (S71-52192), 244–245a (AS11-36-5293), 244b (S74-17457), 244c (SL4-150-5062), 244d (SL4-150-5080), 245b (S74-23458), 245c (SL3-114-1660), 247, 248–249a (AS11-36-5293), 248b, 249b, 249c, 250 (S99-8357), 251a, 251b, 252–253a (KSC-1PP-825), 252b (94-202-8), 254 (78-23630), 254–255 (KSC-79PC-39), 257 (AS11-40-5899), 258–259 (AS17-134-20384), 259b, 260 (S69-40308), 261 (GPN-2001-014), 262a (AS17-145-22285), 262b (S72-49079), 263 (AS17-148-22661), 265 (KSC-72PC-713), 96 (S69-38661)

Nate Bacon Photography: 229d

Nathan Farb/TimePix: 259a

Novosti (London): 34b

Ordway Collection/U.S. Space & Rocket Center: 10b

Photo by Johnny Miller/U.S. Space & Rocket Center: 20b, 22b, 36b, 74, 115b, 118, 131a, 141, 146a, 150b, 150c, 151b–e, 168b, 171b, 177b, 189a, 190, 205, 239b

Photo. No. KN-C23643 12Sep1962 in the John F. Kennedy Library: 44–45

Photo © UC Regents/Lick Observatory: 14b, 63b, 112b, 165b, 225

Ralph Morse/TimePix: 9

Russian State Archives for Scientific–Technical Documentation (RGANTD): 40

San Diego Aerospace Museum: 19, 20a

U.S. Space & Rocket Center: 11, 21, 22a, 24, 30–31, 36a, 45

United States Air Force: 55c

University of Arizona Space Imagery Center: 142–143 (AS11-40-5961, AS11-40-5960, AS11-40-5958, AS11-40-5957, AS11-40-5956), 179–181 (AS15-90-12179, AS15-90-12182, AS15-90-12185, AS15-90-12187, AS15-90-12189, AS15-90-12190, AS15-90-12191, AS15-90-12193), 194–199 (AS17-137-21024, AS17-137-21003, AS17-137-21002, AS17-137-21006, AS17-137-21007, AS17-137-21012, AS17-137-21014, AS17-137-21015, AS17-137-21017)

Willard Clay Photography, Inc.: 229c